WHAT'S IT WORTH?
A HOME INSPECTION & APPRAISAL MANUAL

JOSEPH V. SCADUTO

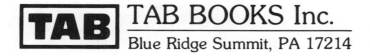
TAB BOOKS Inc.
Blue Ridge Summit, PA 17214

To My Family

FIRST EDITION

THIRD PRINTING

Printed in the United States of America

Reproduction or publication of the content in any manner, without express permission of the publisher, is prohibited. No liability is assumed with respect to the use of the information herein.

Library of Congress Cataloging in Publication Data

Scaduto, Joseph V.
What's it worth?

Includes index.
1. House buying. 2. Dwellings—Inspection.
3. Dwellings—Valuation. I. Title.
HD1379.S33 1985 33.33′2 85-2801
ISBN 0-8306-0761-7
ISBN 0-8306-1761-2 (pbk.)

Front cover illustration by George Robinson.

Contents

Preface

"Buyer Beware" no longer applies to the purchase of real estate. In today's market, you not only need to know but have a right to know of existing or potential problems with a home you are planning to buy. You should also know whether an asking price is justified. This is why astute home buyers are turning to home inspectors and appraisers for professional advice. Many areas of our country, however, do not have qualified home inspectors or appraisers, and it is with this in mind that I have put together this no-nonsense manual on how to appraise and inspect your own home.

I have purposely avoided including confusing facts and figures, and the text is written in language that you can understand. If you use this book as a manual and guide, you will know the correct questions to ask about the condition of major structural and mechanical systems, and what to look for when you inspect and appraise a house. An inspection or appraisal could save you thousands of dollars

because a thorough inspection could uncover serious defects unknown even to the owners. If such is the case, the asking price might have to be lowered or repairs made before the purchase. On the other hand, if there are no serious defects, at least you will have the peace of mind in knowing that you are going to make a sound investment.

Home inspections and appraisals are not meant for buyers only, but also for sellers and owners. A vigilant owner will inspect and appraise his home from the day he moves in until the day he sells. This might be in the form of casual observations on the condition of the hot water tank, to the semiannual ritual check on gutters that need to be cleaned and repaired. For this reason I have included a section on home maintenance as well.

Although it will not make you an expert, this book will be an excellent reference as you consider the purchase of a home as well as over the years of ownership.

Acknowledgments

I am indebted to many people for their cooperation and generous assistance in preparing this book, particularly government officials who have provided me with original prints and invaluable materials about housing in general.

Many thanks to the U.S. Departments of Agriculture; Health, Education and Welfare; Army; Housing and Urban Development; the Department of Energy; and the Wood Heating Education and Research Foundation, Washington, D.C.

I also wish to thank Ms. Rosemarie I. Zunke for her considerable editorial work. A book of this scope would not have been possible without her generous and continuous cooperation. Above all, I am deeply grateful to my wife, Tillie, and my children Stacy and Michael for encouraging me to write this book, and for putting up with me while preparing it.

Introduction

Before you actually examine a house, you should consider several factors that influence the value of property. Probably the most important consideration is location. Even if the house is in great shape, you should be concerned about where it is located. What's the sense in having the best house in the neighborhood when the rest of the homes are eyesores? Remember, the house can be changed but not the neighborhood.

APPRAISAL CONSIDERATIONS

Tour the neighborhood at different times of the day and on different days of the week. Take notes on the condition of neighboring properties. Are the houses well maintained or are there signs of neglect? Are there commercial or public buildings that are a source of aggravation? Is there heavy traffic or teenage hangouts; Both could mean excess noise.

Another consideration is the site orientation of the house. Are there deciduous shade trees on the south and west that cool in summer but let sunshine through in winter? Are there evergreen screens on the north and east sides that provide protection against winter winds? Does the surrounding land slope toward the house? If so, water penetration into the basement is possible. Is the house situated in such a way that solar heating or solar hot water systems could be installed?

The design of the house should also be considered. Are all the rooms laid out in an easy-to-use pattern, or do you have to go through bedrooms to get to a living area? Does the house have sufficient closet and storage space? Is the house large enough to afford privacy for individual family members? Does the house have enough bathrooms? Have security features been built into the house to deter burglars? Do bedrooms have a safe, second means of egress? Do you feel comfortable in the house? Design changes can be made to accommodate new owners, but it might be wise to get an estimate of the costs involved before you make any commitments. Chapter 1 fully discusses the appraisal of homes.

INSPECTION CONSIDERATIONS

After you have decided that the location, the neighborhood, the site, and the design of the house meet your expectations, familiarize yourself with the various components of both structural and mechanical systems to give yourself a better understanding of the house in general. Chapters 2 through 18 describe in detail the inspection procedure.

A house is a combination of individual members that are integrated into systems. There are several major systems of which you should be aware. On the exterior of the house, you will be dealing with three major systems and their individual members. From the ground up, they consist of the foundation, the wall members, and the roof members. Defects in any of these systems or their members can cause problems both on the exterior as well as the interior of the house.

The foundation is made up not only of the visible foundation but also the hidden footing upon which it rests. The wall system consists of the framing as well as the visible siding. Also included in both the foundation and wall systems are openings such as windows and doors. The roof system consists not only of the roof sheathing and framing members but also the roof coverings. In addition, the roof system has interrelated members: chimneys, skylights, plumbing vents, ventilation units, gutters, and downspouts.

The interior inspection will be concerned with major systems like the basement wood framing members. Included in this group are girders, sills, floor joists, and support posts, as well as bracing members such as cross bridging. The interior inspection will also be concerned with the electro-mechanical systems of the house. These include the electrical system, the plumbing system, and the heating system. In some homes you will also have to deal with an air conditioning system. As with the exterior systems, failures or defects in individual members will result in problems directly with the system and indirectly with the house.

TOOLS NEEDED

To do an inspection, certain tools will be need-ed. A bright flashlight to see in dark corners of cellars, attics, and crawl spaces is a must. A screwdriver or awl is necessary to inspect for signs of decay or structural pest damage (termites and other wood-boring insects). A sturdy stepladder will be needed for those houses that do not provide direct access (built-in or pulldown steps) to the attic. An extension ladder can be used to check the condition of gutters and adjacent members. An electrical tester is a necessary tool to check electrical outlets. Binoculars can be very helpful in getting a better look at a roof and chimney. Either a steel ball or a level should be used to determine if the floors are level. The level can also be used to see if the walls are plumb. An extension ruler is important in determining required local building code specifications. A compass is helpful in ascertaining the building's climatic exposure. Knowledge of the house exposure is important in evaluating conditions on the exterior as well as related factors on the interior.

INSPECTION GEAR

Equally as important as the tools are the type of clothing worn to the inspection. Work clothes should be worn because you will be inspecting areas such as unfinished attics, crawl spaces, and basements. These areas are usually dirty and often loaded with dust. In this respect it would be a good idea to wear a respirator in any area that presents a breathing problem. Gloves should be worn during the inspection in areas where direct contact with insecticides and possible contact with rodent or bird droppings might be encountered. Shoes with nonskid soles and ankle-high supports should be worn, particularly if you plan on climbing ladders. A few words of caution should be interjected here. Under *no* circumstances should you subject yourself to any hazards during the inspection. If it is a matter of putting yourself in any physical jeopardy, don't do it.

WORKSHEETS

The last item that you will need for the inspection is a set of inspection worksheets and a pencil.

The inspection worksheets list the important areas to be inspected, as well as what specific things to look for. These worksheets are provided for you in Appendix C. As you do your inspection, use the worksheets to record your findings. After you have completed your inspection, you can use the worksheets to evaluate the true condition of the house and then determine if the asking price is justified.

INSPECTION PROCEDURE

When you arrange the appointment to inspect and appraise the house, certain things should be considered. The owner or agent should be reminded that all utilities must be on and working. It is impossible to test the electro-mechanical systems if there is no power or water supply. The time of day is very important. Choose a time that will allow you at least three hours of daylight. Access to all areas of the house must be made available to you. Failure to inspect a hidden or closed area could prove to be financially disastrous. Just before the inspection, review the checkpoints provided at the end of each chapter. Be sure to bring the tools that you will need as well as the worksheets for recording your findings. Always remember to take your time. Don't rush through such a major purchase.

One additional point that must be stressed is that should you find a serious defect, such as a cracked foundation, do continue the inspection yourself, but hire a professional inspector to get an expert opinion regarding the true condition of any serious defects. It is important however, that you first inquire into the inspector's background and experiences. Turn to Appendix A. It will help you to find a qualified inspector.

INSPECTING THE HOUSE

Starting from the outside and working your way into the house is a good way to conduct an inspection. Defects that are found on the exterior often have an impact on interior members. Don't forget to take notes.

Probably the most common destroyer of homes is water. In your inspection of the exterior and the interior, be on the lookout for signs of water-related damage. As you examine the subject house, consider the various avenues of water penetration. Defects in roofs, gutters and downspouts, foundations, and other areas that provide protection or drainage for the house should be thoroughly checked. For specific examples of each, refer to their respective chapters.

Go over areas of which you are not quite sure. Double-check your work. Look at the house from different angles. Walk around it several times to get different perspectives. You might be surprised to find defects in the structure, such as buckled walls, for example, that might not have been noticeable from one angle but are very pronounced from another. Tell the owner and the real estate agent that you need sufficient time to inspect. If they refuse to allow you at least three hours, it would be wise to tell them that you are not interested. Sometimes people try to hide defects and are afraid that a thorough inspection will turn up some hidden skeletons.

As you work on the house take notes on questionable areas. Don't be afraid to touch and manipulate house components. You want to use all of your senses in the inspection. Not only your eyes, but your sense of touch, smell, and hearing all can increase your awareness of potential problems. Don't be distracted by talkative agents or owners, and don't be afraid to ask questions.

If something is unusual, such as an excessive amount of peeling paint, or if you can't understand something, by all means, speak up. Asking about a defect after you own the property will be too late. If possible, have a friend or spouse with you during the inspection. Two sets of senses are better than one. Sometimes a companion can engage the owner or broker in a conversation and allow you to work quietly and effectively. Use your inspection tools, but at the same time do not cause unnecessary damage to the property. If you don't buy the house, you will be responsible for any repairs that may be needed.

Don't put yourself in any danger. Don't climb dangerous roofs, and don't expose yourself to any electrical hazards.

Appraising a Home

Appraising the value of a home is not as difficult as the "experts" would have you believe. To begin with, most appraisals are only educated guesses, a good reason for people in the business of selling and appraising properties to call the process "guesstimation." You must keep in mine, however, that the value put on a house is not just the result of someone's whim. To make a good estimate, many factors have to be taken into account such as reproduction costs, which require not only knowledge and expertise, but skill and time as well. Let it suffice here that only basic factors and considerations will be covered to enable you to come up with a fair market value of a house.

FACTORS AFFECTING
THE VALUE OF A HOUSE

One of the main considerations is to assess the property's location. What kind of neighborhood is it in? Does the overall quality of homes there warrant the asking price of the house? Drive around to get an idea of its characteristics. Is it close to public transportation, stores, and schools and recreational facilities? What kind of people live in this neighborhood? Will they be compatible with your life-style and attitudes? Will different races, creeds, or nationalities conflict with them? If you have children, consider the age grouping and size of families and how this will affect your family. What about economic factors? Does the professional or occupational means of earning a livelihood match up with yours? Will the taxation and assessment levels be too much of a burden on your budget? Are there zoning or deed restrictions that would prevent you from making improvements on the property? As you drive around the neighborhood, ask yourself whether this is really where you want to live and bring up your family. Is your house going to be the best one in the neighborhood? If so, it will probably be overpriced and difficult to sell. Has the owner overimproved the property to the extent that it no longer belongs in this neighborhood? Owning a $100,000 home in a declining area of lesser valued homes is no bargain, especially when you try to resell it at a later date.

1

If the neighborhood is compatible with your needs, the next step is to determine whether the land that the house is built on is suitable for you and your goals for living in this area. The terrain, the location of the house lot, the size and shape of the lot, and the zoning regulations must all be considered because they could add or subtract from the value of the property.

The terrain and soil should not be so shallow as to allow flooding from heavy rains. If it is, will it require expensive filling in? Does the lot require terracing to prevent washouts, or the construction of retaining walls to safeguard the house? (See Fig. 1-1) Or is it a site that will allow a pleasant view and the use of passive solar energy?

The location of the land is important in that the property may be next to vacant lots or where zoning restrictions should be in effect but are not. If there are vacant lots, check out the zoning laws with the local building department. It would be a shame if you bought an expensive home, and a few years later someone put up a fast food operation next to your property. It has happened! Check with the zoning commission to find out exactly what can and cannot be built on the adjacent land. A beautiful view or the warmth of solar heat could be blocked off by a high-rise structure. It is important to know not only about your land but that of your neighbors as well.

The size and shape of the lot is another factor to be checked. What is the sense of having an acre of land if the frontage is only 75 feet wide? The best shaped lots are square or almost square. In other words, a 40,000-square-foot lot would be 200 by 200

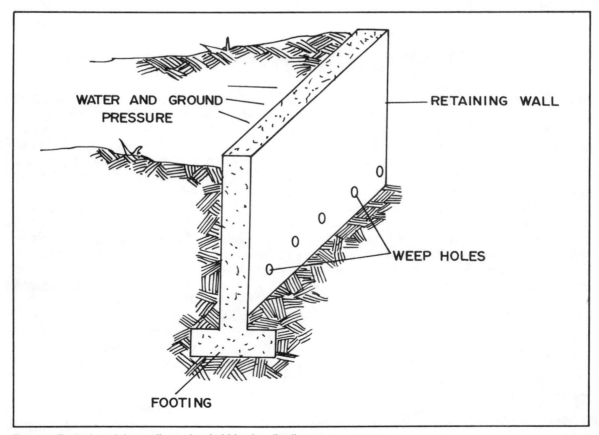

Fig. 1-1. Typical retaining wall, used to hold back soil adjacent to a structure.

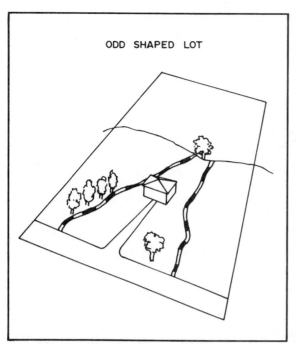

ODD SHAPED LOT

Fig. 1-2. Odd-shaped lot does not permit full usage of a parcel of land. There is little usable land in the rear of the house.

feet or a 20,000-square-foot lot would measure 100 by 200 feet. Try to stay away from odd shaped lots; a pie shaped one, as shown in Fig. 1-2, would allow you to have a huge front yard but nothing in the rear. Corner lots provide convenient access and good light, but you have to put up with a lot of noise and less privacy.

Of course, zoning regulations can also work to your disadvantage. Again, find out whether there are *easements* on the property. These are rights extended to others for access to your land for utility installation, soil removal, flood control, fire prevention, or other local government activities that are necessary for the betterment of the town or neighborhood. Ask the neighbors whether the town exercises its rights to cross the property. What effect would this have on your land? Tire tracks across the lawn for one, damaged plantings for another. Will you be able to install a fence for privacy? Probably not, because most easements call for quick and easy access to the property. This in-

fringement on your privacy has to be calculated into the final valuation of the property.

Although site improvements are discussed in Chapter 5, a final point here must be made about the importance of overimproving property. Good landscaping, which includes foundation plantings and a well maintained lawn, is always a plus, whereas excessive amounts of plantings and/or overgrown shrubs and poorly maintained lawns cut into the price of the house. The latter are curable defects, however, and do not weigh as heavily as expensive site improvements such as digging up yards to install gas lines or public sewer drains. This can be very expensive and should, therefore, be factored into the value of the house as *subsurface improvements*. A swimming pool in the back yard may be an asset for one person but just an additional annual tax expense for someone else. Be sure to figure in such additional tax or improvement costs into the total appraisal figure for the property.

ESTIMATING LAND VALUES

One step necessary to come up with a fair market value for a house is to try to determine the value of the land on which the house sits. Probably the most reliable method is to simply compare it to similar properties in like locations, which were sold during the past year or so. No great skill is needed to find the value of land, particularly if there were recent sales in the area.

First you need an up-to-date source of real estate transactions for the area in question. There are many sources, such as the local tax assessor's records, county public records, real estate brokers multiple listing records, or a local financial news reporting service. In most communities, copies of official deeds are made available at reasonable costs. An even simpler way is to call local real estate companies and tell them you are interested in a piece of land of a certain size. Most of them will be glad to quote prices over the phone with no obligation on your part: a simple, but effective and quick way to get average prices.

After you have compiled a list of several parcels of land that were recently sold, compare their similarities. Are they all approximately the same

Table 1-1. How Comparative Lot Values Can Be Applied to Determine the True Market Value of a Subject Lot.

House Lot #	1.	2.	3.
1. Date of Sale	2 months ago	6 months ago	12 months ago
2. Sale Price	$30,000	$28,000	$27,500
3. Size of Lot	100' × 200'	100' × 175'	100' × 190'
4. Neighborhood	similar	similar	similar
5. Location	good	good	good
6. Site Facilities	good	good	fair
7. Zoning Problems	none	none	none
Subject Lot			
1. Asking Price:	$45,000		
2. Size of Lot:	100' × 200'		
3. Neighborhood:	similar		
4. Location:	good		
5. Site Facilities:	good		
6. Zoning Problems:	none		

Remarks: Subject lot is overpriced. Asking price should be in the $30,000 range to be more in line with current prices.

size and shape? Are there zoning or site problems that could affect the usage of the land? Once you eliminate all undesirable lots, you can compare prices. As shown in Table 1-1, a minimum of three lots should be used in the comparison.

PRICING THE HOUSE

There are three basic approaches to find the current price of property. Of the three—*comparative sales, reproduction costs,* and *income approach*—comparative sales is probably the best method for finding the true value of a house. The income approach is the least efficient, while the reproductive cost approach requires up-to-date information on current construction costs as well as intricate methods of depreciating older established properties. Whichever approach is used, remember that the results are only estimates because the true value of any house or piece of land is also greatly influenced by what the owner is willing to sell it for, and even more so, by what the buyer is willing to pay for it. This final, agreed-upon price is the value of the property.

COMPARATIVE SALES

The greater the number of recent sales that you

use in your estimating, the more accurate will be your final estimate. As with the appraisal process of land, the need to find recent sales transactions will be the first step. Several good sources for such information would be sales data from abstract companies, county tax or record offices, commercial services with computerized sales data, or local real estate firms. Professional appraisal services are very reliable in the current data of recent sales, and a call to one of these agencies could provide you with free but useful information.

Of course, there are other factors that are used: the type of construction, the overall size of the house, the number of bedrooms and bathrooms, a finished basement, a garage, the type of heating system, and the age of the property. Obviously, a house with two bedrooms, one bath, no fireplace, and no garage cannot be equal in price to a house with three bedrooms, two bathrooms, a fireplace, and a garage. So, be sure to use some common sense when you make your appraisal judgment.

The *tax assessment* of the property by the local community is often a rather useful check on the accuracy of the market value of the property, particularly if properties are assessed at 100 percent evaluation. If you find a discrepancy of several thousand dollars between the appraisal done by a local assessor or by a reputable private appraising firm, and the asking price, find out why. You will see that quite often the owners themselves inflate the price of their homes to get as much as they can from un-suspecting buyers. On the other hand, do not be put off by too high an asking price, because it could re-flect an increase in the inflation rate, in which case everything else has gone up in price as well. Ap-plication of comparative sales techniques as applied to a subject property and to comparable sales is il-lustrated in Table 1-2.

REPRODUCTIVE COSTS

The two key figures that you need to know in using the reproductive cost method is the current price per square foot for new construction, and the area of the house in square footage of living area. The first can be gathered by calling up local con-tractors to determine the current figures. They should vary little from one contractor to another. The next step involves a little more work, but it is still simple. Go to the subject house and measure all of the habitable areas, including finished base-ment areas, etc. When you have the square footage, just multiply it by the current square foot costs. (See Table 1-3.) The figure you get should reflect what the house would approximately cost if it were rebuilt at current costs. Keep in mind that this figure will have to be adjusted either up or down depending

upon the age of the house and whether there are any special amenities in the house such as an air conditioning system, several working fireplaces, etc. Generally, depreciation in older homes is offset by good structural and mechanical conditions and by modernizations.

INCOME APPROACH

The income approach really does not apply to single family residences, but it is often used as a basis to check and confirm relative values gained from the other two methods. You will have to com-pute the average rental value of houses. You find this by averaging several rental figures. Current rental figures can be gotten from the rental section of local newspapers. After you have computed the average figure, multiply it by 110, which is a standard fig-ure used by home appraisers to figure current market prices. If the average rent in the area is $900 per month, the appraised value of the house would be $99,000. Keep in mind that this approach is not absolutely reliable because other factors already dis-cussed influence the rental value and thus the end figure.

PUTTING IT ALL TOGETHER

By correlating the three figures that you de-rived from the different estimating approaches and

Table 1-2. Comparative Sales Analysis of Three Properties To Determine Value of Subject House.

Subject Property		Sale #1	Sale #2	Sale #3
Price	$100,000	$105,000	$98,000	$101,000
Date Sold		4 months ago	12 months ago	6 months ago
Land Size	100' × 200'	100' × 175'	100' × 200'	100' × 180'
Land Value	$30,000	$28,000	$27,500	$29,000
Building Size	2000 sq. '	1800 sq. '	1500 sq. '	1800 sq. '
# of Bedrooms	3	3	3	3
# of Baths	3	2	1 1/2	2
Garages	1	2	1	1
Building Age	5 years	10 years	12 years	8 years
Neighborhood	similar	similar	better	similar
Zoning Problems	none	none	none	none
Assessed Value	$99,000	$101,000	$92,000	$100,000

Remarks: as can be seen from the comparison of recently sold comparable homes the asking price of $100,000 is a reasonable figure for this property.

Table 1-3. How To Estimate Reproductive Costs.

Current Costs of Construction Per Square Foot:	$35.00
Square Foot Area of Habitable Areas of House:	2,000
Reproductive Cost of House Minus Cost of Land:	$70,000

tying in the land value with the current assessed value of the property, as shown in Table 1-4, it would indicate that the asking price of $100,000 is justified and a fair market value.

As has been shown, almost anyone can appraise the overall current value of land and property. The location of the house is of prime importance, and if the neighborhood and its site does not suit you, discount the house. The total cost of a house will include not only the cost of the house itself but also the cost of the land. Different appraisal approaches can be effectively used to derive a fair market value for a home. Actually, the comparative cost analysis should be used to determine a true estimated value. Reproductive costs and the income approach should be used to give estimates as a comparison. In addition, the current assessed value of the property will also give you an indication of the true value. By correlating all of these factors and appraisal approaches, you should be able to "zoom in" on the approximate overall prices of properties.

CHECKPOINTS

- Is the community the kind that you want to live in?
- What is the quality of the homes in the neighborhood?
- Are the neighbors likely to be compatible with lifestyle?
- Are the schools your children will attend nearby?
- Are there suitable recreational facilities within walking distance?
- Are there adequate shopping facilities close by?
- Are there zoning or deed restrictions on the property?
- Has proper landscaping been done to prevent soil erosion?
- What about zoning restrictions on adjacent properties?
- Can your neighbors erect eyesores and get away with it?
- Is the lot an odd shaped one or a corner lot?
- Are there any easements on the property?
- Is the lot arranged to suit your privacy needs?
- Are there improvements on the property that conflict with your life-style or needs? (A swimming pool doesn't do anyone any good if it is not used.)
- Is the value of the land comparable to that of other recently sold properties?
- Do similar properties sold recently have similar price tags?
- Is the house assessment close in price range to the asking price?
- Can the subject house be reproduced today for the asking price?
- Does a correlation of the three approaches come close to the asking price?
- Do you feel that the house is worth the asking price?

Table 1-4. Correlate Various Value Estimations for Current Market Value.

Asking Price:	$100,000	
Comparative Cost:	$ 98,000	to $105,000 (range)
Reproductive Cost:	$ 70,000	(minus land cost)
Land Value:	$ 30,000	
Income Approach:	$ 99,000	
Assessed Valuation:	$ 99,000	

Roofs and Related Members

The inspection of a roof entails both a visual examination of the exterior coverings, which is done from the outside, and a thorough checking of the wood framing and sheathing, which is done from the attic. The inspection from the attic is necessary because some defects might not show up during the exterior inspection (leakage that has over a period seriously decayed sheathing and rafters) and can only be detected during a careful check of the underside of the roof.

EXTERIOR

With your binoculars, survey the entire roof carefully, looking particularly at the south side because that is the side most exposed to the awesome effects of the Sun's rays. (See Fig. 2-1.) Check the roof from different angles and distances. Record on your worksheet any defects that you see.

Stand back from the house and check the horizontal line at the roof peak, which is called the *ridge*. Do you see a noticeable sag in its line? If so, this could mean structural damage or failure. Make

a note of it for later scrutiny from the attic. Are there sections of the roof that appear to have sagged or dipped? This too could be a structural defect. Visual clues, such as sagging or dipping, are signs of poor bracing or inadequate support of rafters or roof sheathing. If, upon your inspection from the attic, you see further signs of structural stress, you might want a professional to reevaluate the roof's condition.

The amount of layers of shingles on a roof is important. Most building codes limit the layers to two because it is feared that the weight of more than two layers could cause structural damage to the roof framing members. During your inspection, try to determine how many shingle layers there are. Ask the owner if he knows. If he doesn't, examine the roof line at the *rake* (the side edge of the roof) with your binoculars. If, as in Fig. 2-2, you see the ends of several layers of overlapping shingles, assume that the roof has two or more and so be especially alert in your examination of the underside of the roof from the attic. If you have any questions about the strength of the framing, call in a roofing con-

Fig. 2-1. Shingles on a roof with a southern exposure will quickly develop the deteriorated appearance.

tractor to give you his professional opinion.

While you are looking at the pitched roof with your binoculars, note the type of shingles with which the roof is covered. The most commonly used are asphalt shingles as in Fig. 2-3. If you notice many missing granules, curling edges, cracking and general brittleness, you can be sure that they are in the process of failing. Ask the owner about the age of these shingles. Most asphalt shingles have a useful life of 15 to 20 years. Anything after that should be considered strictly on borrowed time.

More expensive and less common shingles, such as slate and clay tile, are less prone to falling apart and last anywhere from 50 to 100 years. In checking these types, look for missing or cracked shingles. Wood shingles are sometimes used on roofs. Figure 2-4 shows the typical damage found in wood shingles. In your inspection of these, be on the lookout for mildew, decay, and rot, particularly on the north side of the house.

Roofs with level surfaces or with just a slight pitch often have rolled roofing material or tar and gravel coverings. If the subject roof is accessible, and it is not dangerous for you to climb up, by all means check the covering from the top of the roof.

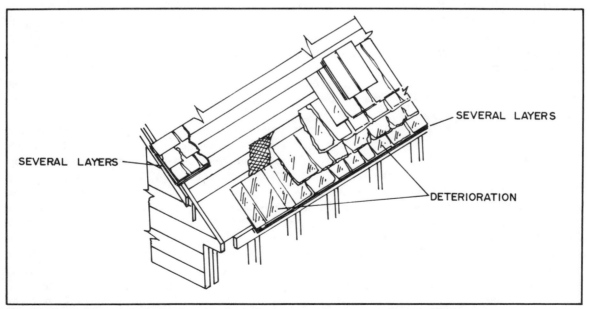

Fig. 2-2. Several layers of overlapping shingles indicates more than one covering of shingles.

Fig. 2-3. Asphalt shingles on a roof. Note deterioration in the valley and adjacent to the chimney. Water penetrations from these two areas is a certainty.

Look for open seams between the layers of rolled roofing. Over a period of time, they open and allow water to penetrate. Exposed nail heads are another entranceway for water and should be covered with a protective coat of roof cement. Remember, tar and gravel take quite a beating from the sunlight and will in time form blisters and patched bare spots, as shown in Fig. 2-5. Be on the lookout for these "symptoms." As with rolled roofing material, look for cracks or openings in the seams. If you notice blisters, be sure not to step on them because broken blisters will most certainly allow water to seep into the house.

With your binoculars, check the *eaves* of the roof (the lower edge of a roof that projects beyond the house) for signs of decay in the wood shingle starter course. (See Fig. 2-6.) Although wood shingles at the eaves tend to rot out in a very short time, some roofers still use these for *starter courses* (first layer) instead of asphalt shingles. Decay in them will bring about further rot of adjacent wood framing. Be sure to check the eaves on both sides of the house, porches, and garages for signs of deterioration. If the wood looks "punky" or is covered with mildew,

Fig. 2-4. Wood shingles will develop mildew, which in turn results in decay and the need for replacement.

Fig. 2-5. Bare spots will, in time, crack and allow water penetrations into the structure.

Fig. 2-6. Wood starter shingles at the eaves will eventually decay. This is the result.

you can assume that decay has set in and will get worse as time passes. Make a note of it for future replacement.

ROOF OPENINGS

Any place where there is an opening in the roof for a chimney or vent pipe, you will find that water can penetrate much more easily than if there were no openings at all. Therefore, be sure to examine each mounted structure and projection carefully, particularly where they meet the roof sheathing. The metal flashing protecting these roof openings easily deteriorates and/or opens up to allow water to enter the house. Be sure to check these areas on a regular basis.

A defective *chimney* is often the source of water penetration. Give the chimney your best attention. First, check the flashing around the base. (See Fig. 2-7.) Is the flashing tight or is it loose and pulling away? Does it look as if it has been plastered over with roofing cement? If so, the flashing might be defective because roofing cement seals it up only temporarily. Next, check the mortar joints between bricks to see that no mortar is missing or deteriorating. Can you see spaces between the bricks? Are the bricks loose and ready to fall out? If the chimney that you are inspecting looks like Fig. 2-8, you will need the help of a mason to restore it. This would be an added cost to consider for your final evaluation.

Plumbing stack vents exit roofs to safely disperse sewer gases. Roof connections should be carefully checked for possible weak links that could allow water to enter the house. Look for openings in the roof adjacent to the vent pipes. The joint between the

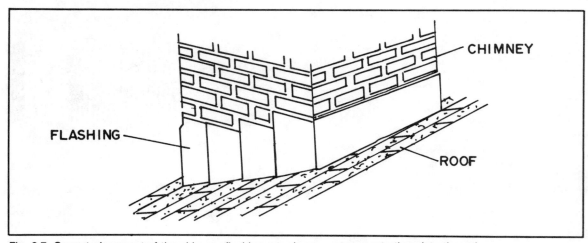

Fig. 2-7. Correct placement of the chimney flashing retards any water penetrations into the attic.

10

Fig. 2-8. This chimney exhibits major damage not only to the cap (top section) but also to all of its mortar joints.

Fig. 2-9. Note elbow at the top of vent. This prevents any accidental entrance of solid objects into the plumbing vent pipe, which could cause serious problems with the venting of sewer gases.

sion or deterioration on the units and for signs of joint failure between the vent and the roof. Water leakage at these joints can be effectively corrected with an asphalt caulking compound.

Skylights, as shown in Fig. 2-10, should be checked for broken or missing glass as well as for signs of water leakage. Wooden frames should be checked for decay and deterioration, and metal units should be checked for corrosion and rust build-up. If the skylight has rusted out or has extensive decay, consider replacing it. Make a note of any deficiencies on your worksheet.

If a TV antenna, as shown in Fig. 2-11, is found strapped to either a chimney or a vent pipe it should be removed. Strong winds can cause serious dam-

Fig. 2-10. A close examination of this skylight shows cracked glass, rusted-through metal, and defective flashing—all will result in water penetrations.

vent pipe and the roof is very vulnerable to leaks and should be sealed if necessary and checked annually. Figure 2-9 shows a typical plumbing vent on a flat roof.

Roof ventilation units should be checked for signs of water penetrations as well. Look for corro-

Fig. 2-11. The damage done to this chimney is directly related to the stress caused by strong winds blowing against the TV antenna.

age by cracking chimney walls and opening vent connections. If the antenna is attached directly to the roof, be sure to check the surrounding roof areas for rusting nail heads, cracks in roofing material, and openings in the roof covering.

GUTTERS AND DOWNSPOUTS

All houses should have gutters and downspouts to carry rain and melting snow away from the house. A house without them invites water in the basement, decay of exterior wood members, and erosion of the foundation soil. The cost of installing and maintaining gutters and downspouts is far less than repairing damage caused by water. See Fig. 2-12.

Gutters are usually made of either wood or metal. Poorly maintained wood gutters decay rapidly and in turn, allow water to damage adjacent wood members. See Fig. 2-13. In your inspection, be sure

to check the joints of gutters very carefully. This is particularly important in corners or places where gutters are spliced together because decay will set in at those spots first. If you have a ladder, climb up *carefully* and check the gutter from one end to the other. With your screwdriver probe the wood. Does the screwdriver penetrate easily? Does the wood appear mushy? Both are signs that the gutter is rotting away. Wood gutters, like metal ones, can be patched. Once they start to deteriorate badly, however, it might be wise to replace them.

Metal gutters are less susceptible to deterioration, except at their seams. Check those for corrosion or rust as well as for holes that need patching. Make a note of any defects.

Gutters should be pitched toward the downspouts so rainwater and melting snow can drain away properly. Check the gutters to see that they are not loose or cluttered with leaves, twigs, and mineral granules from roof shingles. Cluttered gutters as shown in Fig. 2-14 will cause drainage problems, so be sure to go over the maintenance tips in Chapter 21 to avoid this. Look for sags or dips that could cause poor drainage and eventual leaks.

Downspouts transfer water from the gutters away from the house foundation. In checking them, see whether they are properly attached to the gutters. Look for open seams, as can be seen in Fig. 2-15, and check for corrosion or holes in the elbow sections at the base of the downspout. Hold onto a downspout and pull at it. If it moves away from the house the support straps should be renailed to the house. Does the base of the downspout have an elbow leading to a splash plate so that roof drainage can be carried away from the house? Refer back to Fig. 2-12. If the downspout is discharging its water directly to areas next to the foundation, such as in Fig. 2-16, note it on your worksheet.

And what is the best time to check downspouts and gutters? During a heavy rainstorm, of course. If you are lucky, it will be raining on the day of your inspection.

TREES

Although trees close to the house might be ex-

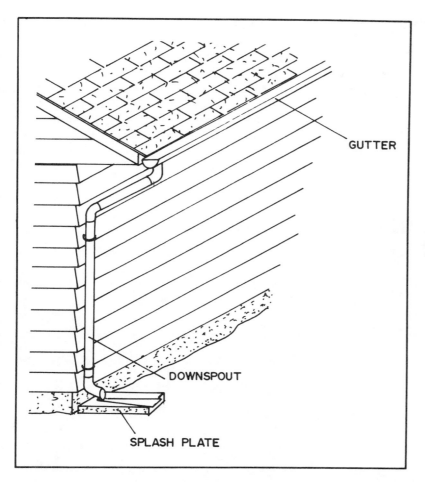

Fig. 2-12. Proper way to discharge roof drainage away from the foundation.

GUTTER

DOWNSPOUT

SPLASH PLATE

Fig. 2-13. The open joint in this wood gutter allows water to cause decay in trim and siding. Proper caulking will reduce this possibility.

Fig. 2-14. Failure to clean gutters of accumulated leaves will result in overflow, with the possibility of damage to the interior of the house.

Fig. 2-15. Note rusted downspout connections and open seam in the horizontal run. Both indicate replacement of the downspouts is necessary.

Fig. 2-16. The results of roof drainage discharging directly to the foundation.

tremely attractive, branches touching the roof can cause rather serious damage to roofing materials and to the roof framing itself. All you need is a high gust of wind, and a heavy branch could break off and strike the roof. Also, too much shade allows mildew to thrive on moist roofing. Falling leaves are the main culprit for blocked gutters, and we know the consequences of this tree related problem. Make a note of trees such as in Fig. 2-17. Pruning overhanging branches or the removal of the entire tree might be necessary to preserve the roof and its related members.

INTERIOR

Many of the ills of the roof can only be surveyed

Fig. 2-17. Overhanging branches cause a variety of moisture related problems. Judicial pruning will overcome any mildew/decay resulting from too much shade.

from the underside of the roof—in the attic. If the subject house has an attic, be sure to examine it thoroughly. Read Chapter 14 for details on the attic inspection.

CHECKPOINTS

- Inspect all areas of the roof.
- Look for sags or dips in roof lines.
- Are shingles losing their granules?
- Look for curling, cracked, missing, or torn shingles.
- How old is the roof? (Check with the owner—if it is 15 to 20 years or older, it is on borrowed time)
- How many layers of shingles are on the roof?
- Examine the southern exposure.
- Look for missing or cracked tiles or slate.
- Check for mildew, decay, or rot in wood shingles.
- Are there cracked, blistered, or open seams in flat roofs?
- What is the condition of the eaves shingles? (Rotting or decaying?)
- Inspect for deteriorating mortar joints in chimneys.

- Check for defective flashing on roof mounted members.
- Note roof joints on plumbing stacks that appear defective.
- Check for signs of water penetration around roof vents.
- Examine the condition of skylights. (Broken glass, missing glass, frame either rotting or rusting?)
- Are TV antennas attached to chimneys or vent pipes?
- Are there gutters and downspouts on the house?
- Do wood gutters appear to be decaying?
- Are metal gutters rusting out?
- Are gutters properly pitched and secured to the house?
- Are the downspouts attached to the gutters, and do they carry water away from the house?
- Inspect for loose straps, open seams, and defective elbows.
- Are there any trees that need to be pruned or cut back?
- Thoroughly check the attic for any signs of water penetration or damage.

Exterior Walls, Windows, and Doors

The exterior walls, windows, and doors are the first line of defense against the elements. Defects in any of them will eventually lead to costly repairs. Rain and melting snow cause decay of wooden members and deterioration of mortar joints and masonry units. It is very important, therefore, that you scrutinize all very carefully. As you walk around the house, try to get an overall impression of the exterior of the house first. Step back and eyeball it from various angles and distances. Are portions of the walls bulging? Can you detect window or door lines that are out of square? Are all the corners of the house plumb? If, after your inspection, you have serious doubts about the condition of the exterior, do call a professional for help.

WALLS

Stand back from the house about 20 feet and sight down each wall from bottom up and from end to end. The corners should line up, and there should be no noticeable dip or sag in any of them. If there is, try to find out from where the ill stems. For ex-

ample, it could be settlement of foundation walls, or from wood rot and structural pest damage. A follow-up investigation inside is essential. Very slight displacement of walls should not alarm you, though, because all houses will have some settlement. (See Fig. 3-1.)

Although various types of house framing systems are found in different parts of the country, the vital members in each framing system are the same. Figures 3-2 and 3-3 show the basic parts of a house wall frame. The *foundation sill* is the first part of the frame to be placed, and it rests directly on the foundation. From here the rest of the house frame develops. The *exterior walls* consist of *wall studs* and *wall sheathing*. Because the vertical spaces between studs act as flues to transmit flames in the event of fire, *fire stops* are installed into the walls. They are wood obstructions placed between studs to prevent fire from spreading in these natural flue spaces. Because most of the framing is concealed, the only places to detect any defects are in the basement and in the attic. Refer to Chapters 4 and 14 for what to look for.

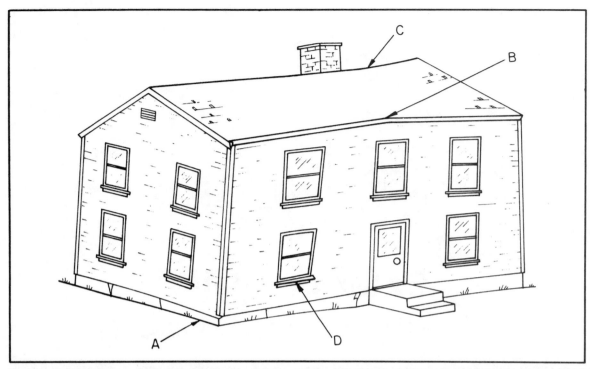

Fig. 3-1. Major displacement of roof, walls, and foundation. (A) foundation with settlement cracks. (B) indicates the major displacement in the eaves. (C) a sagged ridge line. (D) typical window alignment problems. Courtesy of Forest Service, USDA.

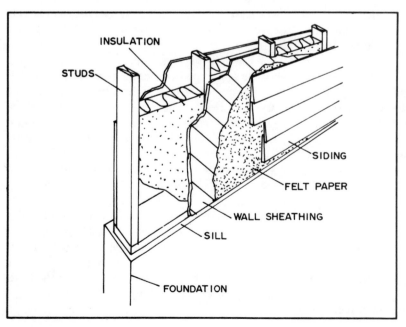

Fig. 3-2. Basic wall framing.

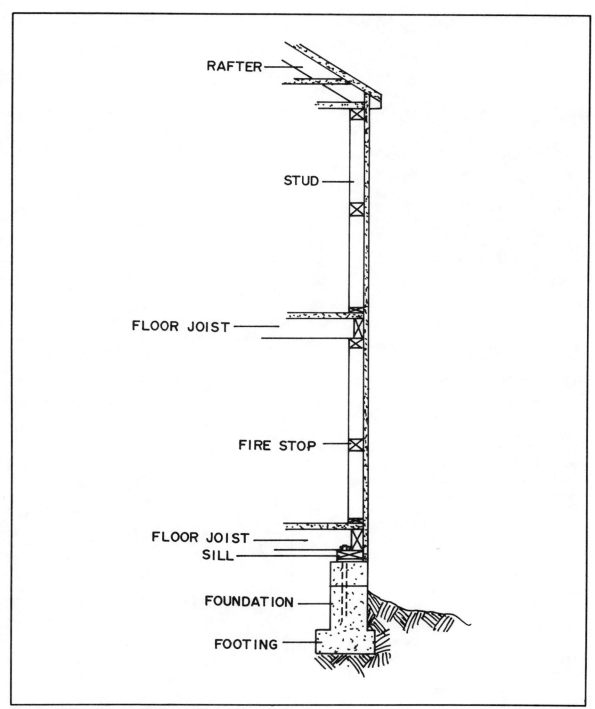

RAFTER

STUD

FLOOR JOIST

FIRE STOP

FLOOR JOIST

SILL

FOUNDATION

FOOTING

Fig. 3-3. The common members necessary to frame a house.

Fig. 3-4. Failure to pay attention to low wood members will result in this type of deterioration.

EXTERIOR COVERINGS

Many different types of exterior siding are used as coverings over the house frame. Wood shingles, wood clapboard, aluminum and vinyl siding, brick, and stucco are the most often seen. Sometimes wood panels, asbestos-cement shingles, and asphalt shingles are used on the exterior of homes. These materials are meant to make the walls weathertight and to create an attractive facade. In addition to the siding, you will also have to check the trim members for any signs of decay or deterioration. (See Fig. 3-4.)

Wood Shingles

Cedar shingles are by far the best quality material that can be used for exterior coverings. They are long-lasting and even more so if they are stained rather than painted. As you know, painted areas will need repainting in a short time--usually every five years or so, depending on the climatic conditions. A stained shingled house can last up to 10 years without laborious scraping and painting. Fig-

ure 3-5 shows what painted siding looks like after several years.

While checking wood shingles, look for cracked, missing, or decaying sections as shown in Fig. 3-6. Take your screwdriver and carefully probe suspect areas. Pay particular attention to spots that are shaded by shrubs and trees. Because the sun does not get a chance to dry covered shingles, decay fungus is likely to thrive there. If you do find seriously decayed and rotted-out sections of shingles, try to reach the wood sheathing behind the shingles. If you find that the sheathing is rotted as well, you may have a serious structural problem and an expensive repair job on your hands.

Wood Clapboard

Clapboard or *bevel siding*, as it is sometimes called, has some distinctive characteristics. The most outstanding is that if does not hold paint readily, particularly if conditions are very moist inside as well as outside. (See Fig. 3-7.) If you are looking at painted clapboard, don't be fooled by its apparent

Fig. 3-5. A combination of lack of maintenance and poor house ventilation has caused this extreme condition of paint peeling. The small gable vents provide little ventilation.

Fig. 3-6. Decaying wood shingles should be replaced before the decay spreads to adjacent wood members.

good condition from a distance; if you look more closely you will most likely see marks of previous scraping and peeling. Make sure to mark down your findings, particularly if evidence of scraping is plentiful.

An older home should always be checked to see whether it has proper *roof* and *wall ventilation*. Figure 3-8 shows the different types of ventilation units usually found on a house. If the siding has many sections of scraped and repainted areas, you probably should count on the drudgery of more scraping and painting in the very near future. Consultation with a contractor to provide appropriate ventilation inside the house may cut down this chronic problem.

The joints of any siding, but particularly those of clapboard, are important to check because they often have open gaps between the siding. The installer may have been careless or gaps may have developed through shrinkage. No matter what the cause, the openings must be caulked to cut back on water damage and absorption by the exposed ends.

Fig. 3-7. Clapboard does not maintain its painted surface and needs constant maintenance. Courtesy of Forest Service, USDA.

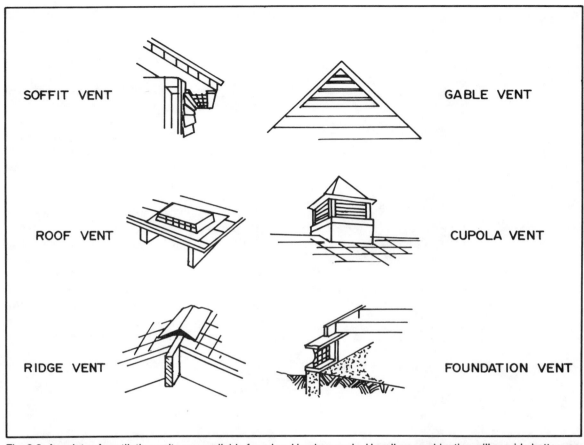

GABLE VENT

ROOF VENT

CUPOLA VENT

RIDGE VENT

FOUNDATION VENT

Fig. 3-8. A variety of ventilation units are available from local lumber yards. Usually a combination will provide better ventilation than just one type.

An open joint is illustrated in Fig. 3-9.

Wood Panels

Wood panels can be made of many different kinds of materials. The most commonly used are those that are made of glued *veneers* of several plies of wood or wood by-products. The key to their integrity is the amount and type of glue used to bond them together. Clearly, for exterior panels you need a high-strength weather resistant glue. Figure 3-10 shows a good example of this type of exterior siding. (Note the lack of gable vents.)

In your inspection of panel siding then, look for tell-tale signs of *delamination* (separation) and glue

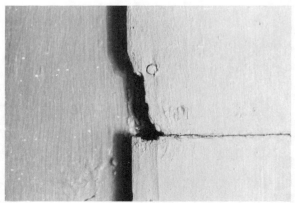

Fig. 3-9. Open joints result in rapid decay of both the siding and the wall framing.

Fig. 3-10. Wood panels are sometimes used in place of standard wood shingles. Don't make the mistake of not providing for gable vents.

failure. In accessible areas, gently pull the edges of the panels. Do the top layers of plywood peel off easily? Check the butt joints between the panels. Do they look buckled and swollen? Do the panels show signs of decay and deterioration? If so, some sections may have to be replaced. Make a note of your findings.

Also check the proximity of any wood siding to the soil. The higher the wood is off the ground, the less chance there is of wood-boring insect damage and decay. (Most building codes, by the way, require several inches of clearance between the bottom of the siding and the soil. If the bottom of the siding is in direct contact with the soil, as shown in Fig. 3-11, note it on your worksheet.) When you purchase the house, be sure to provide for proper grading and clearances to cut down on wood damage.

As you already know from Chapter 2, the southern portion of the house takes a terrible beating from the sun. Walk around the house, and you will know immediately which side is exposed to the south by the dry, brittle, and warped shingles; cracked and discolored clapboards; and blistered, delaminated panels. These areas should always get extra special attention when it comes time to add a protective coat of paint or stain. Figure 3-12 shows the effects of the sun's rays.

Aluminum and Vinyl Siding

Two new entries into the exterior siding field are *aluminum* and *vinyl siding*. Although they both are very attractive and almost maintenance-free, they do pose some problems. To begin with, these types of sidings are almost always put directly over old wood siding. What the manufacturers and in-

Fig. 3-11. Wood in direct contact with the soil, unless specially treated, will rot out in a short time. These shingles are ripe for wood-boring insects.

Fig. 3-12. Shrinking, cracked, and blistered shingles are the results of the southern exposure of this house, as well as lack of maintenance by the owners.

stallers fail to tell the unwary homeowner is that a house needs to breathe. Aluminum and vinyl sidings easily trap moisture which, having no place to go, causes severe damage to all adjacent wood members. If this goes on for any length of time, severe structural damage could result. Because you can't take the siding off, you should make it a point to double-check for sufficient ventilation that will prevent this problem.

Both aluminum and vinyl siding dent easily. Therefore, check carefully all low areas or sections that children or objects may contact. Although either kind of covering can be repaired, it is difficult at times and thus quite costly. Figure 3-13 illustrates what can happen to this type of siding. Also look for loose or sagging sections, which indicates that the material was not properly attached to the house. Note any such deficiencies on your worksheet and bring them to the attention of the owner.

Stucco

Some houses have a *stucco* finish, which is ba-

sically a cement finish on a concrete block or wood wall, applied in several thin coats to make one exterior covering. In time, however, small cracks develop from shrinkage of the material or from slight movements of the house. These cracks will widen and allow water seepage if they are not taken care of. (See Fig. 3-14.) In your inspection of such a covering, be sure to check for cracks, however small, and note the need for repairs. Look for chipped, loose, cracked, or broken sections as well. Be sure to check behind bushes and hidden areas around the perimeter of the house. Usually owners do not check inaccessible areas, and thus the damage can sometimes be extensive.

Veneer Walls

Veneer walls are wood frame walls covered with

Fig. 3-13. Cracked and damaged aluminum siding will cause water penetrations and decay to framing members under it.

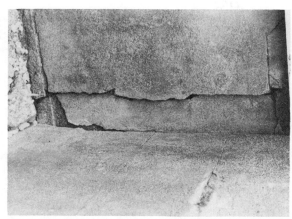

Fig. 3-14. Stucco cracks must be repaired before the damage becomes excessive.

masonry, which is held in place by metal ties that are fastened to wood framing. (See Fig. 3-15.) Shrinkage in the wooden walls or foundation settlement often cause this type of wall to crack. Cracks usually appear first around door and window frames. Failure to correctly repair and seal these will bring about further water deterioration. Be sure to check for damaged mortar joints, broken or missing brick and stones, and areas of walls that seem to be pulling away from the house. Record their location on your worksheet for later repairs.

Asbestos-Cement Shingles

Asbestos-cement shingles, sometimes called *composition shingles*, are made of asbestos fibers and portland cement. Although they are immune to the effects of the weather, resist rot, and are much disliked by wood-boring insects, they are brittle and can be damaged easily. Damage usually occurs on the lower courses of shingles, which often fall victim to children's poor aim. (See Fig. 3-16.)

Asphalt Siding

Another type of siding that you are likely to find on older homes is *asphalt shingles*. When inspecting

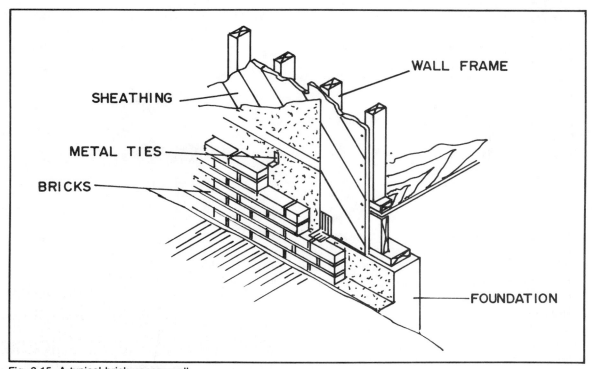

SHEATHING

WALL FRAME

METAL TIES

BRICKS

FOUNDATION

Fig. 3-15. A typical brick veneer wall.

Fig. 3-16. Asbestos-cement shingles are very brittle and crack easily. This is one of the major drawbacks of this type of siding.

asphalt shingles, look for cracked and eroded sections. Take your screwdriver and test the wood sheathing under damaged areas to determine the condition of framing. Figure 3-17 is a good example of this type of siding.

EXTERIOR TRIM

Trim members of a house serve to protect the joints and edges of exterior coverings. They are mostly made of wood. They include *fascia boards* (horizontal board just under the eaves), shutters, door and window sills, moldings, *soffits* (decorative supports under eaves), and any other decorative pieces found on the exterior of a house. Because they are continually exposed to rain, wind, and sun, they too deteriorate and must be checked and maintained.

Trim should be checked particularly in the joints, because that is where water will attack first. Take your screwdriver and press it into the wood as illustrated in Fig. 3-18. If some sections are soft and crumbly, probe all around that section to detect how far the wood has deteriorated. Make a note on your worksheet to caulk and seal any open joints and to repair and replace decayed wood sections.

Check metal trim for missing sections or for those that need painting. (See Fig. 3-19.) See if there are open joints. If so, always try to probe the wood sheathing under the open gaps. Record any defects that will need repairs.

WINDOWS

Windows are checked from both the exterior

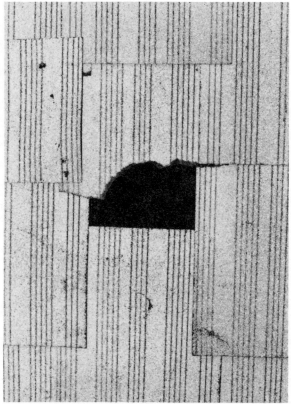

Fig. 3-17. Although asphalt shingles are not brittle like asbestos-cement, they tear easily. Resulting damage to the building is the same.

Fig. 3-18. Low trim areas are one of the first to show signs of decay and deterioration. Be sure to probe all such areas for signs of insect activity.

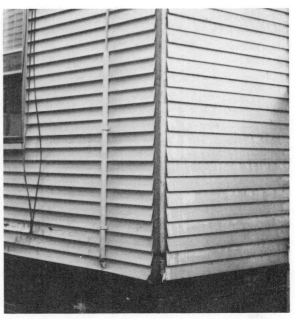

Fig. 3-19. Missing trim will result in decay of those exposed wood members.

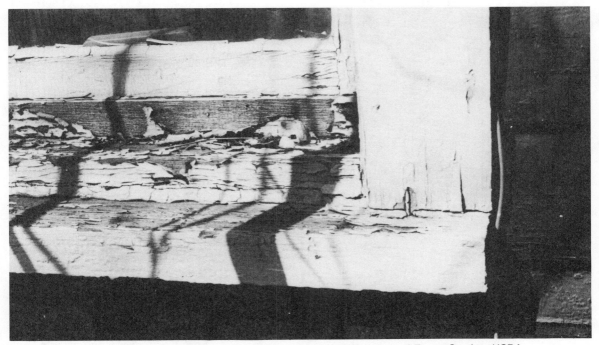

Fig. 3-20. Deferred maintenance will often result in extensive decay. Courtesy of Forest Service, USDA.

and the interior. Outside, check their overall conditions. Are there broken panes of glass? Does the window trim need scraping and painting as in Fig. 3-20? Are there storm windows, and what condition are they in? Are there screens on the windows? Note visible defects on your worksheet.

Metal frame windows are notorious for getting quite cold during the winter. Often water condenses on the inside glass as warmer air from inside the house strikes the panes. This water will store in the frames, and the frames will soon rust and corrode. (See Fig. 3-21.) Metal frame windows also have poor thermal resistance and, therefore, the heat bills are most likely higher than in a house with wooden frames.

If the windows have storm windows, check that

Fig. 3-21. Rusting and peeling paint is common with metal windows. Annual sanding and painting will be required to keep them from deteriorating.

they are tight and do not allow cold air to get into the house. If they are made of wood, check for decay and whether they need painting. Metal storm windows should be checked for pitting, which is often found along the seashore. Excessive pitting will eventually call for replacement of the windows.

Don't be alarmed if you find houses that don't have storm windows, because sometimes double- or even triple-glazed windows are used in lieu of storm windows. The beauty of this type of insulated glass is that it will greatly reduce heat losses and will almost never form condensation. If you find such windows in addition to storm windows, consider yourself lucky, because the savings in heat bills are substantial.

DOORS

Exterior doors differ from interior ones in several ways. They usually are *solid core* and thus provide for less heat loss and better protection against uninvited guests. Furthermore, because they are exposed to the weather their quality is such that they tend to warp and deteriorate less than regular interior doors. Knock on it if you are not sure what type it is: a hollow ring will tell you that it is not a solid core. If you come across a door of poor quality mounted on the exterior of a house, such as in Fig. 3-22, be sure to check for delamination of surfaces, peeling paint, and decayed wood.

In colder climates, it is advisable to have storm doors. They should open and close easily and fit properly. If they don't, a blast of wind is likely to warp the frame out of shape. Generally, check the paint, see whether it needs weatherstripping and whether it has a screen panel for the warmer months. Record areas that need repairs.

Summary. In your inspection of the walls, windows, and doors always be on the lookout for potential defects that may not be a concern at the time of the inspection, but could be later. Particularly important are joints and places where siding, trim, windows, and doors meet. Remember that rain or snow will be your greatest enemy and that you must keep a constant vigil to maintain the exterior in a tight, water-resistant condition. This means semiannual or more frequent inspections and caulk-

Fig. 3-22. Note the lack of an awning over the door and the missing gutter to the right. Both will result in water damage to the door and adjacent wood members.

ing, weatherstripping, and replacement of deteriorated parts.

CHECKPOINTS

- Inspect exterior walls for signs of bulging, dips, or sags.
- Look for out-of-plumb corners.
- On wood siding, check for decay, peeling paint, missing or cracked sections, curling or brittle areas, and open joints.
- Inspect paneled areas for delaminations, open joints, warped or rotting sections.
- Note the proximity of the wood to the ground. A minimum of 6 inches is considered safe against decay and insect attacks.
- Check aluminum and vinyl siding for dents, open joints, sagging sections, and general weather tightness.
- Check stucco wall finishes for cracks, missing or bulging sections.
- Examine veneer walls for cracks in mortar joints or in bricks.
- Look for bulges or pulling away of veneer finishes from framing members.
- Check asbestos-cement or asphalt shingles for missing, broken, or deteriorated areas.
- Check trim members for general weathertightness at joints.
- Note all decay or deterioration of trim members.
- Check windows for broken panes, missing glass, deteriorating wood members, and general weathertightness.
- Check doors for delaminating sections, peeling paint, weathertightness, and general overall conditions.
- Are all storm windows and storm doors weathertight?
- Check overall joints and sections where different building parts meet. Are all gaps/joints properly caulked and sealed?

Foundations

Because the foundation is the supporting member of the entire wall structure of a house, its importance can hardly be overemphasized. Numerous problems, such as water penetration, cold air leaks, and insect and rodent infestations can be traced to a faulty foundation. A defective foundation, in turn, can be traced to poor footings, improper soil grading, a high water table, and poor original construction and design. With this in mind, be sure to take your time outside and be very meticulous in your inspection of the basement and crawl spaces. Refer to the many illustrations in this chapter to aid you in your understanding of what a foundation is and what it is supposed to do.

A foundation can be made of stone, brick, concrete block, poured concrete, or it can be just a plain slab of concrete. A foundation wall is usually laid on a *footing*, which is an enlarged base resting on undisturbed soil, the purpose of which is to spread the transmitted load of a house. (See Fig. 4-1.) In northern climates, the footing is usually below the frost line, which in some locations is 4 feet or more in depth. Many older homes, particularly those with stone foundations, do not have footings, however. This sometimes can create problems. (More of that further on in the chapter.)

EXTERIOR FOUNDATION INSPECTION

Slowly walk around the perimeter of the house and try to determine of what material the foundation is made. Look for cracks and try to discern their patterns, because they signal deterioration and tell you about the general condition of the foundation footing, the water table around and under the foundation, and the type of soil on which the foundation rests.

Stone Foundations

Stone foundation walls are usually 16 inches or more in width. Older ones may have no footings, and parts of the wall below grade level often have no mortar in the joints between the stones. Although footings and mortared joints are essential today, the original designs and construction of builders of yesteryear are superb and have withstood the test of

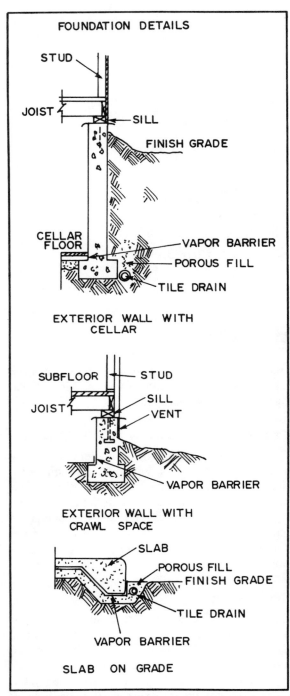

FOUNDATION DETAILS

STUD

JOIST

SILL

FINISH GRADE

CELLAR FLOOR

VAPOR BARRIER

POROUS FILL

TILE DRAIN

EXTERIOR WALL WITH
CELLAR

SUBFLOOR — STUD

SILL

JOIST — VENT

VAPOR BARRIER

EXTERIOR WALL WITH
CRAWL SPACE

SLAB

POROUS FILL

FINISH GRADE

TILE DRAIN

VAPOR BARRIER

SLAB ON GRADE

Fig. 4-1. Foundation details for walls with cellars, crawl space, and slab construction.

time. It is only when ill-advised structural changes to the foundation walls or to the house are made that the foundation may give. During your inspection, check stone foundations for deterioration in mortar joints. Take your screwdriver and gently probe the mortar in several random places. Does it break away easily? If it does, the mortar is no longer functional. Are there holes in the foundation walls? If, so, they should be patched. Crack patterns may point to serious structural problems; usually large cracks that separate the stones and run in a vertical pattern from the top of the foundation to below grade level indicate a high degree of settlement. (See Fig. 4-2.) Be sure to note such findings and check the interior portion of the foundation to see whether there is corresponding damage. Missing or deteriorating mortar should be repaired and wide cracks in walls, particularly at the corners, should be checked by a professional.

Fig. 4-2. A major crack of this size indicates serious problems with the foundation footing. A structural engineer should be consulted to determine the full extent of the problem.

Fig. 4-3. Typical water related damage to brickwork.

Brick Foundations

Many older homes were built on brick foundation walls. If there is damage, it is usually done by water that attacks the mortar joints and often the bricks themselves, as shown in Fig. 4-3. In some cases, soft bricks were used on the exterior of the house rather than the more weather-resistant hard brick. The soft bricks crumble and flake with age. Cracks in brick foundation walls form a *step pattern* when the mortar has shrunk or the mason has done a poor job in laying the bricks.

Another type of crack that tells of a more serious defect is a *vertical crack* that runs through mortar joints and adjacent masonry units. Figure 4-4 illustrates this type of crack pattern. Such cracks indicate serious settlement in the footing, which

should be checked out by a qualified contractor or engineer. If you see cracks that appear to have been previously patched but are still there, settlement of the footing may still be occurring. There is no way of telling, however, unless many test readings over a period of several months are taken. Again, you need the help of a qualified and experienced person.

Concrete Block

Compared to poured concrete or stone walls, a concrete block foundation is undoubtedly of much poorer quality. Even when laid properly with good mortar joints and resting on a secure footing, concrete block still can cause serious concerns. All you need is one weak joint below grade to allow water

Fig. 4-4. A more serious type of crack pattern penetrates in an almost vertical line through brick and related masonry members.

Fig. 4-5. Step crack pattern, shown here in concrete block, is also common in brickwork. Both instances represent a serious structural fault, and a professional should be called in to give a judgement.

to penetrate. In addition, the blocks' hollow cores are perfect for termites to use as "highways" leading to the wooden sill members of the foundation. If you are lucky, the foundation contractor cemented every third course of block to prevent this, but do not count on it.

Concrete block, like brick, may show cracks in both the step pattern and vertical pattern. In Fig. 4-5 you see a step crack pattern in concrete block. If the cracks are small—under 1/4-inch in diameter—you need not be concerned. Larger cracks signal an impaired structure and should be checked by a professional.

Of great concern are horizontal cracks showing up through several blocks, (Fig. 4-6). This is a very serious defect, indicating excessive pressure by soil and water against the wall. If not corrected, the wall could collapse. A professional will have to find the cause and make the necessary corrections. Because this could be quite costly, you should get several

estimates and add the most reasonable one to the cost of the house.

Poured Concrete Foundations

Poured concrete foundations are by far the best of all foundation walls, particularly if the contractor used reinforcing steel rods in the concrete. For most modern construction, poured concrete is used for both the footing and the foundation walls. In northern climates, where frost heaves cause foundation damage, builders even lay reinforcing rods into the footings, as shown in Fig. 4-7.

Poured concrete foundations, like any other type, will over a period of time suffer characteristic defects. Small cracks, the result of years of settling and shrinking, do not pose a structural threat. Vertical, large cracks (more than 1/4-inch wide and 4 feet long), particularly near corners, will eventually impair the safety of the structure in that the end of a wall will settle more deeply than the rest of the foundation. Sometimes you can find this settlement happening to the middle portion of a wall as seen in Fig. 4-8. Both types are serious and should be corrected. This is not the type of repair that an average homeowner should undertake, however, so you might be wise to get some repair cost bids from foundation contractors before you make a commitment to the house.

SLAB CONSTRUCTION

Some houses are built on *slabs*. Slab construction consists of a poured concrete foundation that rests on a footing and has a slab of concrete flooring, usually 4 inches thick. It is either placed directly on the soil or on a bed of crushed stone. Figure 4-9

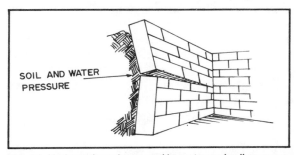

Fig. 4-6. Horizontal cracks caused by water and soil pressure could result in a major collapse of a wall.

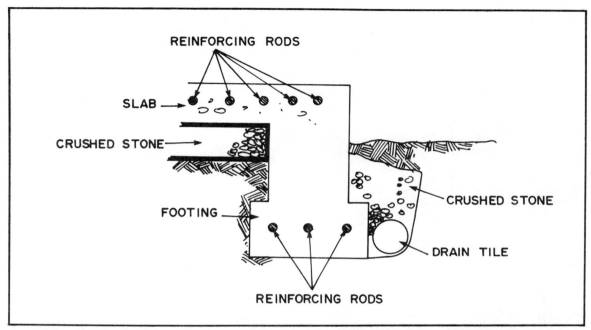

Fig. 4-7. The use of reinforcing rods in poured concrete slabs and foundations adds strength and prevents cracking.

illustrates this type of construction. Slab construction is very difficult to inspect. Very often the foundation is hidden by the grade around the perimeter of the house, and the underside of the slab is inaccessible. If the flooring inside is finished, which it usually is, it is impossible to check for cracks in the floor.

Slab construction has several drawbacks, because the house has no cellar or crawl space. All electro-mechanical units must be installed somewhere in the house or garage (if there is one), and often water and heating pipes are installed directly in the slab. Normal expansion and contraction of the slab will cause pipes to rupture in time. Trying to repair them is useless because the slab has to be broken up in order to get at the pipes. Usually a plumber will merely run new lines on the interior perimeter walls. Remember also that because there is no basement, necessary storage space for household articles is very limited, a fact that should be considered. Finally, slab construction hides termites beautifully. If they do attack, treatment is tricky and expensive. Holes must be

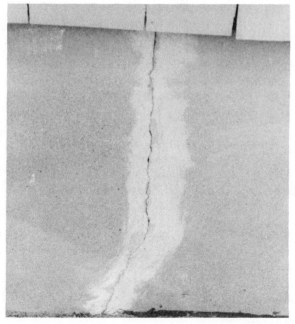

Fig. 4-8. Vertical cracks in poured concrete walls that measure over a 1/4-inch should be considered serious enough to call in an expert.

Fig. 4-9. A house built on a slab. Note the minimum amount of visible foundation.

seldom be seen from the outside. It is only after you have entered the house that you may notice that the doors and windows are poorly aligned and that many of the floors slope or sag. If the exterior walls of a house show pronounced sags or bulges, you can expect the worst inside. All houses have to settle and some settlement should be of little concern.

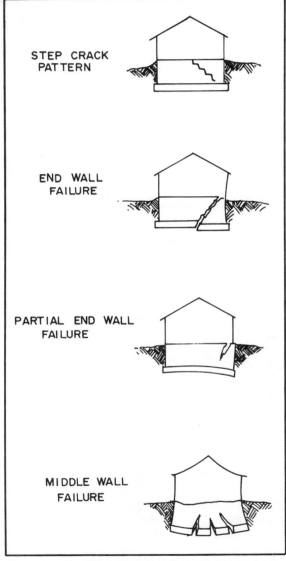

STEP CRACK PATTERN

END WALL FAILURE

PARTIAL END WALL FAILURE

MIDDLE WALL FAILURE

Fig. 4-10. Examples of different types of settlement cracks. All represent serious problems.

drilled into the slab floor to flush out the soil with chemicals and, if luck has it, the exterminator will drill right through a heat or water pipe. Not a very happy prospect.

If you are buying a house built on a slab, be straightforward with the present owner and find out how old the house is, whether he has had problems with buried pipes (usually pipes become a problem after 15-18 years) or with termites, and what was done about the problems. Locate the utilities. Some cities have codes that prohibit heating units in garages or habitable areas of homes. Ask yourself whether you would have enough space for living and storage, and check whether the house has enough space to accommodate all the things that you cannot live without.

SETTLEMENT

The way in which a house has settled can

Uneven (*differential*) settlement, however, should at least alert you to the fact that some trouble may lie ahead. Differential settlement shows itself in cracks in foundation walls, cracks in finished walls and ceilings, floors that slope, and windows and doors that fit poorly. Excessive differential settlement over a period of time could be quite costly to repair. In Fig. 4-10 you will see the common types of differential settlement.

Settlement is caused by the compression of soil under the foundation. Different types of soil react differently under compression conditions. Sandy soils respond quickly and slightly, while clay soils react very noticeably over a long period of time. If the subject house is an older one, you can expect that most of the settlement has already taken place. If the house is relatively new (a few years old), it still may be some time before settlement problems show up. If there is any doubt in your mind, check with the local soil and water conservation office in the town where the house is located. They should be able to answer any questions about the soil conditions and what to expect.

SLIPPAGE

Houses built on hillsides could slip severely. It happens when extended heavy rains saturate the soil. The upper layers of soil slip to the bottom of the hill, sometimes taking houses with them. In California, heavy rains have caused severe losses to homeowners. Houses on a hill usually have a *step foundation* and are reinforced by rods in the foundation walls and footings. Do remember, however, that the side of the hill above the house must be cut back to prevent a steady pressure against the foundation. Figure 4-11 illustrates poor construction practices that could increase slippage problems.

If you are looking at a house built on the side of a hill and you have some doubts, check the surrounding landscape and neighboring homes. Do most of the houses have cracks in their foundations? Has the amount of topsoil decreased because of erosion? Talk to people who have lived in the area for a long time and find out what happens when it rains heavily for a long time. Very carefully double-check the subject house's foundation both on the exterior and the interior for signs of movement or deterioration.

WATER SEEPAGE

Probably one of the biggest, most unwanted headaches that a new owner can have is a leaky basement, particularly if the volume of water is large and the floodings occur frequently. The grade of the lot, the drainage conditions of the soil, the ground water level (water table), and the lack of a gutter/downspout system are all factors that determine the degree of water seepage into the basement.

While you are checking the exterior, look for

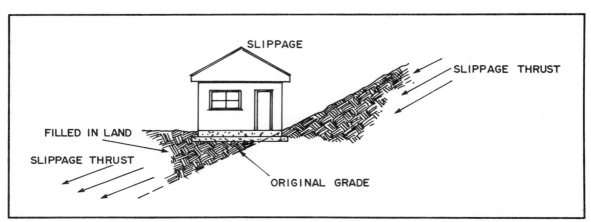

Fig. 4-11. A good example of poor construction that could result in the subject house sliding down the hill.

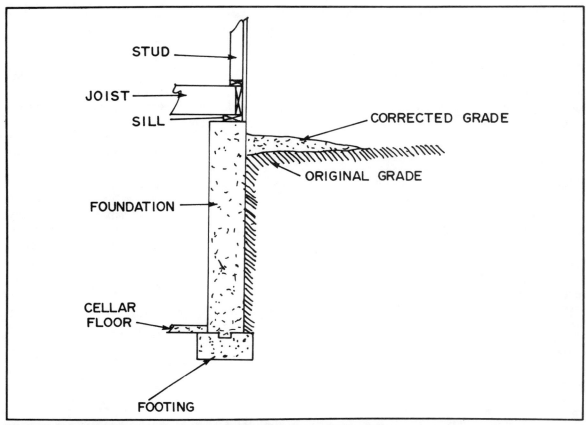

STUD

JOIST

SILL

CORRECTED GRADE

ORIGINAL GRADE

FOUNDATION

CELLAR
FLOOR

FOOTING

Fig. 4-12. This is a good example of proper grading adjacent to the foundation.

areas next to the foundation where the soil has settled and formed depressions. They should be filled and tamped so that surface water can drain away. The soil next to the foundation should be pitched so the ground slopes away from the house, as seen in Fig. 4-12. Surface water (rain and melting snow) can collect in these depressions, and you can be sure that it will work its way down to an opening in the foundation and into the basement.

If the subject house is located on an inclined site, the chances of surface and subsurface water causing problems is great. Here some sort of *surface drainage culvert* should be installed to collect and redirect surface water away from the house. If subsurface water is a problem, then a *foundation perimeter drain pipe*, such as shown in Fig. 4-13, should be considered.

Foundation windows are sometimes located in *wells*. (See Fig. 4-14.) These low areas also need proper grading around them because water will easily penetrate window joints and find a way into the basement. Sometimes a plastic cover will reduce this possibility. Make a note of your findings for future reference.

HIGH WATER TABLE

If the soil on which the house is built has a high water table, you most certainly will have water enter your basement. High water table areas occur where natural subsurface ground water originating from ponds, lakes, streams, or natural springs is present. During spring thaws or when it rains heavily, water bodies adjacent to the house exert hydrau-

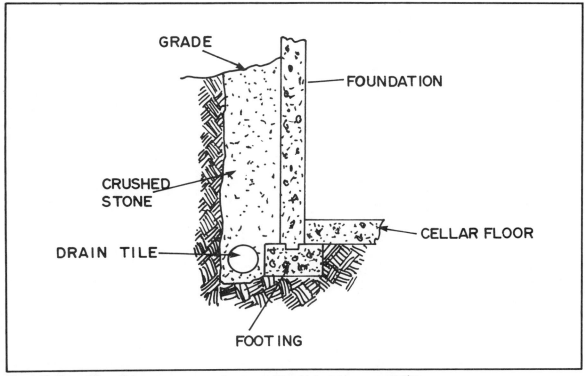

GRADE

FOUNDATION

CRUSHED
STONE

DRAIN TILE

CELLAR FLOOR

FOOTING

Fig. 4-13. Foundation drains are necessary in areas with a high water concentration.

lic pressure on the foundation walls and basement floor. Any cracks or openings in these areas allow free passage of this water. Sometimes this pressure is so great that it can heave and crack concrete.

Quite often the only way to get rid of the water in the basement is by installing a *sump pump*. Figure 4-15 shows a typical sump pump installation. The pump will remove the water and discharge it far enough away from the foundation so that it will cause no harm. If the subject house has a sump pump, be sure to check it by raising the float. If it is in good working order, it will kick over. A pump that is seldom used may become inoperative, because its float rod may have corroded or the electric motor may have rusted out. A preventative measure to assure that the pump will operate properly when you need it is to fill the sump pit with water every two months or so and let the pump empty itself.

Water loves houses that have either no gutters

Fig. 4-14. Plastic domes over foundation window wells help prevent water penetrations to basement areas.

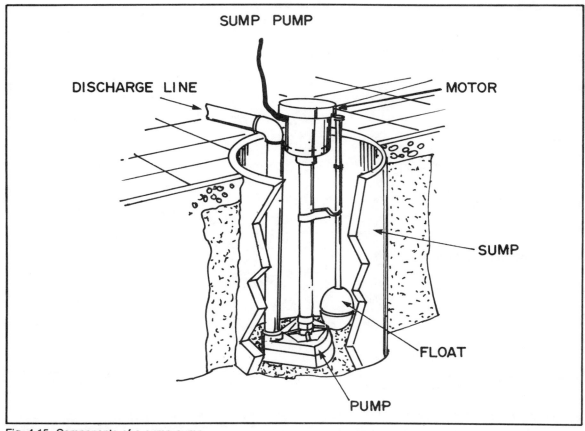

Fig. 4-15. Components of a sump pump.

or downspouts or defective ones because it can accumulate much more easily around the foundation. It just pours off of the roof, and most likely seeps into the basement. (Chapter 2 details correct methods for providing proper roof drainage.)

INSIDE FOUNDATION INSPECTION

After you have checked the foundation carefully outside, the process continues in the basement. First, be aware that there are many sensory signals that from the onset will give you clues to the condition of the basement. One is a musty odor, which is best noticed when you first walk in from the outside. So smell carefully while you study the notes that you have taken on the exterior about the foundation. Defects found there are sometimes visible

inside. Remember though, not all signs mean major problems. Condensation, for example, takes place in every cellar. All that is needed is a good airing out of the basement from time to time. Other signs can lead to faults that have already been repaired, such as a broken pipe. Again, do not be afraid to talk to the owner about something that gives you second thoughts. It is quite possible that the defect has been corrected or can be inexpensively repaired. (It is also a good idea to get a copy of paid bills or the name of the contractor who did the work just in case a problem arises from a poor repair job.)

DAMPNESS

Back to the musty odors—it is often an indication of dampness, which is normal in many basements. Don't confuse normal dampness with water seepage, however. Basements are damp during the late spring and summer months and proper ventilation or the use of a dehumidifier can reduce this. To see whether water droplets on a foundation wall are caused by dampness or from seepage, tape a strip of aluminum foil to the wall. Wait one full day and check the strip. If there is moisture on the surface of the foil, the cause is dampness by condensation. If, on the other hand, the foil surface is dry and the section that was facing the foundation is moist, the condition is seepage. It is also possible to have both dampness and seepage at the same time.

EFFLORESCENCE

If you see white powdery deposits on foundation walls or basement floors, you are looking at *efflorescence*. (See Fig. 4-16.) It is just a fancy name

for mineral salts in masonry units that dissolve in water and pass through to the surface.

After the water evaporates from the surface of the walls or floors, it leaves these deposits of salts. If the layer is thick, you can be sure that there is seepage.

WALLS

Inspecting the walls will require a lot of time and very close scrutiny, so don't rush. Be sure to check both high and low areas of the foundation. Remember that different types of foundation walls have their own peculiar defects and signs of deterioration. When inspecting brick or concrete block walls, look for crumbling mortar joints, cracks in masonry units, scaling sections of block or brick. On stone walls, check the mortar between stones to see whether it still is functional. Crumbling sections or voids between stones should be noted. Look for cracks in poured concrete walls. Any ef-

Fig. 4-16. Efflorescence stains on foundation walls indicate moisture problems. Thick layers of salt residuals mean a steady seepage problem.

Fig. 4-17. Peeling paint from foundation walls is another sign of water penetrations.

41

florescence that you may find on walls, the extent of it, and the location should be noted on your worksheets. Peeling paint on walls, such as in Fig. 4-17, is a sure sign of unfriendly water. Any one of these signs means some degree of seepage into the basement; the difficulty is to tell how much.

FLOORS

Floor joints (where walls join the floor) are likely areas for water to seep in. Check them very carefully, and don't be afraid to get dirty. It will be worth it in the end. Look for efflorescence or water stains on the adjacent wall or floor. If the wall is paneled, look for decay in the lower wood of the panel. Look for cracks in the floor, particularly near the base of support posts. Check for signs of water seeping

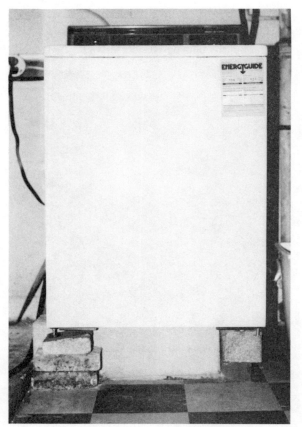

Fig. 4-18. Whenever you see appliances mounted high off of the floor, you can bet there is a water penetration problem.

through these cracks. Note appliances that may have been mounted off of the floor. This is sometimes done if the water seepage is a loyal albeit unwelcome visitor. (See Fig. 4-18.) Look for rust stains at the base of boilers and decay at the base of wall partitions. If the floor is finished, check the condition of the flooring. Have floor tiles been pulled away from the concrete and is carpeting wet or moist? Inspect the base of cellar stairs for signs of decay or water stains. If there is furniture or other large items in the basement, ask the owner for permission to move them so that you may view all areas. Be sure to shine your flashlight into any dim areas. Note your findings. If you find major cracks in the walls or floor, or evidence of serious water seepage, you may want to consult with a professional about the causes and the extent of repairs needed.

CRAWL SPACES

Many homes do not have full basements but are built over an excavation. The space between the ground and the floor of the house is called a *crawl space*. (See Fig. 4-19.) The minimum depth of such space should be 24 inches under the floor joists to allow access to the underfloor by crawling—thus the name. If a crawl space is inaccessible, note this fact on your worksheet.

Assuming that you are looking at a crawl space and that it is accessible, be aware that many defects can be hidden there. The familiar refrain "out of Sight, out of Mind," can be aptly applied here. Too often owners never pay attention to what is going on under the floor, although over a period of time with little or no maintenance, all sorts of problems can develop.

The first thing to check is the condition of the foundation or support piers. Look for signs of deterioration, such as damaged piers or cracks in walls, as seen in Fig. 4-20. Note open horizontal and vertical cracks as well as bowing or buckling walls. Walls and piers at the point where they meet framing members must also be checked. Do foundation walls and the supporting piers look to you as if they have sunk under the weight of the house? If so, mark down your findings and consider having a structural engineer examine them further.

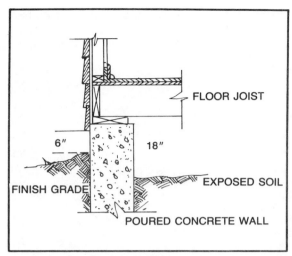

Fig. 4-19. Good construction requires plenty of room between exposed soil and wood members to prevent decay and insect attack.

Even in crawl spaces, it is the damaging effects of water that you have to look out for most. Moisture in such spaces originates from surface water moving through the foundation walls, ground water moving up through the exposed earth floor, or moisture from the house itself. As you inspect the crawl space, check very carefully for evidence of water penetrating or seeping through. Try to pinpoint whence it comes.

By applying *vapor barriers* and installing vent openings, you will be able to cut back the amount of moisture building up in crawl spaces. Figure 4-21 shows what happens when crawl spaces have no vapor barriers and no ventilation openings. Vapor barriers in the form of polyethylene plastic sheets should be spread over the exposed ground to inhibit the natural rise of moisture from the soil. Insulation, with a vapor-barrier backing facing the house side, should be installed between the floor joists to minimize heat loss from the house and to cut back the amount of moisture in the crawl space. No matter how tight the vapor barriers are, however, there will always be a residual amount of water. It is essential to provide vent openings in the foundation walls. In Fig. 4-22 you can see the vent openings, the vapor barriers, and the properly installed insulation. This is how crawl spaces should look.

Because crawl spaces are usually dark and damp areas, don't be surprised to find wood-boring insects or fungus organisms, such as shown in Fig. 4-23. Be sure to take your time and explore every section of accessible wood framing. Keep an eye out for signs of decay or insect activity, and pay particular attention to wood that is too close to the soil or directly in contact with it. Even scraps of wood in the crawl space can give you clues as to whether or not colonies of wood-boring insects were there or still are there. If you find typical termite mud tunnels, break them open and look at the tenants. If you see little white antlike creatures eating happily then you have found an active termite colony. (See Fig. 4-24.) Note all your findings for future repairs and extermination.

Sometimes plumbing pipes or heating ducts are housed in crawl spaces. Both of these should be insulated to prevent freezing and the loss of heat.

Fig. 4-20. Open joints will allow water penetrations into crawl spaces as well as the weather, insects, and rodents.

43

Fig. 4-21. This is a good example of moisture condensation on joists and sill of a basementless house on a wet site. Continued moisture leads to decay of wood and rust of metal. Courtesy of Forest Service, USDA.

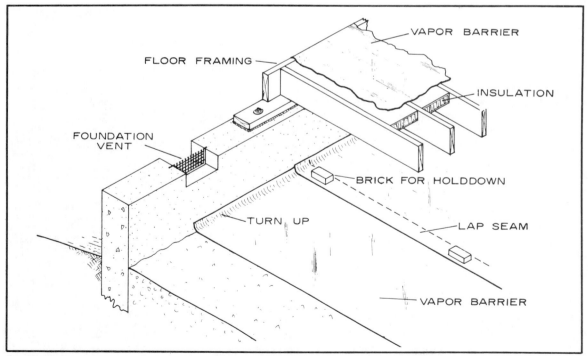

Fig. 4-22. The correct way to protect crawl spaces. Courtesy of Forest Services, USDA.

Fig. 4-23. A good example of fungus growth in an unventilated crawl space. Courtesy of Forest Services, USDA.

Fig. 4-24. An active termite colony. Courtesy of Forest Services, USDA.

While you are examining them, check to see that there are no leaks or spots that are badly rusted and will probably leak. Also look for open joints in the heating ducts, which could cause the heating system to work overtime at your expense. Electrical junction boxes may also be placed in crawl spaces. Check to make sure that they are properly covered and that no exposed wires are present.

CHECKPOINTS

Exterior

• What type of foundation does the subject house have?

• Are there cracks or deterioration on exterior walls?

• Are mortar joints weak and crumbly?

• Note any bowing or horizontal cracks.

• Check for vertical cracks. (Note any over 1/4 inch wide and 4 feet long.)

• Look for major differential settlement.

• Is the house built on the side of a hill?

• Does roof runoff flow away from the house?

• Is the grade sufficient to keep water away from the house?

• Do foundation windows allow water seepage into the basement?

• Is the house situated near a large body of water?

Interior

• Are there signs of dampness?

• Is there a dehumidifier in the basement and is it working?

• Are there signs of water seepage?

• Note any evidence of efflorescence.

• Is there a sump pump and is it working?

• Are there cracks or openings in the foundation walls?

• Are there cracks in the basement floor?

• Do floor joints allow water penetration?

• Are there signs of decay on low wood members?

• Are tiles pulling away from the floor?

• Are appliances mounted off of the floor?

• Do you smell musty odors?

• Ask the owner about previous water problems.

Crawl Space

• Examine foundation walls and masonry piers for signs of deterioration.

• As with the main foundation, have a structural engineer check out bowed or bulging walls, and major vertical or horizontal cracks.

• Look for signs of water.

• Are there properly installed vapor barriers?

• Does the crawl space have adequate ventilation?

• Is the area insulated?

• Are there signs of wood-boring insects or decay causing fungus?

• Are plumbing and heating lines properly insulated to prevent freezing?

• Look for electrical hazards and report them to the owner.

Lot and Grounds

Although you may ask yourself what the lot and grounds have to do with the house proper, their relationship is such that an examination of them is rather important and necessary. Driveways, patios, porches, retaining walls, and landscaping all contribute to or detract from the quality of a house. Poor original design, improper construction, or negligent maintenance can, in a short period of time, cause serious problems with the house. With this in mind, let us examine these areas.

DRIVEWAYS

The surface of a driveway may be paved, unpaved, or covered with crushed stone. Unpaved driveways, as you can well imagine, become muddy and uneven during rainy periods and therefore are rather difficult to use. Make a note to have this type paved with either asphalt or concrete. A paved driveway should be checked for a cracked or deteriorated surface. Also check if it inclines towards the house or garage. If it does, water will surely accumulate around the foundation of the

house or enter the garage. A simple way to correct this is to install a *catch basin* at the end of the driveway as shown in Fig. 5-1.

PATHS

Does the house have paths leading to a detached garage or to the street? If so, check for ruts that could cause an accident. Check whether they slope towards the house or garage. If they do, again, water will form puddles and cause damage. If the edging along the walk or steps is made of wood, check it for rot and insect activity. Figure 5-2 shows a potential tripping hazard in a concrete walk. Left unrepaired, in a short time the entire section will need replacement.

PATIO

A wooden patio should be checked for rot and to see if insects have moved in. Brick patios should be checked for deterioration in the masonry units and if any settlement has occurred. If a patio is next

Fig. 5-1. A catch basin is used to absorb water accumulating around and adjacent to the subject house.

to the house, see if it slopes toward the house foundation members or adjacent low wood units. In the example given in Fig. 5-3, you can see the extent of water and insect damage to wooden members next to a poorly designed patio.

LOT DRAINAGE

A major concern for a homeowner is always the threat of water entering the basement. Carefully check the house lot to see if it is level and if adjacent lots slope directly towards it. If so, surface run-off as well as subsurface water may very well seep through the house's foundation walls. In addition, long periods of flowing subsurface water can seriously damage not only driveways, walks, and patios but also foundations. If you have reservations about the drainage, make sure to get a professional opinion.

The erosion of soil on a lot can be devastating if proper precautions are not taken. One way to cut down on such ground erosion is to provide a heavy ground cover of grass, bushes, and shrubs that will reduce such washing away. If the lot is too steep,

Fig. 5-22. Cracked and deteriorating walks pose a tripping hazard.

Fig. 5-3. Damage caused by poor drainage next to a patio.

terracing would be an effective way of stemming the runoff.

RETAINING WALLS

There is one way to prevent and control soil erosion and that is by building *retaining walls,* such as the one shown in Fig. 5-4. They should be built with *weep holes* to reduce the hydraulic pressure that might build up behind them during spring thaws or heavy rains. These holes are merely openings in the wall that allow built-up water to be released from behind the wall. If you find such a wall and it does not have weep holes, make a note of it. More than likely some deterioration and cracking will take place when lateral pressures develop. In masonry walls, note any cracks or buckling. In wooden walls, record any rot or insect activity.

LANDSCAPING

The landscaping around a house greatly adds to or detracts from the beauty and value of a property. A well maintained lawn with properly placed shrubs and trees will not only add curb appeal to the property but also will cut down on soil erosion, as mentioned before. In addition, shrubs and trees

strategically planted around the house provide shade in the summer and windbreaks in winter. if the subject house that you plan to buy is devoid of beautiful landscaping, take heart; for a few hundred dollars you can add thousands to the value of the property with some simple perimeter plantings.

When looking at landscaping, pay particular attention to trees that are too close to the house. Most trees should be 10 feet away from it, or the roots will be in competition with the foundation for space. Of particular concern are "thirsty" trees such as weeping willows or poplars. As beautiful as they are, their roots are known to penetrate cracks in foundations, open seams in sewer lines, and work their way into swimming pools. (Many a mysterious defect with septic or cesspool systems can be directly related to tree roots seeking water.) In addition to roots, overhanging branches can also cause serious damage to roofs, gutters, and the siding of a house. Chapter 2 discusses this in more detail.

Sometimes you will find foundation plantings of shrubs that are overgrown and completely block off the sunlight from the foundation and/or siding of the house. (See Fig. 5-5.) Such overgrowth not only allows decay organisms to thrive but also provides perfect shelter for insects and rodents. Any

Fig. 5-4. A wooden retaining wall. Note the many vertical joints that act as weep holes to relieve built up water pressure.

Fig. 5-5. A good example of overgrown shrubs adjacent to a house. Lack of sunlight on the house siding will result in decay.

form of vine that is found growing on a house, although beautiful, should be removed. Vines will retain moisture against the siding and will eventually attack the siding itself.

FENCES

Fences are made either of wood or metal, and each has its own peculiar way of fading away. In checking wooden fences, look at the base of the posts, because rot usually originates at the soil line. Figure 5-6 is a good example of this. Probe with your screwdriver to check for decay or insect activity. Then try to wiggle the fence back and forth. If it moves, don't be alarmed; posts can be tamped back into solid plumb position. Check the railings for open splits or cracks that, if not repaired, will

Fig. 5-6. The use of a treated wood post would have avoided this deteriorated condition at the base of the post.

hasten the rotting process. Check the top of wood posts for cracks; they retain water that will cause rot. All of these, if not too badly decayed, can be sealed. Examine the pickets for deterioration and look for broken or missing ones. Note if the fence needs a coat of wood preservative.

Metal fences usually last much longer than wooden ones—if properly maintained, that is. Even the best of metal fences will,in time, need a protective coat of paint. Look for rusty spots and corrosion on the posts or wire fence material. By pulling on the posts, you can check whether they were cemented into the ground. If they are solid and do not move, you can assume that they are. Metal fences, like wooden ones, need annual maintenance to keep them in good shape.

PORCHES

Most houses have some kind of porch or deck attached to them, which inevitably becomes defective over a period of time. There are many details to look at, and the more thorough you are the better you can determine impending decay or imminent safety hazards. The first thing to check is the supports of the porch. As with other wooden members, be sure to look carefully at the wood that is in direct contact with the soil or in very close proximity to it, because it is there that the rotting process begins. Figure 5-7 shows support posts in direct contact with the soil. If the posts are metal, be sure to check for signs of corrosion or rusting. Whether the posts are wood or metal, be sure to still check to see if they are resting on proper footings, namely concrete or a cement block. Sometimes owners place the posts directly into the soil or on a brick with no additional structural support. This results in decay or settlement in a much shorter period of time.

Floor-carrying members such as joists and girders should also be scrutinized for decay, insect infestation, and structural integrity. Are the floor joists securely tied into the house framing with metal hangers or nails? Are all beams and joists carried by sound posts? As you inspect under the porch, probe all wood areas with your screwdriver and note

Fig. 5-7. Posts in direct contact with the soil will rot out and attract various wood-boring insects.

and you won't have to deal with the nuisance of peeling paint every few years. Steps should have railings, and porches should have guard rails for safety, particularly if children are using them. Figure 5-8 is a good example of a porch gone bad. Note the decaying guard rails, the missing railings, the rotting trim and flooring, and the peeling paint.

BULKHEADS

Some homes have basement entrances in the form of *bulkheads*. (See Fig. 5-9.) Defective roof drainage will, in a short time, rot out both the wooden frame and doors of this cellar entrance. Poor lot drainage will also cause decay in the low wood framing members, as well as possible water penetrations to the basement. Wood-boring insects, such as carpenter ants, just love decaying wood bulkheads.

Fig. 5-8. Poor roof drainage has caused extensive damage to this front porch.

on your worksheet any soft spots and defects. While you are there, also see whether the builder used tar paper to cover the tops of the floor joists to prevent them from rotting. The protective tar paper should be between the flooring and the floor joists. If it is missing, you know that the builder did a "fast job."

Steps and flooring materials should be checked for cracks and rotting planks. Walk along the flooring and note sagging or weak areas as you pass over them. Do the steps sink under your weight? All flooring and steps should be sturdy enough to support both live and dead loads and several pieces of furniture without structural deflection. Because outdoor steps and flooring do not hold paint well, these wooden members should be treated with preservative penetrating stains rather than covered with paint. A good oil-based stain will preserve the wood,

Fig. 5-9. Wooden bulkheads need annual maintenance and are noted for leaking. The replacement of a wood bulkhead with a metal one would result in a tighter fit and less maintenance chores.

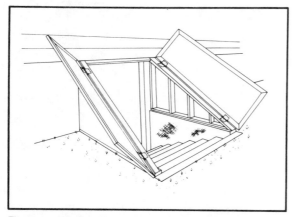

Fig. 5-10. This shows a typical metal bulkhead.

Before you know it, their offspring will be making headway into your house. It is for these reasons that metal bulkheads, as depicted in Fig. 5-10, are being used more and more. They are easier to maintain and are not on anyone's menu.

CHECKPOINTS

• Check for cracks or deterioration in driveways.

• Does the driveway decline towards the house?

• Are there ruts in paths that could cause accidents?

• Look for settlement cracks in concrete patios.

• Check for rot or insect damage to wooden members of patios.

• What is the overall grade like? Is it level or inclined?

• Inspect for weep holes in retaining walls.

• Look for cracks or tipped sections of masonry walls.

• Check for decay in wooden retaining walls.

• Inspect the grounds for erosion of topsoil.

• Are shrubs and trees too close to the house?

• Will tree roots or branches be a problem?

• Inspect wood or metal fences for signs of deterioration.

• Check wood posts, rails, and pickets for decay or insect activity.

• Note any rusting or corrosion on metal posts or fencing.

• Inspect all porch and deck components for signs of decay or insect activity.

• Record all safety hazards on porches or decks.

• Look for cracked, missing, broken, or loose flooring and railings.

• Note whether the porch needs painting or staining.

• Check wooden bulkheads for water damage.

• Probe rotted bulkhead wood for evidence of wood-boring insects.

• On metal bulkheads note the need for painting.

Garages

Not all houses have garages; those that do either have an attached garage that is part of the house framing, or a detached one that is not at all connected to the house. Whichever kind it is, a thorough inspection is necessary to determine its condition. This can be done after you have finished checking the exterior of the house.

DETACHED GARAGES

You may think that because detached garages are not physically part of the house, an inspection is not necessary. On the contrary. If you value a dry and safe place for your car, a garage should be in just as good a shape as a house. It, too, can have serious structural defects that should be corrected, or it, too, may accommodate wood-boring insects that could send their offspring into your very nearby home. So, take the time and effort to check it as carefully as you would a house.

Roof Members

As with the house, water seepage is the major focus of your attention. An examination of the roofing material is the first step. Try to get a good view of all sides of the roof. Step back from the garage and use your binoculars. If you have a ladder and the roof is not too high, climb up to get a closer look. Sometimes roofing materials are deceptive in appearance. From a distance, they may look fine and intact. If you look more closely, however, you may find that the reverse is true. (See Fig. 6-1.) While you balance on the ladder, check the gutters and the adjacent wooden members. Are the gutters decaying and in need of replacement? Has water backed up and caused damage to fascia boards? Take your screwdriver and probe suspect areas. If the wood is punky, you will probably need to replace the gutters. If the garage has metal gutters, check the joints for possible leaks and look for corrosion or deterioration. Pay close attention to the condition of the downspouts, and particularly the ends of them. Does rainwater flow away from the garage as it should? Or does it allow water to accumulate around the garage foundation, as in Fig. 6-2. Make a note of all defects.

Fig. 6-1. Close-up of garage roofing in advanced stages of deterioration. Note the opening in the wood framing that allows water penetrations to the interior.

Fig. 6-2. An example of a plugged-up drywell. When this downspout discharges its water, flooding around the base of the garage foundation occurs.

Garage Doors

The base of the garage door frames is another place where decay sets in first. Probe these low wood areas, as well as any other low wood sections, to see what kind of shape they are in. The builder may have installed the door jambs directly into the soil as shown in Fig. 6-3. Here you can expect both water damage and insect activity. Sometimes wood siding also touches the soil directly or is in close proximity to it. Figure 6-4 shows the results of this error.

Garage doors also need to be in good condition. Check the base of the doors. A door of good quality will have a piece of protective weatherstripping between the wood and the ground. This not only protects the exposed wood but also cuts down on

Fig. 6-3. Door jambs directly in the soil are an open invitation to termites.

Fig. 6-4. Wood siding in contact with the soil will rot rapidly and attract a host of insects.

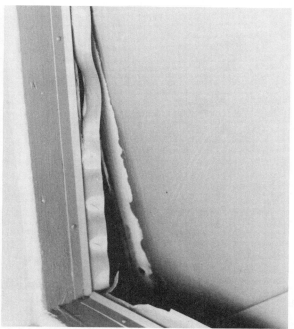

Fig. 6-5. Damaged weatherstripping allows heat to escape and unfriendly things to enter the garage.

drafts. Note the lack of weatherstripping not only at the base but also on the sides of the doors. Figure 6-5 shows damaged weatherstripping that should be replaced. Failure to correct this defect will result in lost energy dollars. In Fig. 6-6, you see an example of a garage door without weatherstripping. Note the wide gap between the door and the frame. As you continue to check the door, look for cracked panels, broken or missing glass, and defective locks. Test the doors by lifting them up and down. Do they move easily, or do you have to be a weightlifter to get in and out of the garage?

Walls

As you walk around the garage, eyeball the sides to see whether wall displacement has occurred. Because garages are not built with the same care that houses are, you may find some structural defects. Footings and foundations for garages, particularly for older structures, were not always built to last forever. Frost heaves, settlement, and general deterioration often cause serious damage to the

Fig. 6-6. Installation of weatherstripping on this door will cut down on cold air penetrations into the garage.

Fig. 6-7. This garage is structurally unsound. Expensive repairs will be needed to correct the problems.

up on your ladder and test the integrity of the wood by probing with a screwdriver. Is it rotting out and in need of replacement? Are there indications of insect activity? Can you see daylight from the underside of the roof? If so, the roofing material should be replaced. Are the roof framing members still structurally sound, or do they need to be replaced?

Interior Walls

If the garage walls are unfinished, check each stud individually for deterioration. Pay particular attention to the base of the studding. While you are doing this, also look at the foundation sills. With your screwdriver, probe every few inches to see if there is any damage. As you walk around, gently push outward on every third stud. Does the wall give way to your pressure? If so, the structure may need additional bracing. If you find that you can move sections of the walls, double-check each corner to see if there are diagonal braces. (See Fig. 6-8.) If there are none (many do not have them although they should), have a carpenter install them for you should you purchase this property. These cross braces will prevent the walls from shifting, particularly under heavy loads of snow on the roof or stored goods in lofts.

Should the inside walls be covered with a finish material, such as plaster or plywood panels, you will have to limit your inspection to visible clues. Check for cracks or broken sections of walls. If you find openings, use your flashlight and try to see what the framing is like under the finished walls. Occasionally, you will find such damaged areas only on the rear wall of a garage—most likely caused by someone parking "by ear" instead of by sight. If this is the case, you may wish to double-check the outside rear wall again to see if it has suffered structural damage. After all, a wall can only take so much crashes.

Lighting

Usually, detached garages do not have lighting. If you are in one that does have it, however, turn the lights on and off to see whether or not they do indeed work. Note obvious defects such as old

foundation. Do the walls bow or sag? Does the garage look like the "Leaning Tower of Pisa?" Are the windows and doors difficult to open and close? If the subject garage looks like the one pictured in Fig. 6-7, you may want to have a builder quote you a price on a replacement.

Upon entering the garage, you should systematically follow up on your findings from the exterior inspection. Defects in roofing materials may have caused damage to adjacent inside framing. Any problems with the exterior side walls, doors, and windows should be followed up with a thorough eye on the inside.

Roof Framing

Check the rafters and roof sheathing for water seepage. Look for evidence of mold or fungus growth on these wooden members. If possible, climb

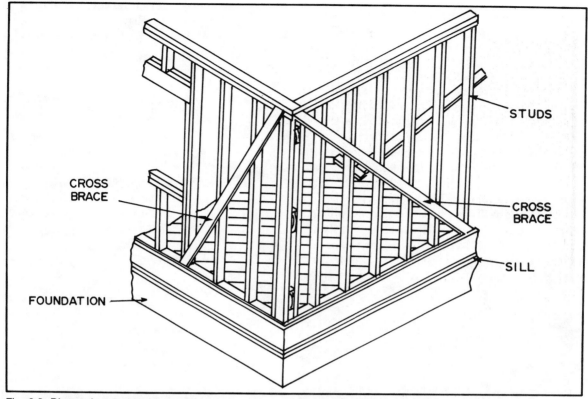

Fig. 6-8. Diagonal cross bracing prevents the garage walls from racking.

spliced wires, open junction boxes, and hanging wires such as in Fig. 6-9. If the electrical work appears to be a typical "handyman" arrangement, get a licensed electrician to go over it and give you his professional opinion.

A final word on detached garages: although such a garage is not attached to the house, it still is part of the property. You are paying a percentage of the selling price for this structure. If you find serious defects with it, tell the owner or his representatives. Costly repairs or replacements should be factored into the selling price. If you do not, you may pay thousands of dollars more than you had originally planned.

ATTACHED GARAGES

Because an attached garage is an integral part of the house, it requires a much different approach than the inspection of a detached one. Here fire and

Fig. 6-9. Electrical hazards, such as this hanging wire, should be repaired to prevent anyone from injuring themselves.

safety hazards are the number one concern in addition to all the other inspection principles discussed under "Detached Garages."

The entrance from the garage to the house should have the following safety features: the door itself should be fire resistant (metal clad), it should be self-closing and have a tight seal to prevent garage fumes from entering the house, and it should have a dead bolt lock to prevent unlawful entry into the home. The garage floor should be lower than the house slab, again to prevent toxic gases from getting into the house. Figure 6-10 shows the type of door needed for attached garages.

Walls and ceilings that are adjacent to living areas need to be covered with fire resistant materials, such as stucco or 5/8-inch sheetrock. Cracks or broken sections should be recorded and

Fig. 6-11. Storage of flammable materials in garages is a foolhardy practice that could lead to serious consequences.

repaired as soon as possible. Exposed combustible materials on walls should be removed or properly fireproofed to prevent potential fires. Both walls and the ceiling should be insulated to keep heat losses to a minimum.

Storage of gasoline, oil-based paints, and paint thinners should not be allowed in attached garages. Fire hazards as depicted in Fig. 6-11 should be recorded for future removal. Also, some people like to store firewood in their garages because it is easier than having to go out in the cold to the old woodshed. This practice is not only dangerous as far as a potential fire is concerned, but also foolhardy because the owner himself may be carrying wood-boring insects into his home.

Houses that do not have a full basement usually have their heating plant in the garage, which is

Fig. 6-10. Garage doors that lead into living areas of a home should be metal clad.

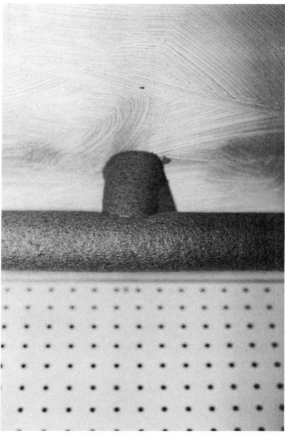

Fig. 6-12. Fully insulated pipes in a garage. This sound practice prevents heat losses and cuts down on the chances of freeze-ups.

cracks are okay, but they should be caulked and sealed to prevent water from coming in. Major cracks or heaved sections should be checked out by a professional to determine the cause and the possible solution.

While you are in the garage, be on the constant lookout for evidence of water seepage. (See Fig. 6-13.) Water stains, efflorescence on walls, and corrosion on low sections of metal posts all indicate water entering the garage. Double-check the pitch of the driveway. If it declines toward the garage, the installation of an exterior catch basin should be considered.

No matter where they are located, wooden members always taste good to wood-boring insects.

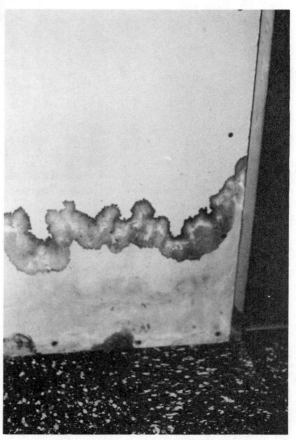

Fig. 6-13. Water stains on this garage wall indicates major water problems and should be investigated closely to find the causes.

probably the worst place to have a boiler or furnace. The possibility of an oil or gas leak from a fuel line is always present. Gasoline vapors could ignite from the burner pilot light, or an out-of-control vehicle could crash into the heating unit and cause an explosion. Be sure that you check for proper ventilation that can carry off toxic fumes. If a boiler or furnace is in the open, make a note to have it partitioned off from the rest of the garage. Because pipes in garages are more vulnerable to freezing, you should check to see that they are fully insulated, as in Fig. 6-12. Make a note of all the problems that you can foresee.

Garage floors, like basement floors, should be checked for cracked or heaved sections. Minor

Fig. 6-14. Note on your worksheets any obvious water accumulations.

As with detached garages, also check for them in attached ones. Pay particular attention to those areas that get wet from flooding, rain, or condensation as shown in Fig. 6-14.

Crawl spaces over the garage or to the side of it should also be checked. If the garage has an access door in the ceiling, be sure to use a sturdy ladder to reach it. Go about checking it as if you were in an attic. (Read Chapter 14 for details on how to inspect an attic.) While you are in the crawl space, be sure to record the amount of insulation and ventilation, if any. Figure 6-15 shows a garage gable with no gable vent. As you know, this is a good way for condensation problems to develop. Mark down on your worksheet this and any other defects that you find.

CHECKPOINTS

Detached Garages

• Inspect roof shingles for broken, missing, or deteriorating sections.

• Examine gutters and downspouts for defects.

• Check fascia boards for decay.

• Examine low wood members for decay or insect activity.

• Operate the doors to see if they work.

• Do doors need weatherstripping?

• Can the doors be locked to keep out uninvited guests?

• Check for cracked panels, broken panes, damaged or decaying sections.

• Inspect all sides of the outside for structural displacement.

Fig. 6-15. Ventilation is important in garages as well as the main house. Note the lack of ventilation on this garage gable.

• Check for bulging, loose, or deteriorating sections of siding.

• On the inside of the garage, check all exposed framing members for decay or deterioration.

• Examine foundations for defects.

• Inspect for possible electrical problems.

Attached Garages

• Check for possible fire hazards.

• Inspect the door from the garage to the house. Is it fireproofed?

• Are the walls and ceiling adjacent to living spaces fireproof?

• Note unsafe storage practices for combustible materials.

• If the heating unit is in the garage, have safety precautions been taken to prevent a fire or an explosion?

• Examine the floors and walls for signs of water penetration.

• Probe suspect wood areas for decay or insect activity.

• Inspect crawl spaces for insulation and ventilation as well as possible water leaks.

Structural Pests and Wood Rot

Termites are destructive insects with ferocious appetites that cost Americans millions of dollars each year, not only for repairs but also for attempts to control their numbers. Because knowledge of nesting and feeding habits can only help you save money and grief, be sure to study the next few pages carefully before you go on the quest for termite damage.

There are two major kinds of termites—*subterranean termites* and *nonsubterranean termites*. The subterranean kind is found in every state except Alaska, but is particularly prevalent in the southern half of the country (Fig. 7-1). The non-subterranean kind (Fig. 7-2) is restricted to the southern half of the country and the Pacific Coast states. Both will cause extensive damage to homes.

Subterranean termites live in nests in the ground, close to a source of wood, and build tunnels upward into wooden structures above them. Non-subterranean termites do not need contact with the soil; they just fly directly into the house and settle in for the duration. Both types of termites are divided into three *castes*: a royal *couple* (sexually

mature male and female), adult *workers*, and adult *soldiers* who defend the colony in times of danger. Figure 7-3 shows the three different castes.

SUBTERRANEAN TERMITES

Subterranean termites live in the soil, from which they derive moisture. They chew tunnels through wood, from which they derive sustenance. Because they prefer a diet consisting mostly of wood, they will construct, if necessary, tubes adjacent to the soil to get to wooden members of a house. Subterranean termites will even construct tubes through cracks in slabs, through expansion joints in floors, in the voids of concrete blocks, through cracks in foundation walls, and even (as illustrated in Fig. 7-4) across the face of foundation walls.

Formosan termites are an imported species of subterranean termite. At present (thank goodness) they only exist in the Gulf Coastal states, although some have been recorded in the Carolinas. The major difference between this termite and our native species is that they are larger and more aggressive, they are able to penetrate chemical barriers that nor-

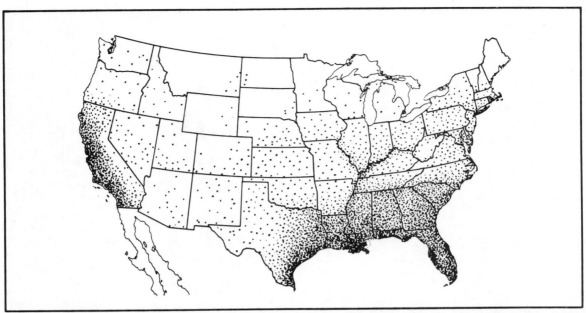

Fig. 7-1. Relative hazard of termite infestation in the United States is indicated by density of stippling. Courtesy of the Forest Service, USDA.

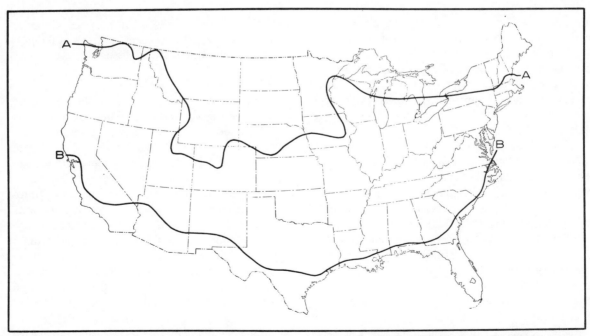

Fig. 7-2. This map shows the location of the two major groups of termites: (A) below this line to line B subterranean termites can be found. (B) below line B nonsubterranean termites are prevalent. No major termite colonies exist above line A. Courtesy of Forest Service USDA.

Fig. 7-3. This figure shows the three different castes of termites: (A) winged reproductive, (B) adult worker (C) adult soldier. Courtesy of Forest Service, USDA.

Fig. 7-4. Termite tubes across a foundation wall. Courtesy of Forest Service, USDA.

mally stop our native termites, they form larger colonies, and they cause more damage. At this writing, there is no chemical treatment that will permanently stop them.

NONSUBTERRANEAN TERMITES

The two major kinds of nonsubterranean termites are *dampwood* and *drywood termites,* both of which can live without contact with the soil. Their colonies tend to be smaller than those of subterranean termites and thus the damage they cause is not quite as extensive. At present, no major sightings of them have been found in the northern states.

REPRODUCTIVE OR SWARMING TERMITES

Swarming termites are the young males and

females of either the subterranean or nonsubterranean colonies that are sent out from the parent colony to reproduce and start new colonies. Sometimes homeowners will confuse swarming ants with termites. Figure 7-5 shows a typical flying ant, which is different from a termite. It is important for you to know the difference between the two. Swarming ants represent the reproductives of carpenter ant colonies. Like swarming termites, they leave established colonies to form new ones. There are three ways in which you can distinguish between the two:

• By the shape of the *body*—the ant has a narrow wasp-waist. The termite is straight down the sides with no wasp-waist.
• By the *wings*—termites have two pairs of wings of equal length whereas the ant has two pair

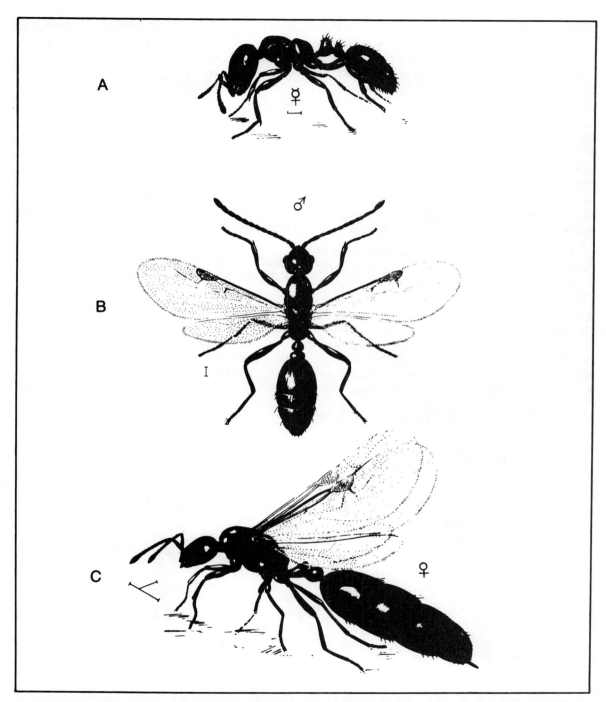

Fig. 7-5. Carpenter ant reproductives: (A) side view without wings, (B) top view of reproductive, (C) side view with wings. Courtesy of Forest Service, USDA.

of wings of which the front pair is much longer than the back pair.

• By the *antenna*—a termite's antenna is straight and looks like a string of little beads. The ant's antenna bends at right angles and doesn't look like beads.

Figure 7-6 shows the major differences between swarming ants and swarming termites. If you find either species in your house, an established colony exists somewhere in the building.

HOW TO RECOGNIZE THE PRESENCE AND WORK OF TERMITES

Large numbers of winged reproductive termites that emerge or swarm from soil or wood are likely to be the first signs that a termite colony exists. Discarded wings also point to the existence of a well established colony nearby. If you see such wings beneath doors and windows, be alert because termites may have tried to escape from within the house.

The presence of flattened *shelter tubes,* as shown in Fig. 7-4, is another sign of termite infestation. These tubes are from 1/4- to 1/2-inch or more wide.

Termites use them as passageways between the wood and the soil from which they draw moisture. The tubes also protect them from the drying effect of direct exposure to air.

Termite damage to wood is not noticeable on the surface. Termites are skilled at hollowing out wood without damaging the outer covering. The only way to determine whether termites are presently active or were so in the past is by probing with a tool such as a screwdriver. If the tool penetrates easily and the wood appears hollow, you can assume that termites have been at work. In Fig. 7-7 you see the base of a piece of trimwork that has been visited by termites.

CONDITIONS FAVORING TERMITE INFESTATION

Termites love moist, warm soil that contains an abundant supply of food, namely wood or other cellulose material. They often find it beneath houses where the space below the first floor is poorly ventilated and where scraps of lumber, form boards, or roots are left in the soil. Most termite infestations in houses occur because wood touches, or is too close

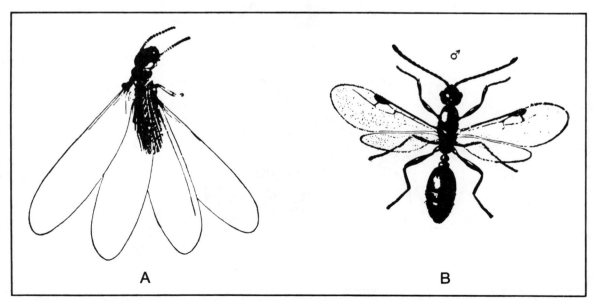

Fig. 7-6. Showing the major difference between reproductives of termites and carpenter ants: (A) reproductive termite, (B) reproductive carpenter ant. Courtesy of Forest Service, USDA.

Fig. 7-7. Wood damaged by termites.

to, the ground, particularly at porches, steps, or terraces. Cracks or voids in foundations and concrete floors make it easy for termites to reach wood that is not in direct contact with the soil. Figure 7-8 demonstrates how termites can gain entrance to a house.

PREVENTING TERMITE ATTACK

All wood scraps, roots, stumps, and other wood debris should be removed from the surface of the soil beneath porches and in crawl spaces. Grade stakes, form boards, and any other such construction lumber should be removed to prevent termite attack.

To prevent an unfavorable moisture build-up in the soil beneath a house, the soil surface adjacent to the foundation should be sloped so that surface water can drain away from the house.

Foundation walls and piers should be made as impervious to termites as possible to prevent attack

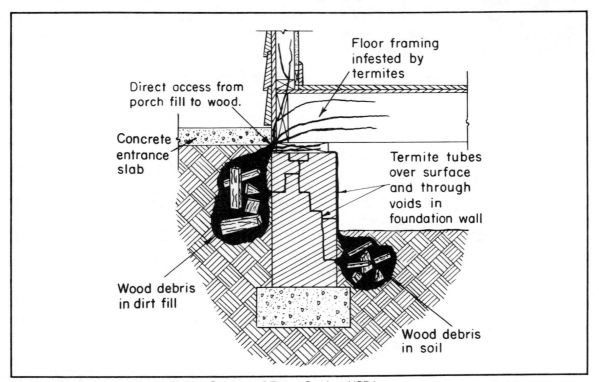
Fig. 7-8. Termite entrances to a house. Courtesy of Forest Service, USDA.

Fig. 7-9. Potential termite entrance in cracked foundation.

on woodwork. Poured concrete foundations should have no cracks. Cracks as small as 1/32-inch in width will permit passage of termites. The foundation crack shown in Fig. 7-9 is an ideal way for termites to enter this house. Hollow concrete block or hollow brick foundation walls should have the top course and all joints completely filled with concrete. Where these openings are left unsealed, there always exists the potential for termite entrance. Wooden posts or piers used for foundations should be treated with an approved preservative. Failure to do this will only result in termite activity or decay.

CONCRETE SLAB CONSTRUCTION

One of the most susceptible types of construction, and one that gives a false sense of security, is the concrete slab construction that is used in many parts of the country. (See Fig. 7-10.) Termites can gain access to a house over the edge of the slab, or through expansion joints, openings around plumbing, or cracks in the slab. Infestation in houses with this type of construction is most difficult to detect and control. If you are buying a house that is built on a slab, it might be wise to consult with a profes-

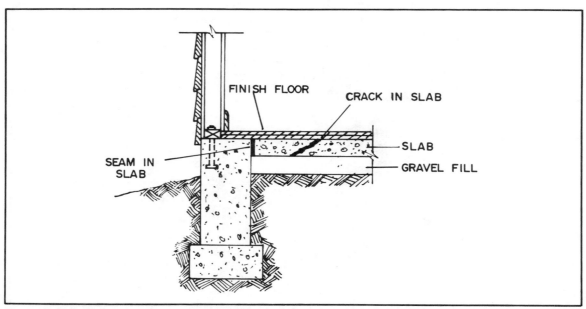

Fig. 7-10. Slab construction. Seams in slab or cracks make easy entrance for termites.

sional exterminator. (See Chapter 4 for more information on slab construction.)

INSPECTING FOR TERMITES

To check for termites, you have to look at exterior as well as interior areas. Outside, check foundation walls for termite tubes. If the house perimeter has shrubbery, be sure to move the shrubs so you can really see the foundation. Look for cracks that could allow termites a free ride. Sometimes poured concrete or hollow block foundations have a thin stucco coat over them. In time this stucco finish pulls away and leaves a gap between it and the foundation. No matter how small this gap is, there is always the chance of some hard working termites squeezing by for a free meal. Take your screwdriver and tap suspect areas. Make a note of any that may need preventative repairs.

Most outside woodwork is susceptible to termite attack. Therefore, porch steps should rest upon a concrete base that extends at least 6 inches above grade, as illustrated in Fig. 7-11. Door frames should not extend into or through concrete or asphalt floors or driveways, and foundation windows should be at least 6 inches above the soil. Figures 7-12 and 7-13 show why. In a very short time the wood decays and termites are drawn to it.

Probe all suspicious wood with your screwdriver. If your screwdriver sinks into the wood easily, and the interior portions appear channeled out (as in Fig. 7-14), you have found the work of termites. Note on your worksheets all such areas. If

Fig. 7-12. Termite damage in door jambs in direct contact with soil.

Fig. 7-13. Termite damage to foundation window.

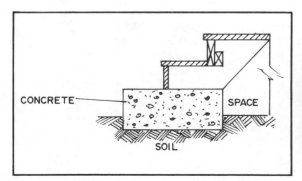
Fig. 7-11. Sound construction practices prevent termite entrance.

Fig. 7-14. This shows what wood looks like after a termite attack. Courtesy of Forest Service, USDA.

you find extensive damage, an evaluation by a professional may be necessary.

CRAWL SPACE INSPECTION

Because crawl spaces and the underside of raised porches account for a large portion of all termite infestations in houses, it is important for you to get into these areas to check for signs of termite activity. If you are lucky, the opening will be large and easy to use, such as the one depicted in Fig. 7-15. Unfortunately, most crawl spaces are more difficult to enter and get about in than the one shown here.

Keep in mind that the main reason why these spaces are potential termite havens is because they usually are dark and dank. Poor ventilation and condensation/moisture problems are ideal conditions for our little friends. In addition to providing ventilation, you should also give some thought to va-

Fig. 7-15. Access door to a crawl space.

Fig. 7-16. Correct way to cover crawl space's exposed soil to prevent condensation problems. Courtesy of Forest Service, USDA.

por barriers. Figure 7-16 shows you how to cover over the exposed soil found in most crawl spaces.

During your inspection, be on the lookout for low wooden members. Sometimes you will find wood supports that are in direct contact with the soil. Probe all these questionable wooden members to test their condition. Note on your worksheets any wood debris that should be removed. Be on the lookout for termite shelter tubes. If you see any, break them open to see if anyone is at home. If you see what appear to be white ants, you now have your first encounter with termites.

BASEMENT INSPECTION

The inside inspection for termites is generally done in the basement. Partitions and posts should be checked carefully. Probe the base of these units with your screwdriver to test for termite activity or damage. In older homes, you may find wooden sup-

port posts rather than the more modern metal units. (See Fig. 7-17.) Usually these wooden posts extend past the cement floor and rest directly in soil. As you know by now, this is an ideal way for termite penetration. Cracks in the cement floor under partitions or wooden posts are another way termites can make easy entry. Be sure to seal up any cracks once you buy the house.

It is next to impossible to detect termite activity or damage in finished basements. Basements that have been turned into recreation rooms with finished ceilings, walls, and floors are an exterminator's nightmare. There is no way of telling what is happening without tearing out some of the finished coverings. If you are lucky, there is a suspended ceiling and you will be able to lift the ceiling tiles to check those accessible areas. Sometimes finished rooms in basements have access doors to electrical service panels and for plumbing or heat shut-off

Fig. 7-17. Use of wood posts increase the risk of termite attack.

valves. If this is the case, be sure to inspect carefully in those areas. Note any areas that were not visible or accessible for future reference.

In unfinished basement rooms, you should check the foundation sill very carefully. Start at one corner and work your way around the perimeter of the basement. Probe with your screwdriver every 6 inches, but be sure that you do not puncture any live wires or water pipes. If you do find damage in sections of the sills, you should probe adjacent floor joists and girders to see if the damage has spread to them. Figure 7-18 shows a typical floor framing arrangement. If the damage in the sills and adjacent wooden members is extensive, a structural engineer should be consulted to evaluate the present condition of the framing.

Another area for easy termite penetration is the base of the cellar stairs, where stringers (support members for the treads and risers) might extend into the concrete floor. Termites can easily chew their way up the stringers to other structural members. Probe the base of the wooden stairs as described in this chapter. Weakness caused by termite dam-

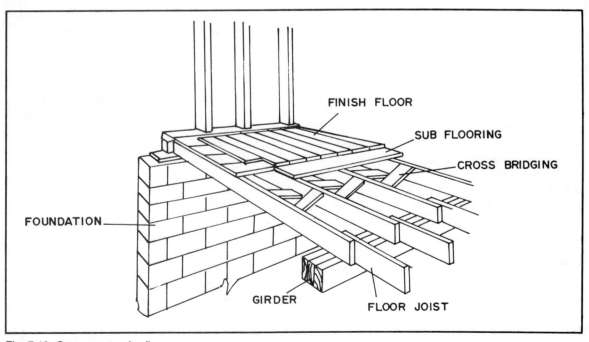

FINISH FLOOR

SUB FLOORING

CROSS BRIDGING

FOUNDATION

GIRDER

FLOOR JOIST

Fig. 7-18. Components of a floor.

age could lead to a serious hazard for anyone using the stairs. Note any repairs that might be needed.

Finally, water pipe and electrical conduit entrances are common termite avenues. All plumbing and electrical pipes should be clear of any exposed soil in basements and crawl spaces. Wooden blocks or stakes connected to the soil should not be used to support them. Where pipes penetrate concrete walls or floors, the openings should be sealed with cement or a roofing grade sealer to prevent termite entry. Be sure to examine these areas for any tell-tale signs.

BEETLES AND ANTS

Termites are not the only insects that make their living by chewing wood. *Powder-post beetles* and *carpenter ants* also cause serious damage to buildings. The damage inflicted by these insects differs from that of termites. Powder-post beetle damage is characterized by the presence of a fine-to-coarse powder that is packed tightly in galleries made in the wood. Damage by carpenter ants can be recognized by the presence of hollow, irregular, clean chambers cut across the grain of partially decayed wood.

POWDER-POST BEETLES

Like termites, powder-post beetles cause damage to wood that costs millions of dollars annually to repair. Both hardwoods and softwoods are subject to infestation and damage. These beetles may attack wood used in the construction of homes, or in the manufacture of seasoned wood products, such as furniture.

Inspecting for Powder-Post Beetles

You can look for signs of powder-post beetles while you are hunting for termites. The most obvious sign of powder-post beetles are the small round emergence holes in the infested wood. Adult beetles exit through these flight holes after they have done their work. One word of caution, however, not every emergence hole means that the wood is infested at the time of the inspection. Many of

Fig. 7-19. Powder-post beetle flight holes. This figure shows an old inactive infestation.

the flight holes that you may come across could be the hallmark of beetles that left many years ago. Shine your flashlight on the holes. Newly formed holes have a light, clean appearance whereas older ones are much darker in color. Figure 7-19 is a good example of old inactive flight holes.

Another way of telling if the infestation is still active is by looking at the *frass* (the fine powder left by the beetles). If it is from an old infestation, the frass will be caked and have a pale yellowish color. Newly formed frass will be very light in appearance, similar to that of fresh sawdust. In Fig. 7-20 you will see recent flight holes as well as some serious structural damage to a foundation sill.

CARPENTER ANTS

Hollow, irregular, clean chambers cut across the

Fig. 7-20. An active infestation with the resulting damage. Note the light color around the flight holes indicating recent activity.

sections of wood that show signs of decay. In checking gutters, be sure to look at adjacent wood members. Check the roof overhang where shingles meet the gutter. Unexplained piles of sawdust are always a warning signal. Other typical places to check are portions of wood framing, siding, or trim that are in contact with the soil. Large open seams in trim members and at the base of wooden columns are prime candidates for carpenter ants. Figures 7-21 and 7-22 show two good examples of these potential nesting sites.

During your inspection, be sure to probe any areas of concern. If the wood falls apart after you stick your screwdriver in and ants come streaming out, you may have found a nest. Also look for ant traps in the house. These commercial baits are

grain of partially decayed wood and fine to coarse wood fibers discarded by the ants as they build their nests, are all signs of carpenter ants at work. Also, numerous large black ants, 1/4- to 3/8-inch long, crawling indoors or outside indicate carpenter ant activity. Flying ants in the house and the remains of discarded wings found near windows and doors are also sure signs.

Carpenter ants will nest anywhere in the house as long as they can find wood that is moist or softened by decay. Rotting gutters and steps, deteriorating wood in attics, and moist wood in and out of the house provide a suitable nesting site for these wood borers.

Inspecting for Carpenter Ants

In your inspection, pay particular attention to

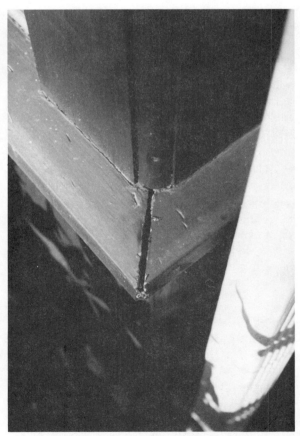

Fig. 7-21. Potential carpenter ant infestation in this open and decaying seam.

Fig. 7-22. The base of this decaying wood post is an excellent nesting area for ants.

when the problem is only simple rot. Therefore, it is important for you to be able to tell common wood rot from insect damage.

Four primary types of damage by wood-attacking fungi are commonly found in homes: *sap stain, mold, decay,* and *soft rot.* They convert wood into simple digestible products, and by doing so reduce the weight and strength of the wood. Thus, framing members of the house will become structurally deficient.

SAP STAIN

Sap stain can be identified by its discoloration of the wood. The blue stain-type is the most often encountered, but the color may range from brown to almost black. Sap stained wood is more permeable to water; thus, outside wood is more subject to decay. (See Fig. 7-23.)

MOLD

Molds cause discolorations of various shades and in advanced stages will penetrate deeply into wood and thereby increase the wood permeability. If you find heavy mold concentrations, you can assume that adjacent wood has decayed extensively. Figure 7-24 shows various stages of mold and the results to wood framing.

DECAY

There are two types of decay: *brown* and *white rot.* Wood with brown rot takes on a brown color and tends to crack across the grain. Wood that has white rot will lose its natural color and appear whiter than normal, but will not crack against the grain. Figures 7-25 and 7-26 show the two types of decay.

SOFT ROT

Soft rot can be identified by being much shallower than the other types of wood rot. If after scraping off the surface rot you find wood that has almost normal hardness, you have a case of soft rot. Because soft rot does not penetrate deeply into the wood, it should not be a major concern for you.

usually found in bathrooms and in kitchens because ants usually track through these areas for moisture. If you do see these traps, you can assume that there is some activity in the house. And finally, if you see ants walking around the house as though they own it, you might as well hunt for their nests because the chances are that they have made their home in yours. Record all of your findings and note whether you think that a pesticide treatment might be necessary or not.

WOOD ROT

Sometimes people confuse common wood rot with different types of structural pest damage. Quite often unscrupulous pest exterminators will try to sell an extermination job to an ignorant homeowner

Fig. 7-23. A good example of sap stain. Note the discoloration in the wood. Courtesy of Forest Service, USDA.

INSPECTION OF WOOD ROT

The cost to protect homes from serious decay can be minimized if homes are inspected on a regular basis and repairs are made to correct any defects. Unfortunately, this is not what the average homeowner does and therefore most homes suffer from some form of decay or rot. In your inspection of the subject house, check areas both on the outside and the inside, particularly places where wood is exposed to water.

Exterior

Check roofs, roof edges (fascia, soffits, rafter ends), joints in and adjacent to windows and door frames, and appendages such as porches, steps, and rails. Look for areas that may have signs of repeated wettings, such as in Fig. 7-27. Crawl spaces (as you know) merit special attention, so be sure to inspect and probe for any signs of deterioration. Record all your findings on your worksheets.

Interior

Inspect the attic for signs of wood decay. Pay particular attention to areas around chimney and vent openings in the roof. Check gable louver vents and adjacent wooden members for signs of water damage. Inspect wooden members in the basement directly below the kitchen and bathroom. Probe all sills, girders, and joists. Pay special attention to the base of wooden posts, partition walls, and the low

Fig. 7-24. Various stages of mold deterioration is illustrated in this figure: (A) initial stages from rusting nailhead, (B) secondary stage of mold decay in siding from rusting nail, (C) decay of wood shutters, (D) decay in siding, (E) advanced stages of decay on wood, (F) discoloration and decay to exposed wood. Courtesy of Forest Service, USDA.

Fig. 7-25. A good example of white rot. Note the areas exhibiting cracks following the grain. Courtesy of Forest Service, USDA.

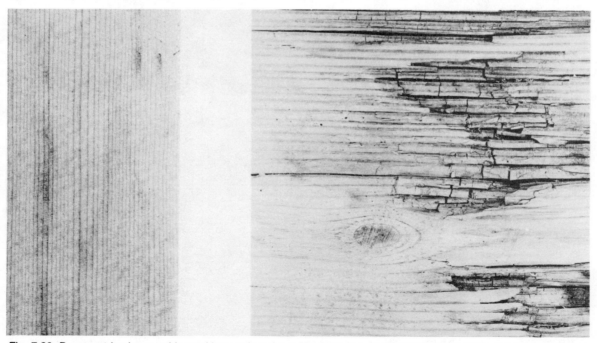

Fig. 7-26. Brown rot is shown, with cracking against the grain. Note the discoloration of the grain. Courtesy of Forest Service, USDA.

ends of stairs. Examine the map in Fig. 7-28 to determine the level of potential for decay in your area.

CHECKPOINTS

Termites/Exterior

- Check all wood in direct contact with soil.

- Note termite tubes on foundation walls.
- Inspect crawl spaces for telltale signs.
- Probe all suspicious areas with a pointed tool.
- Check cracks in foundation walls.

Termites/Interior

- Look for discarded swarmers' wings.
- Check for termite mud tubes.

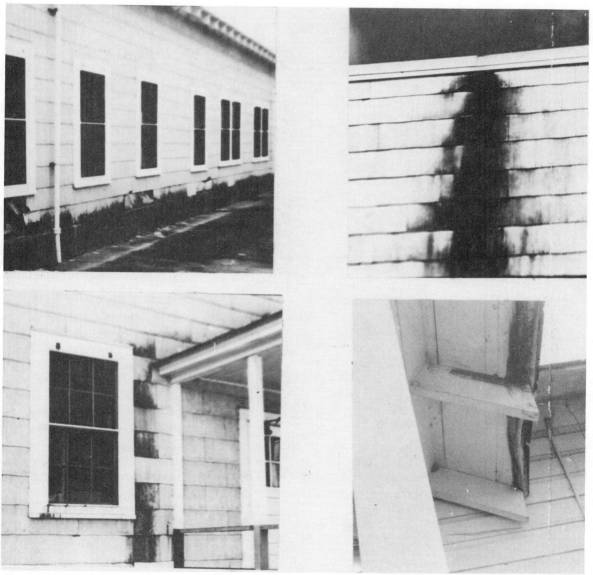

Fig. 7-27. Areas of a building that are subject to repeated wettings. Courtesy of Forest Service, USDA.

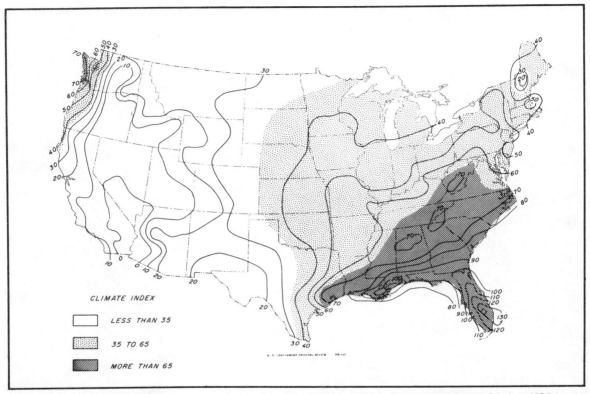

CLIMATE INDEX

LESS THAN 35

35 TO 65

MORE THAN 65

Fig. 7-28. This map indicates areas of high moisture and potential for decay. Courtesy of Forest Service, USDA.

• Inspect the bottom of wooden posts, partition walls, and the base of cellar stairs.

• Probe all sills, joists, and girders.

• Look behind access panels in finished rooms.

• Check around water or utility pipes for signs of activity.

Powder-Post Beetles

• Look for clusters of small holes in wooden members.

• Probe damaged areas for signs of insects.

• Check the frass (wood powder) to see if it is fresh.

• Examine exit holes to see if they are new.

Carpenter Ants

• Look for piles of unexplained sawdust.

• Check for discarded swarming ant wings.

• Are there large black ants in the house?

• Probe all suspect areas.

Rot

• Check for discoloration in wood members.

• Probe suspected areas, particularly ones that are subject to periodic wettings.

• Check for structural integrity of framing members in crawl spaces and under kitchen and bathrooms.

• Probe sills, joists, and girders for signs of decay and rot.

Electrical Wiring

As you well know, the electrical system in a home can either be a good servant or a dangerous enemy. For it to be a good servant, your home must be properly wired. All too often, however, houses are not correctly wired. Be on the look-out for wiring that does not meet code specifications. Wires installed by a handyman can cause serious injury or even death. Many fires are caused each year because electrical codes were violated and installations faulty. Clearly, if owners were aware of the defects in their systems, loss of life and destruction of homes could often be avoided.

The purpose of this chapter is for you to be able to identify trouble spots in the total electric service. You do not have to be trained or be an expert with electricity to detect defects. By the time you have read this chapter thoroughly—not once but several times—and have gone over the summary at the end of the chapter, you should have a very good idea of what to look for when you check an electric service.

EXTERIOR

Start your inspection on the exterior of the house. Figure 8-1 shows a typical *service entrance*. Count the number of wires entering the house from the utility pole to find out whether there is sufficient voltage. Three wires—two carrying 120 volts each and one neutral wire—provide the standard 240-volt service needed for a modern home. This is illustrated in Fig. 8-2.

Examine the *entrance head* visually. It should be at least 10 feet above the ground to prevent accidental contact with people. The *conductor wire*, which extends along the side of the house, should be securely attached. In addition, many local codes call for a metal *conduit* to protect the lower section from accidental damage—usually 6 feet above the foundation. A good example of this is shown in Fig. 8-3. While you are examining the main line, also check the electric *meter*, which may be located adjacent to it. Sometimes they are located in the basement, and if this is the case check it while you are there. Is the gauge spinning rapidly? If so, check to see if any unusually high amount of electricity is being used at that time. If there are no major appliances in operation, the system may be defective.

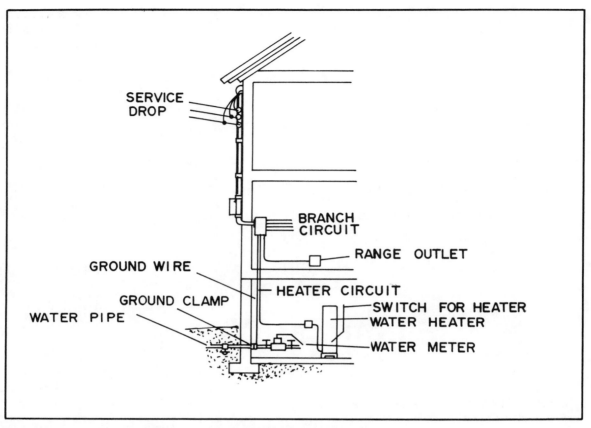

Fig. 8-1. This is a good example of a typical service entrance to a house.

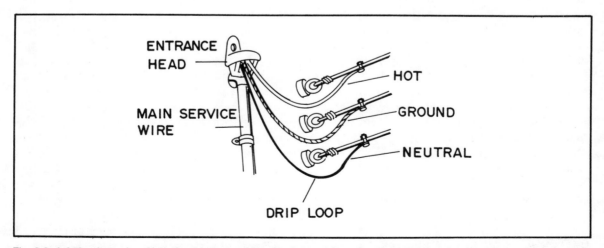

Fig. 8-2. A 240-volt service. Note the drip loop, which sheds water from the wires and thereby prevents water from entering the service conduit.

Fig. 8-3. Protective metal conduit on lower portion of service wire.

Ask the owner to show you the bills for the past few years. If they are comparatively high, find out why and see if the reasons are plausible. Unless the high amount of consumption is explained, you may find yourself paying for electricity that you have not used.

INTERIOR/BASEMENT

After the initial inspection of the exterior electrical system, you will be ready to inspect the interior system. First, before you even approach the main service box, you must see if the system is properly grounded. *Grounding* is the connection of the electrical service to the earth, a precaution necessary to prevent damage from lightning and to minimize danger from shocks. Find the main water pipe coming in from the street. There should be a wire connection at the *street side* of the water meter, as shown in Fig. 8-4. It is very important that the ground connection is on the street side of the meter. If it is on the house side of the water meter, the ground circuit would disconnect upon removal of the meter and become a shock hazard.

Here is what to watch for in your inspection of the ground connection: see if the ground connection is properly secured to the water pipe. Sometimes an amateur mechanic, in the process of doing household repairs, will disconnect the ground and forget to reconnect it. This can be seen in Fig. 8-5. Also look for signs of corrosion or deterioration, which could indicate a poor connection. Exam-

Fig. 8-4. Grounding cable connection to the street side of the water meter.

Fig. 8-5. A grounding cable disconnected from the water pipe. This potentially hazardous situation should be corrected by a licensed electrician.

ine the water pipe to be sure it is a metal water pipe and not plastic. Grounds are meant to be attached to metal pipes or rods that are several feet in the ground.

Once you are sure the condition of the ground is okay, find the main *service panel,* in which the main *fuses* or *circuit breakers* are usually located. The *branch circuit fuses* or circuit breakers may also be located within this box. The first thing that you want to do is test the *main disconnect switch,* although not before you have put on all available lights, including those in the basement. Once they are on, return to the main service panel and pull the main disconnect switch. Figure 8-6 shows the main disconnect switch. All of the lights in the house should go out.

If not, a serious defect exists in the system. This must be found and corrected by a licensed electrician. You should also pull the main switch to see whether it will indeed disconnect. Often main switches become inoperable due to corrosion or nonuse. If it does not disconnect, be sure to record it and have the owner correct it before you move in.

If the branch circuits consist of circuit breakers, you should check each individually by tripping them from the "on" to the "off" position as demonstrated in Fig. 8-7. (All circuit breakers should be tested semiannually to make sure that they are in working order.) You may notice some doubled-up circuit breakers that are for individual appliances such as electric dryers and electric hot water tanks. When you trip these, they should go off

Fig. 8-6. The main disconnect switch shuts off all power to the house.

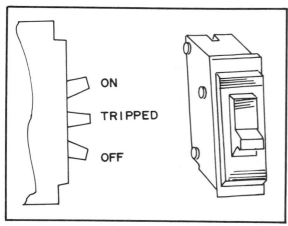

Fig. 8-7. Circuit breaker showing the on, off, and tripped positions.

simultaneously. If they don't there is a serious defect. Again, it should be recorded.

Another kind of circuit breaker is the *ground fault interrupter* (GFI). GFI's are supersensitive circuit breakers that monitor the current flow in the wires of a circuit. If a fault exists, the GFI will cut off the power to the circuit within 1/50 of a second. This could save lives, because a continuous flow through your body can be lethal. The latest electrical codes require GFI's in outdoor and bathroom circuits, because these areas are where mishaps are likely to occur. GFI's have their own test and reset buttons. Figure 8-8 shows the ground fault interrupter circuit and its test button. A GFI should be tested on a monthly basis. As soon as it is noticed that they do not operate properly, an electrician should be called to make the necessary repairs.

Older-type panel boxes usually contain fuses rather than circuit breakers. In Fig. 8-9, you can see the different types of fuses in current use. Fuses are equally safe and adequate as circuit breakers of equivalent capacity, provided fuses of the proper size are used. Often homeowners replace fuses in a circuit designed for a 15-amp fuse with a 20- or 30-ampere fuse. If a circuit wired with a No. 14 wire (current capacity 15 amperes) is fused with a 20- or 30-ampere fuse, an overload could occur, because more current will pass through the circuit than the No. 14 wire can safely carry. The wire heats up and

could cause a fire. Make sure that each wire is fused properly.

By following along each wire that comes out of the service panel, you will be able to determine the design requirements of the fuses or circuit breakers. The lettering on the wire insulation tells the type of fuse or circuit it should have. A No. 14 wire should only be fused with a 15-amp circuit or fuse, and a No. 12 wire should take a 20-amp circuit or fuse. *Under no circumstances* should a 30-amp fuse or circuit breaker ever be connected to either a No. 14 or No. 12 wire. Refer to Table 8-1 for a correct wire load guide.

TYPES OF WIRE

Electric current is carried in different types of wire. Knowledge of the types of residential house wire will aid you in your inspection.

Knob and Tube Wire

This type of wire is commonly found in older

Fig. 8-8. Ground fault interrupter circuit. Note the test button below the on-off switch.

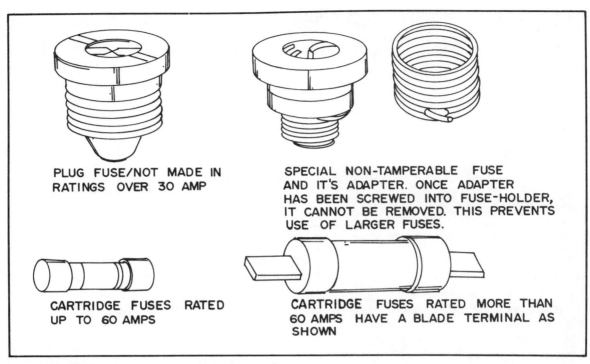

Fig. 8-9. Illustration of the various kinds of fuses in use today.

homes. It is obsolete and often dangerous. Installation consists of two parallel strands of insulated black wire strung several inches apart on porcelain knobs, protected by porcelain tubes. This type of wiring tends to be brittle and hazardous in exposed areas. Another disadvantage is that new wire cannot safely be spliced into it. Figure 8-10 is a good example of this potentially dangerous wiring.

Romex and BX

The two basic types of electrical wire found in

most homes are: *flexible armored cable* called *BX* and plastic covered wire, commonly called *romex*. (See Fig. 8-11.) Both of these types meet the National Electric Code safety requirements. If installed correctly, they will present no physical hazards to either the home or the persons residing in it.

Lamp Cord

Common lamp cord is sometimes used to provide extra outlets or to extend an existing outlet. Both of these practices are dangerous, because lamp

Table 8-1. Correct Size Fuse for Copper or Aluminum Wire.

Wire Amperage Rating	Wire Size/Copper	Wire Size/Aluminum
15 amp	No. 14	No. 12
20 amp	No. 12	No. 10
30 amp	No. 10	No. 8
40 amp	No. 8	No. 6
55 amp	No. 6	No. 4
70 amp	No. 4	No. 2
100 amp	No. 2	No. 0

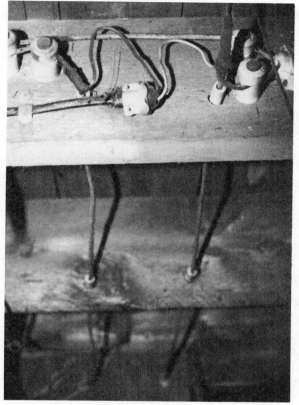

Fig. 8-10. Old knob-and-tube wiring is still used in some homes today. It is considered dangerous by most electricians and removal of it from the home would be wise.

cord is only suitable to replace a cord on a lamp or other similar small appliances. When overloaded, this flimsy cord will heat up and cause a fire. Sometimes homeowners try to hide their makeshift wiring under rugs, as shown in Fig. 8-12. If you see any such dangerous wiring, note the location and tell the owner. If you buy the house, be sure to have an electrician provide correct outlets in these areas.

Aluminum Wiring

A special word of caution about the use of aluminum wire in the general lighting circuits of a home is necessary here. Fires and deaths are evidence of the fact that aluminum wire heats up much more quickly than copper wire and is therefore an unsatisfactory conductor of electricity.

Copper-clad aluminum wire (aluminum wire with a thin coating of copper) is a reasonable compromise, but copper is still the best conductor. In your inspection of the general wiring (wires branching off of 15- and 20-amp circuits), check to see whether aluminum wire was used. You can tell it is aluminum if you don't see any copper.

If you do find aluminum wiring, you must next check to see if the proper receptacles were used. Wall outlets as well as switches for aluminum wiring are marked CO__ALR or CU__AL. Both markings mean that the device is specifically designed

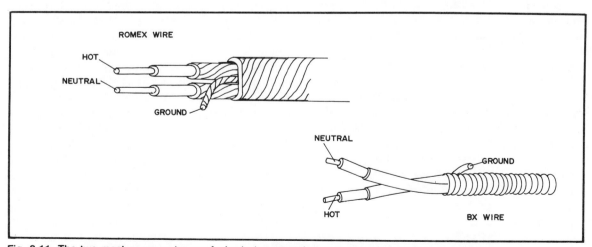

Fig. 8-11. The two most common types of wire in homes today. Note the ground wire on each type.

Fig. 8-12. Placing wires under rugs is a potential fire hazard and should not be allowed in the home.

WIRING ADEQUACY

Although wiring adequacy can be pretty much determined by reading the main disconnect on the main circuit or fuse panel, this is not always true. Often the main will read 100 amps but when it is pulled, the fuse or circuit breaker will show a 60-amp fuse or breaker. It is also important to check the size of the main wire leading into the house. A 100-amp service will require a No. 2 wire, but you may find a higher, less safe wire instead. This type of shoddy workmanship is found on low quality construction and in areas where local building inspectors are lax on their inspections. The National Electric Code specifies that newly constructed homes be provided with a minimum of 100-ampere three-wire service. If the subject house has a 60-ampere or lower main, it is recommended that it be rewired for at least a minimum of 100 amperes. Actually, the cost between 100 and 150 amperes is negligible, and the higher rating should be considered. As you are inspecting the main line, carefully examine the printing on it. If you are lucky, you may be able to read the size of the wire.

for use with either copper or aluminum wire.

If aluminum wire was used, it should have been sized larger than the usual sized copper wire. For example, if No. 14 copper wire is recommended for a 15-amp fuse, a No. 12 aluminum wire should have been used. If you find that the house does have aluminum wiring, and that it has the correct type of switch and outlet receptacles with the required wire size, the system should be safe.

If you still have some doubts about the safety of the wiring, look for some telltale signs. Going from room to room, check each outlet and switch for uncharacteristically warm cover plates. This is a definite sign of a problem. Note an unusual amount of nonfunctioning outlets and switches. And of course, if you smell anything smoldering or see smoke coming from any receptacle in the house, you know you have a problem. In a case like this, first inform the owner and if you do purchase the house, be sure to have the wiring checked out by an electrician.

INSPECTING BEHIND THE COVER PLATE

Now an important word about inspecting behind the protective cover plate of the service panel. (See Fig. 8-13.) Remember that it is very dangerous to take the protective cover off and expose yourself to the live wires shown in Fig. 8-14. Many important clues to the true condition of the electrical service, however, can only be detected by checking the following areas for defects. Sometimes a handyman homeowner decides he needs an extra circuit and provides one by doubling-up on an existing circuit. This only overloads the circuit and invites a potential fire. By checking behind the panel, you are able to see if some of the circuits are *dummy circuits*. These circuits contain a fuse and may appear to be functional but, in fact, are not even wired. Often an owner will put a fuse into an unwired fuse holder just to give the appearance that the service has the required amount of fuses or circuits.

portant. A general rule of thumb is that a separate 20-amp general purpose circuit is recommended for every 500 square feet, or a 15-amp circuit for every 375 square feet, of floor space. In addition, you should have at least two 20-amp appliance grounded-type circuits for the kitchen and the laundry room, independent of normal lighting fixtures.

If an electric stove is part of the house, a separate 50-amp circuit should be provided just for the stove. Individual 30-amp fuses or circuit breakers should also be part of the service for an electric clothes dryer, electric hot water tank, and central air conditioning. If the house does not have these appliances, you will not need the additional 30-amp circuits. See Table 8-2 for a list of individual appliances requiring separate circuits.

Fig. 8-13. An electric service panel with its protective covers in place.

Other defects that can be found behind the cover panel include signs of corrosion in the box or on the wire connections. Water sometimes drips down the external masthead and works its way into the panel. Corrosion will interfere with correct electrical contact and could cause electrical problems with the service. Note any such corrosion and double-check the tightness of the external masthead.

Check for signs of melting insulation on the electric wires. This is an indication of undersized wire connected to fuses or circuit breakers that are too large for the wire. This usually occurs with 30-amp fuses used with either No. 14 or No. 12 wire. (A 30-amp fuse should be connected to only No. 10 wire.) Be sure to replace such overfused circuits with appropriately sized fuses.

NUMBER OF CIRCUITS

The number of circuits in the panel box is im-

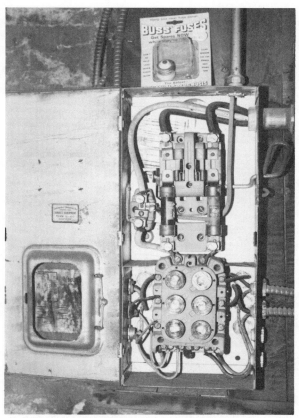

Fig. 8-14. The protective covers removed and the live wires exposed. Only a professional should expose himself to such danger.

Table 8-2. Correct Fuse Size for Appliances According to Electrical Code.

It is customary to provide a separate circuit for each of the following appliances.	
Electric Stove:	50 amp fuse
Water Heater:	30 amp fuse
Washing Machine:	20 amp fuse
Clothes Dryer:	30 amp fuse
Garbage Disposal:	20 amp fuse
Dishwasher:	20 amp fuse
Furnace:	15 amp fuse
Water Pumps:	15 amp fuse

SAFETY

During your inspection of the basement, be sure to note on your worksheet any visible safety or electrical hazards. Panel boxes should only be accessible from the front, and the doors should be such that

Fig. 8-15. An open junction box with exposed live wires is a hazard. A protective cover should be provided.

no accidental contact with electrical current could be possible. All switches, outlets, and junction boxes should have covers to protect against the danger of electric shock. Figure 8-15 shows an open junction box with live wires. Also note any frayed or bare wires that could constitute a safety hazard. Check for the improper use of lamp cord and the running of live wires under rugs, both of which pose serious potential fire hazards.

INTERIOR/LIVING AREAS

In your inspection of the living areas of the house, be sure to check each room for electrical outlets. A convenience outlet located every 6 feet of running wall space is required to provide flexibility in furniture placement and cut down on the use of long extension cords. Many communities require that each room have at least two outlets. Keep in mind that this is a bare minimum requirement. In kitchens, outlets every 4 feet of counter space provide quick plug-in of appliances. In bathrooms, outlets and switches must not be reachable from the tub or shower. All outlets must be covered with a protective plate to prevent the contact of wiring with the body, combustible objects, or splashing water.

Be on the lookout for "octopus" wiring arrangements. This is a plug inserted into an outlet to allow you to use a multiple of portable appliances at the same time rather than the amount normally used. Figure 8-16 shows this type of improper arrangement. This type of wiring is no substitute for the lack of sufficient outlets. Note any such wiring and be sure to have an electrician add sufficient outlets to prevent circuit overloading.

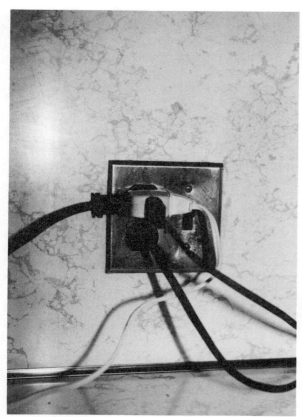

Fig. 8-16. Octopus arrangements should be corrected with additional circuits.

When checking outlets, you must see if they are functional and properly grounded. Use an electrical *circuit tester*, as shown in Fig. 8-17, to do this. These types of testers can be purchased in most electrical supply stores for a nominal fee. Grounded outlets should have three slots. The third slot (the semicircular slot) is the *grounding connection*. If the circuit tester lights up when its leads are inserted into the parallel slots, the outlet is functional. To test for proper grounding, one lead of the tester is inserted into the hot side of the outlet (usually the smaller of the two elongated slots), and the other lead is inserted into the third slot. If the tester does not light up, the outlet is not grounded. Ungrounded outlets are extremely hazardous and must be corrected. Note any difficiencies on your worksheet.

Summary. You inspect electrical systems to detect obvious evidence of insufficient power supply, to ensure the availability of adequate and safe lighting and electrical facilities, and to discover and correct any obvious hazards. Should you be in serious doubt—electricity is technical and complicated—do not hesitate to consult with a professional home inspector or a licensed electrician. It is always better to be safe than sorry.

CHECKPOINTS

Remember that under no circumstances should you touch any exposed wiring or probe with tools in electrical panels.

Exterior

- Is the service drop a three-wire or two-wire?

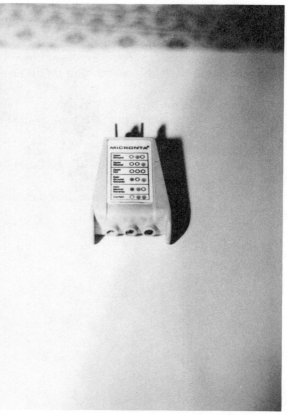

Fig. 8-17. An electrical tester is an invaluable tool to assist you in determining the condition of electrical outlets.

(Note that a two wire service only provides 120 volts, which is considered inadequate.)

- Is the service wire from the entrance head down to the meter secured to the building?
- Does the electric meter appear defective?
- Is the insulation on the service wire intact? If not, is there any exposed wiring?
- Are there obstructions in contact with the overhead wires? (Tree limbs sometimes cause problems with wires.)
- Are there openings in the building that will allow water to affect the electrical service?
- Are there outside outlets or lights? (If so, are they watertight and functional?)
- Are exterior circuits provided with ground fault interrupters (GFI's)?

Interior/Basement

- Check the electric service ground to see whether it is disconnected or loose.
- Is the ground connected to a metal pipe?
- Does the main disconnect shut off all electrical circuits?
- Are all circuit breakers working?
- Are there ground fault interrupters in the system and are they working?
- Is there overfusing in the service box?
- Are the wire sizes appropriate for the fuse or circuit breakers?
- Do individual appliances have their own separate circuits?

- Is there old knob and tube wiring in the house, and is it deteriorating?
- Has lamp cord wire been used to provide additional outlets?
- Is there aluminum wiring in the house? Does it appear safe?
- Are there open junction boxes with exposed wires?
- Are there openings in the main panel box that could allow someone to come in contact with live wires?
- Are there exposed live wires hanging from the ceiling or on the floor?

Interior/Living Areas

- Do the living areas of the house have sufficient outlets and lighting?
- Are all switches and outlets properly grounded?
- Do the kitchen and bathrooms have sufficient and safe outlets?
- Are all outlets in good working condition?
- Are there "octopus" arrangements with outlets?
- Does the bathroom have a ground fault interrupter and is it working?
- Is there use of lamp cord for outlet wiring?
- Are there cords under rugs or flooring?
- Do appliances have their own separate circuits?
- Do all overhead lights have switches?

Heating

Heating systems fall into two basic categories: *central heating* systems and *space heaters*. Each has advantages and disadvantages. In this chapter you will read about the three basic central heating systems, namely warm air, steam, and hot water. (References to space heating units such as fireplaces, wood-burning stoves, and electrical heating have been made in Chapters 12 and 16.)

All central heating systems consist of burners, combustion chambers, heat exchangers, distribution systems (ducts or pipes), heat outlets (registers or radiators), and automatic safety and temperature controls (gauges and thermostats); most use either gas or oil, and some use electricity, wood, coal, or solar energy to generate heat. Systems differ from each other in the manner in which they produce heat and are categorized accordingly.

WARM-AIR SYSTEM

In a warm air system, a furnace heats air that is then distributed to the rooms in the house via ducts. (See Fig. 9-1). The older *gravity-type* warm air heating system makes use only of the specific gravity difference of warm and cold air (warm air is lighter and therefore rises). The modern version, a *forced* warm air system, operates on the same principle, but adds a fan or blower to increase air movement. Because of the fan or blower, heat is delivered much more quickly to all areas of the house. This solves the drawbacks in the gravity system, where heat is slow in coming and may be insufficient in rooms that are too far away from the furnace. Figure 9-2 illustrates a modern forced warm air system.

Start your inspection by first finding the *thermostat*. Usually you find it on the first floor in a dining room or den. Turn it up to about 80 degrees, then return to the basement. One of the first areas to check is the *duct distribution system*. Look for individual dampers in branch ducts. In Fig. 9-3 you can see a duct with the damper in the closed position. Consider dampers in the ductwork a plus, because they help to control the amount of heat for each room. By closing or opening these dampers, you will be able to control the flow of heat through

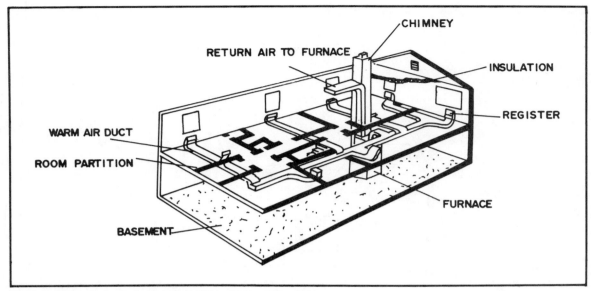

Fig. 9-1. A forced warm air system showing ducts and registers.

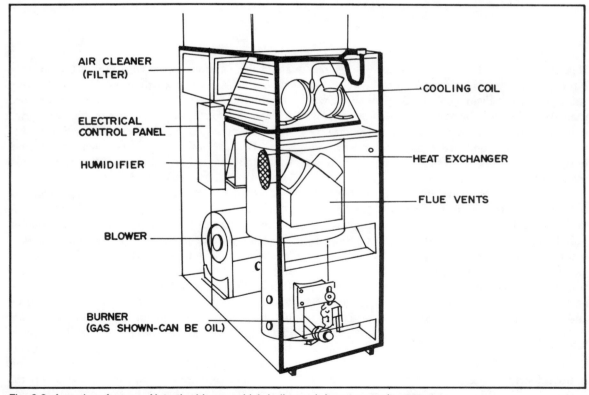

Fig. 9-2. A modern furnace. Note the blower, which indicates it is not a gravity system.

Fig. 9-3. Dampers in the duct system help control the flow of warm air. The damper is in the closed position.

them. While checking the ducts, look at the joints connecting individual ducts. Are there any open gaps through which heat is leaking into the basement? Also check the duct connections to the registers. Are they connected properly or is heat escaping into the basement? While the furnace is going, go back up to the living areas and check each room to make sure that there is a register and that sufficient warm air is discharging into the room. Note rooms that do not have registers or emit an insufficient amount of air. Figure 9-4 shows a floor register with its cover off. Note the amount of dust that has been allowed to build up. Periodic vacuuming would prevent this.

If the system is a forced warm air system, you will find a panel section that contains the fan or blower. Remove the cover so you can check it thoroughly. Look over the fan belt of the blower. Is it deteriorating and in need of replacement? Press your thumb against it. If there is more than 1/2-inch in slack, it should be adjusted and tightened for better performance. If there are oil cups in the motor, check to see if they need oil. Examine the fan for excessive dirt on the fan blades. There should be a filter adjacent to the blower unit. Check its condition. Filters should be cleaned or replaced as soon as they show signs of dust accumulations. Dirty filters impair the easy flow of warm air. In Fig. 9-5, an interior view of the compartment shows a filter that has seen better days. This filter should have been replaced several months ago. Below it is the blower.

Fig. 9-4. A floor register for a warm air system. Accumulations of dirt and dust will hamper the system. Periodic vacuuming prevents this.

Fig. 9-5. Filters should never be allowed to get this dirty. A dust-clogged filter prevents proper operation of the system. Note the blower directly behind the filter.

Some homeowners have humidifiers installed into their forced warm air systems to lessen the dryness of the heat. This is a serious mistake because the ever present moisture in the furnace seriously corrodes all metal parts in the furnace. Figure 9-6 shows a humidifier installed in a furnace plenum. Note the water stains and the corrosion on the humidifier and furnace jacket. Extensive rusting out of the metal parts could allow water to reach the heat exchanger. Once the heat exchanger is damaged, it must be replaced usually at a cost of several hundred dollars. Because the average homeowner or buyer is not capable of checking the condition of a heat exchanger, it would be wise, if in doubt, to have a heating specialist examine it.

STEAM SYSTEM

Although steam systems are, for the most part, no longer installed in new construction, you will still find them in older homes. Unlike a warm air system that uses a furnace to heat air, a steam system uses a boiler to generate steam. A good illustration of

a steam boiler is shown in Fig. 9-7. A steam boiler is partially filled with water—usually 3/4s—and the rest is air. The water is heated until it becomes steam, which then rises in the pipes (without the aid of a pump) until it reaches the radiators. Air in the radiators is expelled through air vents, as shown in Fig. 9-8. When steam comes in contact with the radiator, it turns back into water and returns to the boiler.

Steam systems are classified according to their pipe arrangement and their methods of returning the condensate (water) to the boiler. The two major types of systems are the *one-pipe air vent* and the *two-pipe return trap* system.

In the one-pipe system, condensate, pulled by gravity, returns to the boiler in the very same pipe in which steam rises. Radiators in this system have

Fig. 9-6. A humidifier can often cause more damage than good. Note the water stains on the unit and the corrosion on the furnace jacket.

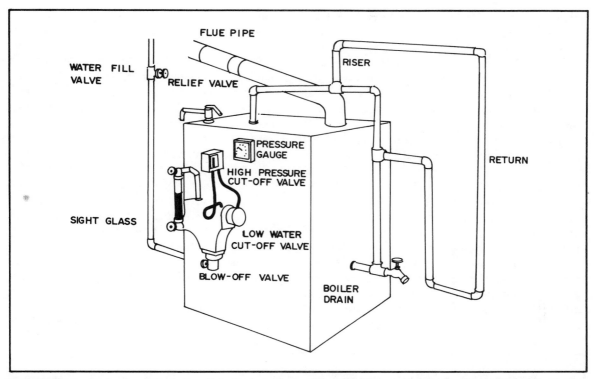

Fig. 9-7. Components of a steam boiler. Note the important safety valves (low water cut-off valve and the high pressure cut-off valve).

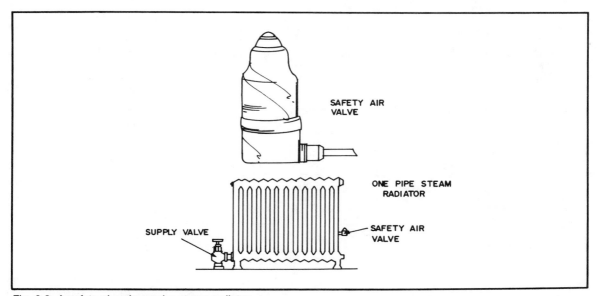

Fig. 9-8. A safety air valve and a steam radiator.

valves that permit air venting. Figure 9-9 shows a typical one-pipe system.

In the two-pipe system a thermostatically controlled air return trap permits the flow of water and air from the radiator, but prevents steam from leaving it. This is more economical than a one-pipe system, which will lose some of its heat through the venting process.

A steam system does not need pumps or fans to circulate steam, a decided advantage. Furthermore, because no water remains in the pipes when the system is at rest, there will also be no frozen pipes. The disadvantage with this type of system is that it is slow to respond to a call for heat. Some older systems take from 20 to 30 minutes to fully build up enough steam to heat a large house.

As with the warm air system, the first thing you should do is turn the thermostat up high to fire the system. In your inspection of the steam boiler, you will want to be very concerned with the water level gauge. (See Fig. 9-10.) This gauge reads the level of water in the boiler, usually half to two thirds of the way up the gauge. Should it be full of water, this would indicate that there is too much water in the system. If, on the other hand, the water level in the gauge is low, it means that the boiler needs water. Operating the system with too little or no water will crack the boiler. Operating it with too much water can cause leaks in the radiators. Both are situations you want to avoid.

The second important feature in the system is the *low-water cutoff control*. This is illustrated in Fig. 9-10, and also in a close-up shot in Fig. 9-11. This safety device shuts down the burner when the water level in the boiler is too low. It is either mounted on the exterior portion of the boiler or is part of the interior of the boiler. The interior units are self-cleaning, and there is nothing that has to be done to maintain them. The device mounted on the exterior has to be serviced monthly, however. There is a *blow-off valve*, that when opened will test the performance of the control. Looking at Fig. 9-11,

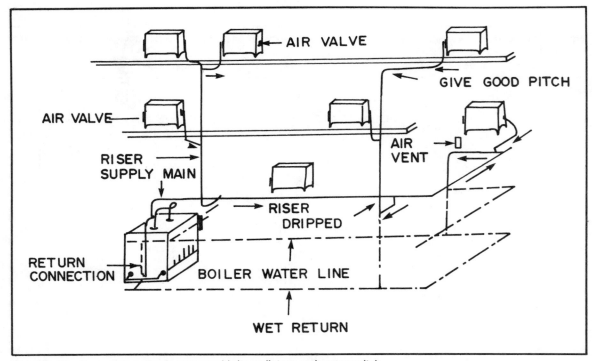

Fig. 9-9. Gravity one-pipe steam system with its radiators and proper pitch.

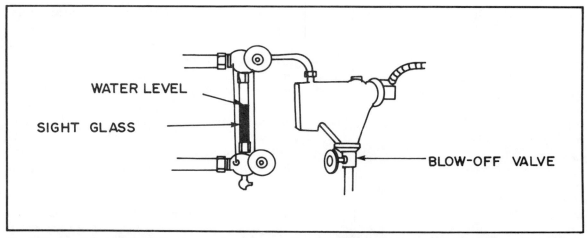

Fig. 9-10. A typical water level gauge on a steam system. The water level is approximately where you would want it on your gauge.

you will see the blow-off valve with a tag attached to it. If the boiler has such a blow-off valve test it by opening it up. Sometimes owners have not done it in years, and when you open the valve a liquid sludge may drip out. If you find such a neglected valve, note it on your worksheet for future replacement.

As the system is operating, check every room in the house to see that each room has a radiator and that the individual radiators provide sufficient heat. Sometimes the valves on the radiators are clogged with dirt or paint, and an inexpensive replacement can make the difference between a cold and a warm room. During your inspection of the radiators, be sure to check the inlet valves to see if they are working and not leaking. Note the lack of a handle on the inlet valve shown in Fig. 9-12.

HOT WATER SYSTEMS

A hot water system operates on the principle of circulation and recirculation of heated water. In this system the boiler, the piping, and all of the radiators are filled with water. Water heated in the boiler is moved through the pipes to the radiators, where the heated water gives off some of its heat. The cooler water flows back to the boiler to be reheated and recirculated. Figure 9-13 shows a forced hot water system.

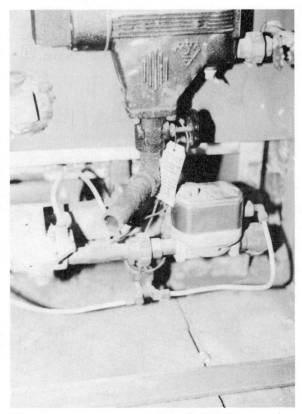

Fig. 9-11. The low water cutoff valve. Note the extensive amount of corrosion on the fittings. This unit is probably not functional and will need replacement.

Fig. 9-12. An inlet valve. Note the missing handle, which makes it all but inoperable.

When water is heated it expands and increases in volume. Therefore, an *expansion tank* is needed. (See Fig. 9-14.) A tank will either be *open (gravity system)* or *closed (forced hot water system)*. Either type must be of sufficient size to accommodate the change in water volume within the heating system. The open tank must be placed at least 3 feet above the highest point of the system and requires a vent and overflow pipe. The open tank is usually in an attic, where it is protected from freezing. Figure 9-15 shows an open expansion tank in a one-pipe gravity system.

Again, there are two basic types of hot water heating systems—gravity and forced hot water. Like the gravity hot air system, the gravity hot water system tends to be inefficient and is no longer installed in new homes. Because the system depends solely on hot water rising to displace cooler water, larger pipes are needed—about 3 inches in diameter—while the piping in a forced hot water system is usually 1 inch in diameter.

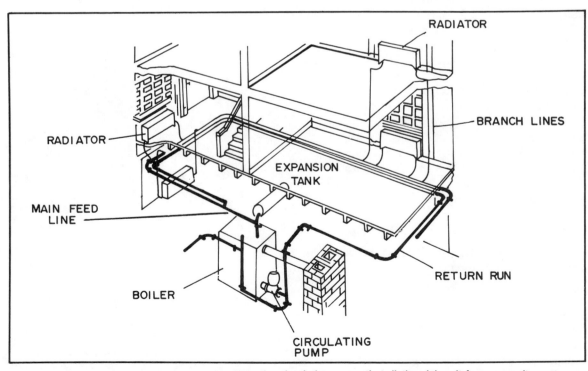

Fig. 9-13. A typical forced hot water system. Note the circulating pump that distinguishes it from a gravity system.

Fig. 9-14. A typical expansion tank found in most forced hot water systems. Note the drain valve for draining the tank.

In a forced hot water system, a circulating pump is used to circulate the heated water back through the pipes and to the radiators. In Fig. 9-16, you can see a circulating pump with three oil cups. These cups should be oiled at least once a year with a light lubricating oil. Some heating systems in larger homes may have more than one circulating pump. In these systems, different levels or areas of the house are zoned off, and each has a separate thermostat that will operate the individual circulating pumps only when heat is required.

One of the major advantages of the forced hot water system is that it is fast responding, and because hot water remains in the pipes after the boiler has shut down, there is less heat fluctuation. One of the disadvantages is, however, that because water is always present in the pipes, their joints easily corrode and frozen pipes are a possibility.

As with the other types of systems, first turn up the thermostat to fire up the boiler. If you see a circulating pump on the boiler, you know that it is a forced hot water system and not a gravity-type. Check the circulating pump's oil cups to see whether

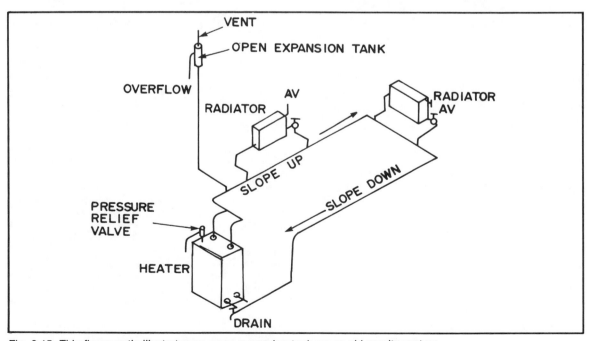

Fig. 9-15. This figure aptly illustrates an open expansion tank on an old gravity system.

Fig. 9-16. This circulating pump has three oil cups that need annual lubrication (a few drops of a light lubricating oil).

they need oil. Examine the pipes leading into and exiting from the pump for signs of corrosion or active leaks. Listen for unusual sounds that the pump might make while it is running. Squeaking noises may indicate faulty bearings and should be checked by a serviceman.

Next check the expansion tank itself and its riser pipe for signs of water leaks and corrosion. Note the absence of a *cleanout plug* on the tank, which is needed to drain it and to recushion the tank with air.

While the boiler is operating, go through all of the rooms in the house to see that each room has a radiator and that each radiator supplies sufficient heat for the room that it is in. Pay particular attention to oversized rooms with only one radiator because they may be cooler than normal sized rooms during the coldest months of the year. Check each radiator for an *air valve* which, when in the open position, will release unwanted trapped air. A radiator full of air will not become fully heated. Also check the shut-off valves and fittings at the base of radiators for active leaks and signs of corrosion. Note all your findings.

COMBUSTION CHAMBERS

All boilers and furnaces have a *combustion chamber* for burning fuel. In your inspection, no matter what type of system you are examining, be sure to check the condition of the combustion chamber. If you are lucky, you will find a door that will open and allow you to get a fairly good idea of the condition of the inside of the chamber. Sometimes these doors are sealed, such as in Fig. 9-17, and you will not be able to tell much about the shape of the

Fig. 9-17. A sealed combustion chamber door. Water stains under the door indicate a possible problem that should be checked by a serviceman.

Fig. 9-18. The interior of the combustion chamber. Note the crumbling condition of the walls. Repairs should be undertaken to prevent damage to boiler walls behind the combustion chamber.

chamber. In this case, it would be worthwhile to have this inaccessible area checked out at a later date by your serviceman. If there is an accessible door, by all means open it for a thorough inspection, but first be sure to shut off the control switch for the burner. This switch is usually right on the boiler. If there is none, check either the cellar stairway or the first floor hall leading to the cellar for such a switch. As you inspect the interior of the chamber, note deterioration in the chamber walls, such as seen in Fig. 9-18. Missing or crumbling firebrick can cause flame impingement upon the heating unit's metal frame, which could then crack. If the heating unit is a boiler, look for signs of water dripping into the chamber or evidence of previous leaks. If you have any suspicion about the condition of the chamber, have a professional examine it for you.

FLUE PIPES

Both boilers and furnaces are required by law to be connected to a chimney so that harmful gases can escape to the outside rather than into the house. Flue pipes are joined to the heating unit and the chimney. Their connections should be tight to prevent flue gases from escaping into the house. So that heating gases can be properly discharged, a flue pipe should pitch up toward the chimney at a minimum of 1/4-inch per foot; in your inspection, note dips and a poor pitch. Also, tap the bottom of the pipe with your screwdriver. If it sounds as if it is packed with soot and carbon deposits, make a note to have it cleaned before the next heating season. Carbon and soot deposits will cause rust to eat through the pipe. (See Fig. 9-19).

Fig. 9-19. This is a good example of what carbon and soot deposits can do to metal flues. Annual cleanings would have prevented this deterioration.

Fig. 9-20. An oil burner. Burners such as these should be cleaned and serviced annually.

BURNERS

A burner is simply a device that mixes and ignites fuel and air in a combustion chamber. The two types of burners that you will most likely encounter in any type of system are an oil-fired or a gas-fired burner.

In Fig. 9-20, you see a typical oil-fired burner. Although servicing should be left to a competent serviceman, you still can check for clues to its present condition. While the burner is operating, listen for unusual sounds that may indicate a faulty transformer or fuel pump. Gently rock the burner back and forth to see that it is properly attached to the combustion chamber. Loosely mounted burners do not fire properly and are costly to operate. Examine the fan for dust and dirt build-up that would impede its operation, as well. Note air leaks around the burner connections to the boiler.

A gas burner, unlike an oil burner, has fewer moving parts and therefore requires to be serviced and inspected only every 2 or 3 years. An oil burner requires servicing every year in order to function properly. Another important difference between the two is that the gas flame in the burner should be blue, whereas in an oil burner the flame should be a sun yellow. If you come across a burner flame that does not correspond to these colors, be sure to have it checked out for possible defects. Figure 9-21 is an example of a gas burner.

As you examine the gas burner, watch the flames for a minute or two. Are they steady or do the flicker? (Fluctuating flames are indicative of a burner malfunction and should be noted on your worksheet.) While the burner is operating, shut off the emergency switch on the boiler to see if it is functional. If the burner continues to run, the switch

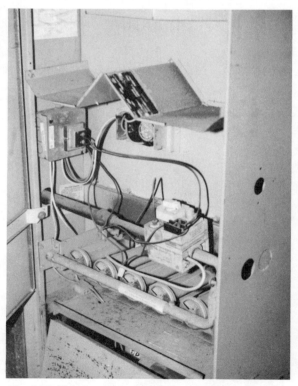

Fig. 9-21. This figure show a gas burner in a warm air furnace. Unlike oil burners, they do not need annual servicing. Servicing and cleaning every 3 years in most instances is sufficient.

is faulty and will need replacement. Also look for excessive amounts of corrosion on the burner, particularly on the burner jets. Build-up of rust particles clogs the burner jets and makes them inoperable. A simple cleaning will overcome this problem.

DRAFT UNITS

Both gas and oil have specific types of draft inducing elements in their breeching pipes. A gas *draft diverter*, as shown in Fig. 9-22, is a good place to check for problems with the gas exhaust. While the system is running, put your hand near the draft diverter. You should not feel an outward flow of hot exhaust gas against your hand. If you do, dangerous gases are not being vented correctly. Have the draft diverter and its chimney connection checked by a serviceman.

Oil-fired systems require a draft regulator on or near the flue pipe. Figure 9-23 shows a draft regulator in a flue pipe. Be sure to check its condition. Is it operable? Is it rusting out and in need of replacement? If you don't find one, note it on your worksheet. A draft regulator is needed for proper combustion.

THERMOSTATS

A thermostat is an electrically operated, temperature sensitive switch that is used to automatically turn on and turn off the heating system. All central heating systems have at least one thermostat, which should be mounted on an inside wall, approximately 4 feet above the floor. No cold drafts should affect it, and neither should it be affected by warm air or heat. A thermostat in direct line with a door opening to the outside will kick on the heating system every time you open the door in winter. If it is located above a radiator or a warm

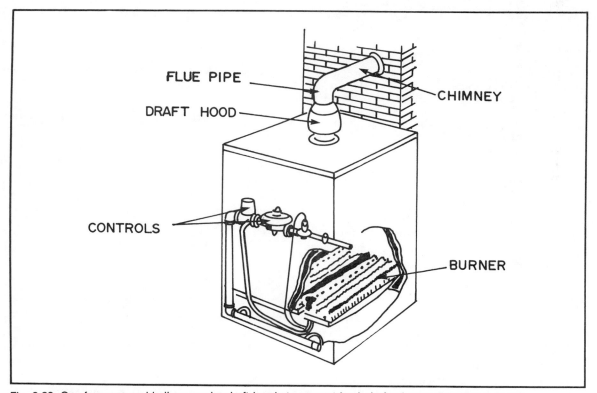

Fig. 9-22. Gas furnaces and boilers require draft hoods to prevent back drafts that would affect the pilot.

Fig. 9-23. Oil-burning appliances use a draft diverter to control air flow in the chimney. Note the missing screw on the top of the draft control plate. This is needed to properly adjust the unit.

air duct, on the other hand, it will be fooled by the heat and not kick on at all when it should. Note any obstacles placed next to the thermostat; they will block the free natural flow of air and thereby prevent the unit from operating properly. Consider having a day-night thermostat installed to cut heat costs.

SAFETY CONTROLS

All three systems have control valves and gauges that shut off the system in an emergency. Steam and hot water controls read water temperature and steam pressure, while warm air system controls read air temperature and control fan operation. In addition to those, the two basic fuels

(gas and oil) also have specific controls that you must inspect as well.

Warm Air Controls

There are two basic controls in a warm air system (not including the thermostat): a *fan control* and a *high temperature control*. The purpose of the fan control is to simply blow off built-up warm air in the system until the temperature in the heat exchanger drops from a present temperature of approximately 120° F to about 85° F. The high temperature limit control is a safety control that will turn off the burner if the temperature in the heat exchanger gets too high—usually around 175° F. The best way to test these two controls is by running the system. If the fan doesn't turn on after the burner has been operating for a while, or if the heat coming from the registers is too intense, then assume that the controls are faulty and some adjustments must be made. Be sure to bring this to the attention of the owner.

Steam Controls

The low-water cutoff and the water-level gauge controls have already been discussed in this chapter. In addition to these two controls there is also a *pressure relief valve* and a *high temperature limit switch*. The relief valve is a safety valve that automatically discharges when the operating pressure is too high, usually around 15 psi. The high pressure limit switch is connected to the burner. When the pressure in the boiler exceeds a predetermined setting, the switch will shut down the burner. As with the warm air system, make sure you run it in order to test these important safety valves.

Hot Water Controls

As with the steam system, a hot water system employs a relief valve as a safety control. It will discharge hot water when the predetermined pressure is exceeded. On a hot water boiler the maximum pressure is usually 30 psi. There is also a high limit temperature control that prevents the boiler water from exceeding a preset temperature. If the

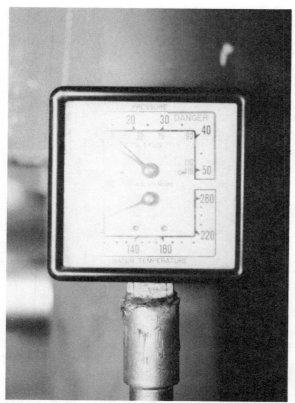

Fig. 9-24. The high limit control valve is used on hot water systems to prevent pressure or temperature problems.

mocouple, which is a standard safety device that will close and prevent the flow of gas in case of an emergency. Figure 9-26 shows a gas burner with its gas pilot and thermocouple unit. A close-up view of the pilot and the thermocouple can be seen in Fig. 9-27. Note the lack of any such safety device on the subject system and be sure to have them installed once you own the house.

OIL FUEL INSPECTION

In an oil-fired system, check the tank for leaks and corrosion. Sometimes you will find a plug that was installed to stop a leak. This is usually only a stop-gap. If the bottom of the tank is rusting away, you may need a replacement. The cost, including installation, is usually a few hundred dollars. Men-

relief valve is dripping water at the time of the inspection, note it on your worksheet for further investigation. When you have the system cleaned and serviced, be sure to have the serviceman run a test on the limit control to make certain it is functional. Figure 9-24 shows the high limit control.

Fuel Controls

Both gas and oil have specific controls that stop the flow of fuel to the burner. Be sure to check that these control valves are present in the system. On an oil system, look for *firomatic safety valves*, which shut down the system if there is a malfunction. There should be three of them: one on the fuel tank, one on the oil burner, and one over the heating plant. Figure 9-25 shows a firomatic over a furnace.

On a gas-fired heating system, look for a *ther-*

Fig. 9-25. A firomatic oil safety valve. Its purpose is to automatically close in an emergency.

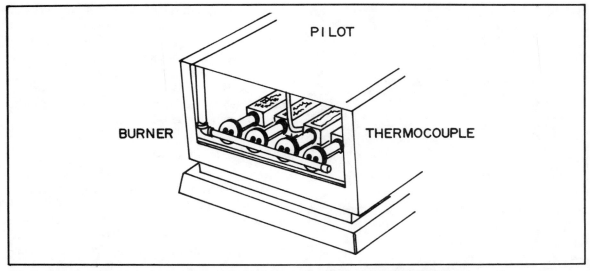

Fig. 9-26. Gas-fired appliances use a gas pilot and a safety valve called a thermocouple.

tion this fact to the owners, perhaps they may replace it for you. Be sure to check the oil outlet and oil filter for leaks. Also note how close the oil storage tank is to the boiler or furnace. It should not be closer than 5 feet. Can you read the oil gauge on the tank? It is important that the gauge is working. Check the outlet pipe to see whether the re-

quired firomatic is on the oil line. Is the tank accessible? Homeowners love to build partitions around the tank or pile household goods against it. A tank should be visible and accessible for inspection and repairs at all times. Figure 9-28 illustrates a typical oil tank installation.

After you are finished inspecting the oil tank,

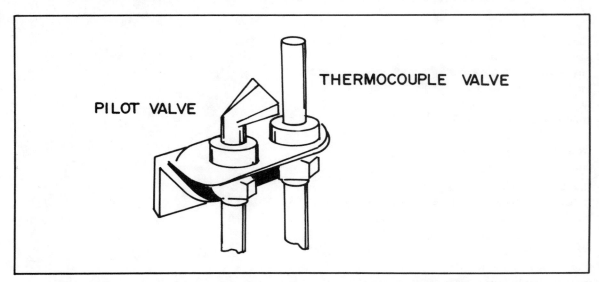

Fig. 9-27. A close-up of these two parts of a gas burner. The thermocouple automatically shuts down the burner during a malfunction.

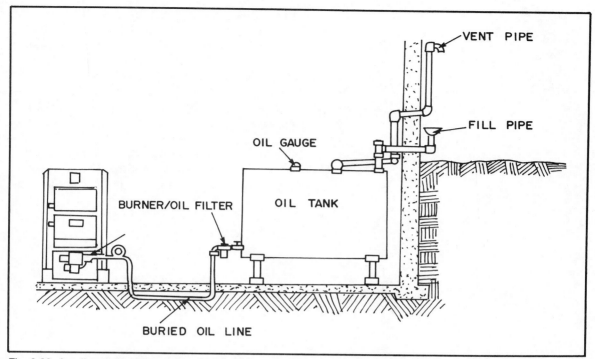

Fig. 9-28. An oil tank must be at least 5 feet from an oil burner. Note the location of the vent pipe to the oil fill pipe. It should always be above the fill pipe to prevent venting problems.

turn your attention to the oil burner. If the owner is present, ask how often the burner is serviced. Oil burners should be cleaned, inspected, and serviced annually. Look for signs of poor maintenance like deposits of soot and carbon on or around the burner. This indicates poor firing of the burner and more than likely a need for a good cleaning and tune-up. Look for leaks from the fuel pump or oil connections. If the fuel line coming from the oil tank to the oil burner is not protected, note it on your worksheet. An exposed line can be accidentally damaged by someone stepping on it. Note the lack of a firomatic on the T-connection of the fuel line in Fig. 9-29. In a fire, this line would continue to discharge oil.

GAS FUEL INSPECTION

In a gas-fired system, check the gas lines for rust on pipes and fittings. (See Fig. 9-30.) Run your hand along suspect areas. Do you smell gas? If so,

Fig. 9-29. An oil filter without a firomatic safety valve. Be sure to report any such findings to the owner.

111

Fig. 9-30. A typical gas line installation. Be sure to check for any signs of gas leaks and/or rusting pipes. If either is noted, be sure to have the necessary repairs done.

have the local gas company check the possibility of a gas leak. Check the gas line next to the boiler or furnace. Is there an easy to use gas shut-off? If not, make a note of it and have one installed. Smell around the gas burner and fittings. Is there a gas odor? Even the slightest whiff should concern you, and the owner should be made aware of it. If you do purchase the house, you should consider installing a *gas alarm*. This relatively inexpensive gadget will alert you to the slightest leak.

SERVICE CONTRACTS

Once you buy the house, you should contract with a fuel company to service and maintain your heating system on an annual basis. One of the first things that you should ask for is an *efficiency audit* of the entire system. The completed audit will give you a very good idea on how efficient or inefficient the system really is. Tests are made on the burner, the combustion chamber, and the flue pipe to determine the rate of combustion. The results are used to fine tune the system for its most economical operation. The charge is usually small compared to the savings in fuel. Keep in mind that a poorly maintained system will deteriorate much more rapidly than a properly serviced one and that the costs of maintenance wane in the face of the costs for major repairs.

CHECKPOINTS

Warm Air Systems

- Do all living areas have registers?
- Are there air ducts connected to all registers?
- Do all ducts have dampers?
- Are the ducts insulated?
- Are there openings in the ducts or connections to registers?
- Any signs of corrosion or rusting on the ductwork?
- Is there a humidifier in the system, and is it showing signs of deterioration?
- Does the system have filters, and are they are in need of replacement or cleaning?
- Is the fan belt for the blower loose or deteriorating?
- Do oil cups need oil?
- Are ducts too close to combustible materials?
- Is the system an old gravity feed furnace?
- Are the fan control and high limit controls working?

Steam Systems

- Do all rooms have radiators?
- Are radiator air vents functioning, or are they defective?

- Do radiators and piping bang when the system is in operation?
- Are radiators or piping leaking?
- Are safety valves and gauges damaged?
- Is there rusting or corrosion on the boiler or piping?
- Are there water stains around the boiler?
- Does the low water cutoff valve work properly?
- Is the combustion chamber intact?
- Are the pressure relief valve and the high limit switch working?

Hot Water Systems

- Do all rooms have radiators?
- Are the air release valves on the radiators working?
- Are there leaks in the radiators or in the piping?
- Does the circulating pump need oil?
- Are there signs of corrosion or rust on the boiler or its piping?
- Is the combustion chamber intact?
- Is the breeching pipe in good repair?
- Is there loose or crumbling insulation on the boiler or piping?
- Is the system an older gravity feed one?
- What is the condition of the relief valve and the limit control valve?

Burners

- What kind of fuel is being used?
- How old is the burner?

- Are the visible defects?
- Are there unusual sounds coming from the burner while it is operating?
- When was it last serviced?
- Are there any leaks?

Thermostats

- Are they located too high or too low on a wall?
- Is the thermostat too close to a window or door?
- Are there obstacles blocking the free flow of air around the thermostat?
- Is the thermostat too close to a source of heat?

Oil Storage Tanks

- Are there leaks at the oil filter lines?
- Is there corrosion and rusting on the underside of the tank?
- Is the oil line going from the tank to the burner protected?
- Is the oil gauge in good repair?
- Are there emergency shut-offs on the oil line or filters?
- Are all firomatics working and in good repair?

Gas

- Does the burner have a thermocouple?
- Do you smell any gas odors from the burner or the pipes?
- Any corrosion on gas pipes?
- Consider buying a gas alarm for the house.

Plumbing

The plumbing system of any house has three components: an adequate potable (clean) water supply, a satisfactory drainage system, and ample fixtures and equipment. Its function is to supply sufficient amounts of hot and cold water and to drain all waste water and sewage to a public or private disposal system.

Because a great deal of the plumbing is hidden between walls or under floors, it is very important that you check very carefully the exposed plumbing members located in the basement. Signs of defects in water lines or drainage pipes can usually be found there. If the house has a private waste disposal system, be sure to question the owner about its condition and maintenance. It is also vital to have the owner tell you exactly where the tank is. Defects in plumbing systems cannot only be costly to repair but also hazardous to the occupant's health. Be sure to familiarize yourself with all the components of the plumbing system, as shown in Fig. 10-1. Codes are easily violated. Use the diagrams and photographs to help you better understand the system.

To check the plumbing system, you will spend most of your time in the basement, although some parts can be checked in the bathrooms and kitchen. (Chapter 15 details what to look for in these areas.)

MAIN WATER LINE

Your first job is to find the *main water line*. This is usually located at the base of the interior foundation wall with the water meter and the house electrical grounding device. Figure 10-2 shows what you are looking for. Here is where your actual inspection begins. Look for the main shut-off valve, which should be located between the water meter and the foundation wall, although sometimes it is on house side of the meter. Not having a main shut-off valve could be a problem. If there is a leak at the meter and you don't have a shut-off before it, you could end up with a flooded basement. Not having a shut-off after the meter can be bothersome, especially if the branch shut-off valves are not working. Note the lack of a main shut-off valve and consider hiring a plumber to install one.

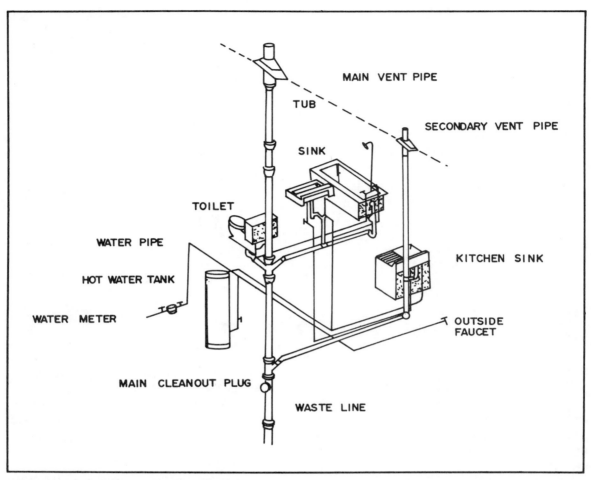

Fig. 10-1. Components of a plumbing system.

The next thing you should do is see if the main water line coming into the house is lead. In many older houses, the main lines are lead pipes. They are a health hazard because of the leaching of lead into the water supply. Lead can be distinguished from copper or brass by its gray color. Take your thumb and gently scratch the surface of the pipe; copper or brass will show a shiny copper color; lead will be a dull gray. Brass or copper will also have threaded or soldered fittings. If the line is lead, and you should buy the house, consider having a plumber install a new water line. Other types of pipes found in homes are plastic, galvanized iron, and stainless steel, all of which are safe.

Check the water meter for leaks or signs of corrosion and see that the main shut-off shows no signs of deterioration. Ask the owner whether the main shut-off valve is working properly, and test it by shutting it off and back on again. Often, particularly in older homes, the main valve is frozen in the open position. Should it be inoperable, an additional one should be installed by a plumber.

The size of water pipes is also important. The main coming into the house should be a minimum of 1 inch; smaller pipes just won't provide the necessary water pressure. The main line in the basement should be a minimum of 3/4-inch. From this main line, follow it to each branch line. Branch lines

Fig. 10-2. The main water line with a shut-off valve. Note the electrical grounding cable on the water line.

that feed fixtures will almost always be 1/2-inch in diameter. While you are checking them, be on the lookout for corrosion and deterioration, particularly in the joints.

BRANCH LINES

Check all branch lines for shut-off valves that will stop water from entering fixtures. Sometimes there are no shut-off valves in the basement, but you will find them directly under the individual fixtures that they service. Figure 10-3 shows bathroom fixtures with shut-off valves. Test all valves by turning them off and on. Make a note of any that aren't working.

Water lines should be checked to see that they are properly supported by pipe hangers or straps of sufficient strength and number to prevent sagging. Hot and cold water lines should be approximately 6 inches apart unless they are insulated. If they are not insulated, the hot line may transfer heat to the cold water line.

Note any water pipes that pass in front of windows or areas where cold drafts could affect them. Make a note to have them insulated so they won't freeze. It is also wise to insulate hot water lines in the basement to prevent loss of heat. Insulating

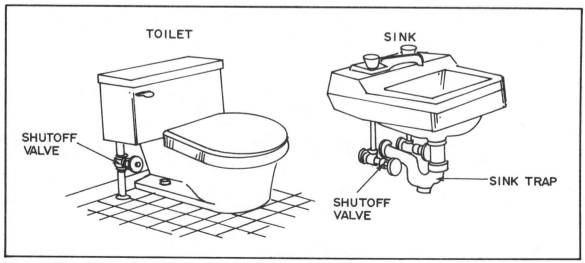

Fig. 10-3. Shut-off valves under various fixtures is important, particularly if there are none in the lines feeding these fixtures from the basement.

117

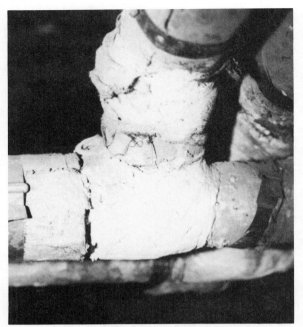

pipes is particularly important in unheated garages or crawlspaces. In Fig. 10-4, we see pipes that are insulated with older-type asbestos insulation. This type of pipe insulation should be removed and replaced with nonhazardous material by a qualified contractor. Note any such findings for future removal.

In your inspection of branch lines, look for possible cross connections in the water pipes. Figure 10-5 is a good illustration of this potential problem. Cross connections in the piping are sometimes present when an older well water pipe is connected to a newer town installation. A drop in the town water pressure could allow polluted well water to pass into the system through an open or defective valve. Cross connections are sometimes at junctions between drinking water pipes and pipes carrying water for the heating system. Note questionable connections and have them double-checked by a plumber.

Fig. 10-4. The use of asbestos insulation is hazardous. Be sure to have a qualified contractor remove such dangerous material from any pipes in the house.

TRAPS

While checking the water lines in the basement,

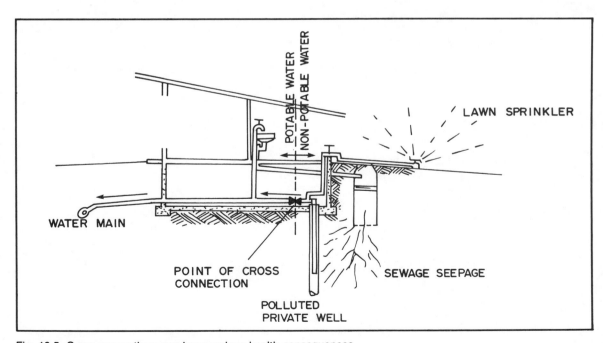

Fig. 10-5. Cross connections can have serious health consequences.

you are likely to come across traps connected to the first floor fixtures that prevent sewer gases from entering the house. Figure 10-6 is a good example of a standard trap. As you examine these traps, look for signs of rusting, corrosion, or leaks. Check the wooden members adjacent to the traps for water stains. You can take your screwdriver and probe this wood; if gentle probes penetrate easily and moisture oozes out of the wood, these stains could be an indication of a current leak. To make sure, go to the bathrooms and kitchen on the upper levels and fill the fixtures with water. Flush these and return to the basement to look for leaks. If you have a spouse or friend with you at the time, have them do the draining while you check from below. Listen carefully for dripping water. Sometimes the defect is simply an undetected drip that over a long period of time could cause serious wood damage. Use your flashlight to check hidden areas and don't be afraid to run your hand along any suspicious places for signs of water. Make a note of fixtures that do not appear to have traps connected to them. (See Chapter 15 for details on inspecting plumbing fixtures.)

WASTE LINES

Traps are also connected to waste lines. They are usually 2 inches in diameter, although smaller ones of 1 1/4 inches are sometimes found. These branch waste drains connect with a larger main drain, which is usually 4 inches in diameter. This 4-inch drain connects to the public or private disposal system. In checking the waste lines, you should look for signs of water or waste leakage. Look also for water stains and open or cracked pipes. Figure 10-7 shows a damaged waste line that is clearly a health hazard to the inhabitants of the house.

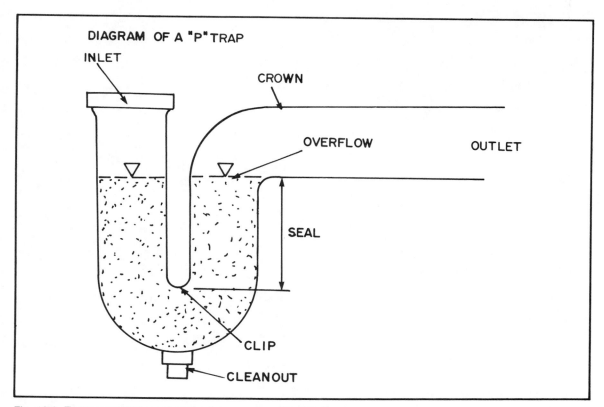

Fig. 10-6. Traps prevent the entrance of sewer gases into the house.

Fig. 10-7. Cracked and open sewer lines present a serious health problem and should be corrected by a licensed plumber.

In your inspection of the main waste line, check to see if there is a cleanout plug. This access plug will allow a plumber, if necessary, to enter the main line in order to clear any blockage. Many times the cleanout plug is inaccessible or buried under the concrete floor. If the plug is visible look at it carefully, and if you see a gnarled plug you may have a drainage problem that could require the costly services of a plumber every few months. Find out from the owner whether there have been problems with the drainage system and why. Sometimes tree roots get into the underground pipe and block it. Also, children and even adults flush items that cannot possibly discharge from the pipe. If you see water stains or the remains of sewage near the cleanout plug, ask the owner for a reasonable answer. If he

can't come up with one, you may wish to give the house some second thoughts.

Open cleanouts are a health hazard. Sewer gases can back up into the house and cause serious ailments to the inhabitants. In some sections of the country, water rats enter houses through open or broken cleanouts or pipes. In Fig. 10-8, you can see a damaged cleanout plug connection. Note any such defects and have the owner correct them.

The material used for drainage pipes varies from location to location. Often houses will have a combination of cast iron, plastic, galvanized iron, or copper. Sometimes you will come across old lead traps as seen in Fig. 10-9. These old lead traps and

Fig. 10-8. Note the opening in the cleanout plug. This open and damaged section of pipe can allow sewer gases as well as human waste back into the house, with resulting health hazards. Be sure to record any such potentially dangerous area for future correction.

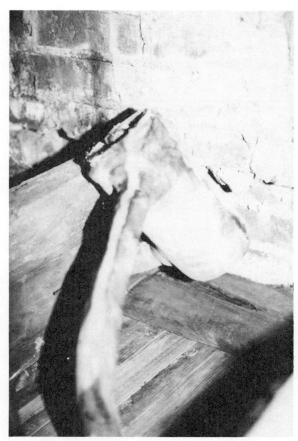

Fig. 10-9. Old lead traps are best replaced. Repairing them is almost impossible.

would remain in the pipe and cause blockage problems. Figure 10-10 indicates the correct pitch for proper drainage. Record on your worksheet any improper pitches, dips or sags.

VENTING

One major defect often found in plumbing systems is improper venting. Venting prevents loss of a trap seal. (See Fig. 10-11.) This seal in a plumbing trap may be lost because of a siphonage problem. One way you can tell that there is no venting or improper venting of a fixture is to listen for gurgling or sucking sounds after a fixture is drained. These sounds indicate that a fixture does not have a vent pipe extending to the exterior (usually through the roof). Often handyman plumbers install new bathrooms and kitchens and, although they install the discharge waste pipes correctly, they forget about the important vent pipes and end up with fixtures that "play heavy metal" every time they are flushed. Another way of telling whether the fixture is vented is to be on the lookout for foul smelling odors coming from the fixtures themselves. The odors are probably sewer gases floating past the unprotected traps. Note any doubts on your worksheet and, if necessary, hire a plumber to double-check it for you.

PRIVATE DISPOSAL SYSTEMS

Many communities do not provide public disposal systems for household wastes. In these instances, homeowners use either a *cesspool* or *septic tank system*. Both are satisfactory ways of handling discharge or liquid and solid wastes from residences.

A cesspool is a hole in the ground, lined with stone or hollow core blocks. Its construction allows liquid sewage to leach into the soil while retaining the solid wastes. A septic system consists of a watertight tank that serves as a holding area for sewage. The settled sewage in the tank decomposes, while the liquid wastes rise to an outlet pipe and flow into a drainage field. In Fig. 10-12, you can see a typical septic system.

Private disposal units should be cleaned periodically, usually every two or three years, and

drainage lines, although not hazardous, may be brittle and easily damaged. Although they may not be leaking at the time of the inspection, make a note on your worksheet for future replacement. Modernization of bathrooms and kitchens makes their replacement necessary, because few plumbers will tie new fixtures into these archaic pipes.

The pitch of the house drain is important. Check the underside of the bathroom and kitchen from the basement and follow the drain-waste lines to where they exit from the house. These pipes should pitch toward the sewer line at the rate of 1/4 inch for every foot of run. A flat pitch will not allow liquids to discharge fast enough and too steep of a pitch will allow liquids to discharge too fast. At either of these two incorrect angles, solid materials checked on an annual basis to see that they are operating properly. The owner should tell you how often the holding tank has been pumped out over the past several years. If it has not been cleaned for a long time, you just may have some serious problems. A system is very costly to replace (anywhere from a few to several thousand dollars).

The tank is buried usually 20 feet from the house. If you are lucky, the cover will be visible, and you will be able to remove it to inspect the interior

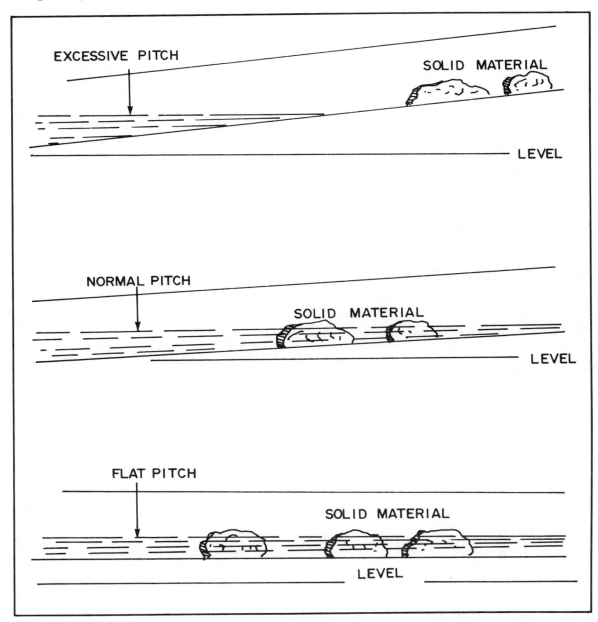

Fig. 10-10. Correct pitch of a house drain is important to prevent build-up of solid wastes.

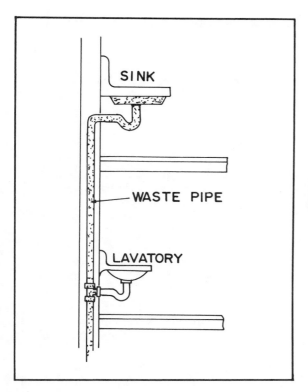

Fig. 10-11. Without proper venting of fixtures, trap seals will be lost due to the suction of draining water. Gurgling sounds or heavy suction sounds indicate venting problems.

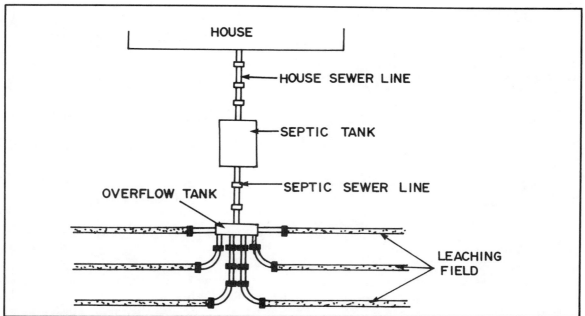

Fig. 10-12. A typical septic system.

Fig. 10-13. A septic tank with its cover off. Note the accumulations of waste materials around the discharge pipe.

Water Piping

- Is the main water pipe a lead line?
- Is there a main shut-off valve, and can it be shut off?
- Are there shut-off valves in the branch lines?
- Are there signs of defects in the water meter?
- Any signs of corrosion or deterioration in water lines or their fittings?
- Are water lines properly supported?
- Are the pipes insulated?
- Are there indications of cross connections in water lines?

Drainage Pipes

- Do all fixtures have traps?
- Are there signs of deterioration or leaks in the traps?
- Do all drainage pipes pitch properly?
- Any signs of deterioration in the drainage lines?
- Are all drainage pipes properly supported?
- Are there cracks or openings in the drainage pipes?
- Is there an accessible cleanout plug for the main sewer line?
- Is the cleanout plug missing or damaged?
- Does the system have proper venting to the exterior?
- Any signs of sewage backup in the basement?

Private Disposal Systems

- Is there a septic or cesspool system?
- When was the last time that the holding tank was pumped out?
- Check with the owner about previous problems with the system.
- Is the grass above the system lush in com-

of the tank. (See Fig. 10-13.) Often the cover is buried, and you will have to ask the owner permission to dig for it. If, upon removal of the cover, you discover that the tank is loaded with solid wastes, the chances are that the leaching field is deteriorating. As the new owner, you may be faced with replacement costs.

During your inspection of the exterior, look for typical defects associated with private systems. Lush green patches of grass, wet and soggy soil, strong odors, standing puddles of water—any or all of these above or adjacent to the system could mean trouble. Record all your findings and discuss them with the owner.

parison to the rest of the yard?

• Are there strong odors emanating from the tank area or the leaching field?

• Is the cover accessible?

• Does the ground above the field appear wet and soggy?

• Is there standing water over the tank or the field?

Domestic Hot Water

The domestic hot water for a family is usually supplied by a tankless system working off of the house boiler, an oil-fired hot water tank, a gas-fired hot water tank, or an electric hot water tank. Each of these has its own peculiarities and must therefore be scrutinized very carefully.

TANKLESS SYSTEM

By far the least economical and least efficient is the tankless hot water system. (See Fig. 11-1.) A copper heating coil inside the boiler heats the water. The trouble with this type of system is that the boiler must work all year round in order to provide hot water. Because a boiler has a life expectancy of 25 to 30 years (working only during the winter months), you know that this added burden greatly reduces its life expectancy. Clearly then, if the subject house has such a system, be sure to find out the boiler's age. If the unit is 25 years old or older, it is likely that it is inefficient and may need repairs, or in a short time may need replacement.

While checking out a tankless system, look at the exterior of the boiler jacket carefully. You will find a metal plate near the top of one side with two water pipes extending from it. These are the cold and hot water pipes. Sometimes you will find a mixing valve on the boiler. Such a valve on the boiler can be adjusted during the summer so that the boiler will be used only to provide domestic hot water and not heat. If you see one, make a note to check with the heating serviceman to get specific directions on how to use it.

Rusting, water stains, and signs of corrosion on the plate or the bolts that hold the plate to the boiler indicate that there is a defect somewhere. Look at the cold inlet and the hot outlet pipes. Are there signs of leaks or deterioration in the pipes or joints? Heavy accumulations of rust on pipes and the boiler could mean a leak that is held in check by the packed-in, corroded metal. Do not probe! The slightest disturbance will reopen the defect, and you will be responsible for the repairs. If you see heavy concentrations of rust and corrosion, assume the worst: namely, that a leak exists.

In order to properly inspect the hot water

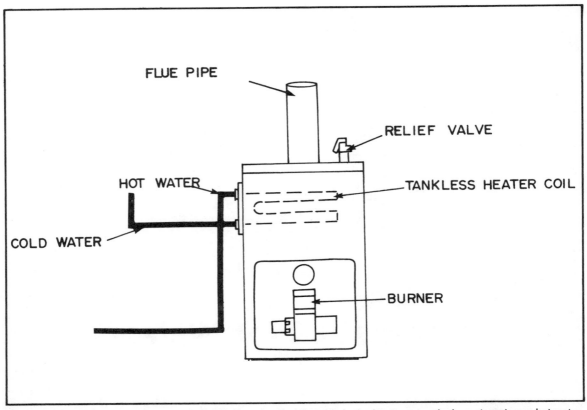

Fig. 11-1. A typical tankless hot water system. Keep in mind that this is the least economical way to get your hot water.

system, you should go to each bathroom and the kitchen and systematically turn on all the hot water faucets. Run these faucets simultaneously. Does the flow of water slacken when you have more than one hot water faucet on? The water should be clear and free from rust particles and other sediments. If it is not, the coil or the hot water lines are most likely constructed by mineral deposits. Replacement of the heating coil in the boiler is costly and varies from region to region. You could expect to pay anywhere from a few hundred dollars to several hundred, depending upon the extent of the defect. Replacing hot water lines will be less expensive.

OIL-FIRED, HOT-WATER TANKS

Sometimes an oil-fired boiler will have a separate oil-fired hot water tank. Like the boiler, the tank has its own burner. Figure 11-2 shows a typical oil-

fired hot water tank and its burner. Burners must be cleaned and serviced annually. To find out when the burner was last serviced, look at the tank; you may find a card attached to a pipe that will tell what was done and when. If there is no such card, ask the owner. While you examine the burner carefully, be on the lookout for oil leaks at the pump or fuel line connections. Also check whether the oil line is exposed. It should be protected against anyone accidentally stepping on it.

Safety valves are similar to those found on oil-fired heating systems. Look for firomatic safety valves on the oil storage tank, on the oil burner, and over the hot water tank. In Fig. 11-3, you see a firomatic valve mounted on a ceiling. In case of excessive heat, these valves will automatically close so that oil is not pumped into the heating chamber. The firomatic directly above the hot water tank

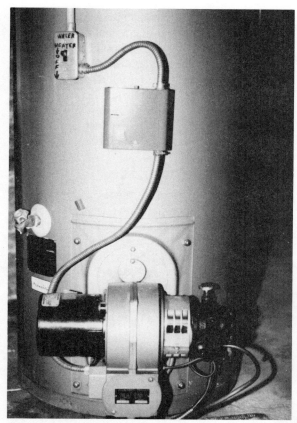

Fig. 11-2. An oil-fired hot water tank requires annual maintenance of its oil burner.

The pitch of the flue pipe should always be upwards towards the chimney at the rate of 1/4 inch for every foot of the horizontal run. Be on the lookout for flue pipes that dip or drop down, especially because flue gases cannot be properly expelled from such pipes. Flue pipes easily load up with soot and carbon deposits and should be dismantled and cleaned annually. Heavy soot concentrations also cut down on the efficiency of the tank; be sure to include this maintenance feature into your annual servicing schedule.

ELECTRIC HOT-WATER TANKS

Electrically operated hot water tanks differ from oil- and gas-fired units in that they usually last

closes off the electricity to the burner. While the burner is going, reach up and turn the valve off. The burner should shut down. If it doesn't, it is defective and must be repaired.

GAS-FIRED, HOT-WATER TANKS

Gas-fired hot water tanks are similar to oil-fired hot water tanks in that they must be properly vented to a chimney or flue leading to the outside. Check the flue pipe for signs of deterioration, loose connections, and pitted metal, any of which would mean poor maintenance and possibly the need for replacement. In Fig. 11-4, you see a disconnected flue pipe that also has a poorly sealed connection to the chimney. Both of these defects represent a safety hazard to the inhabitants and must be corrected.

Fig. 11-3. Firomatic safety valves, such as those found in oil-fired heating systems, are also required over oil-fired hot-water tanks.

Fig. 11-4. Disconnected flue pipes discharge dangerous fumes into the basement. Be sure to reconnect any such defects.

will be slow and will inconvenience the family. A standard rule of thumb is that a family of four needs a minimum 40-gallon gas- or oil-fired hot water tank. An electric tank should hold a minimum of 55 gallons for a family of four; anything less would be inefficient. If the hot water tank in the basement does not meet your family's needs and must be replaced, be sure to add the expense of replacing the tank to the overall cost of the house.

TEMPERATURE SETTINGS

Temperature settings are also important enough to be checked by you. Operating temperatures range from a low of 120° F to almost 180° F. Anything from 160° F and up is not only wasteful, but dangerous. For example, a faulty shower valve could scald someone showering. Actually, 120° F is more than adequate for most household uses. Check the temperature setting valve, which is normally found at the base of the tank as shown in Fig. 11-5. If it

Fig. 11-5. Temperature settings on hot water tanks are important. Note the setting on this dial is at normal. Higher temperatures shorten the life of the tank.

longer, and they do not need a flue pipe because they do not produce harmful exhaust gases. They do need a 30-amp circuit however, so check to see that one direct 30-amp circuit is used for the tank. No other appliance should be tied into this circuit. Because the *recovery rate* (time it takes to replace used hot water) of these tanks is quite low when compared to gas and oil units, most electrically operated tanks usually have larger capacities.

TANK SIZES

The size of hot water tanks is important. A too small tank will not provide an adequate hot water supply and will run inefficiently. Its recovery rate is set on high or at a setting above 140° F, you can assume that the tank is running inefficiently. High temperature settings also shorten the life of a tank. Note your finds on your worksheet.

DRAIN VALVE

While the tank is operating, listen for rumbling or banging sounds that could indicate an excessive amount of sediment build-up. Tank manufacturers recommend that the tank be drained of roughly 1 gallon of water every few months in order to cut down on sediment buildup. This is particularly true of regions that have a high mineral content in their water supply. A note of caution about the drain at the bottom of the tank: if it has not been drained for years and you attempt to drain some water at the time of the inspection, the valve might not reset properly when closed. Be careful when you test the valve (you are only

inspecting--you do not own the house), or the result may be a flooded basement. It is often better hold off testing it until you are the owner of the house. In the event that it won't close, have it repaired at your own expense. (See Fig. 11-6.)

REVERSED PIPES

Look at the top of the tank; you should see water fittings that are marked HOT and COLD. The cold water feed line enters the tank through the COLD inlet, and the water heated by the tank leaves through the pipe connected to the HOT water outlet. (See Fig. 11-7.) Sometimes plumbers inadvertently reverse the water line installation. Check to see whether this is the case by touching each pipe about 3 feet away from the tank. If the cold water line is hot, the connections are reversed and the tank is running inefficiently. Here the cold water that enters the tank does not enter through the dip tube, which

Fig. 11-6. Drain valves at the base of hot water tanks should be opened on a semiannual basis to get rid of accumulated sediments. Note the corrosion and rust on the tank jacket.

Fig. 11-7. Reverse pipes on the top of the hot water tank will work, but will cost extra energy dollars. Be sure to check to make sure each pipe is in its right location. Note the relief valve on the tank without an extension pipe.

would normally bring the cold water down to the bottom of the tank. Rather, the cold water enters the tank at the top, mixes with the hot water, and thereby cools it. The homeowner has probably increased the temperature setting to compensate for the lower temperature of the water, which in turn increases the fuel consumption and decreases the life of the water heater. Clearly, the reverse installation should be corrected.

RELIEF VALVE

While you are scrutinizing the top of the tank, check to see whether there is a *relief valve*. This is a safety device that is both temperature and pressure sensitive. It will be located somewhere near the top of the tank, as seen in Fig. 11-8. If you find that the relief valve is on the cold water inlet pipe a potential hazardous situation exists. Make a note of it and have it corrected once you buy the house.

If the temperature or pressure builds up too high, the relief valve will discharge water to relieve the problem. These valves can be periodically tested by lifting the lever handle on the top of the valve. If water does not discharge, it should bereplaced.

Also, the relief valve should have a length of pipe attached to it that discharges the hot water into a container on the floor. If a relief valve, as shown in Fig. 11-8, should discharge hot water when someone was standing near it, the person could get scalded. If you find such a defect note it for future correction.

INSULATION

Because the cost of energy is continually rising, it is always wise to be on the lookout for ways to save. Mark down on your worksheet if the hot water tank or water lines (particularly the hot water lines) are insulated. Figure 11-9 demonstrates prop-

Fig. 11-8. A relief valve is meant to blow-off hot water when a predetermined pressure is met. Note the proximity of the vertical post to the relief valve. In an emergency, it won't release and an explosion could occur.

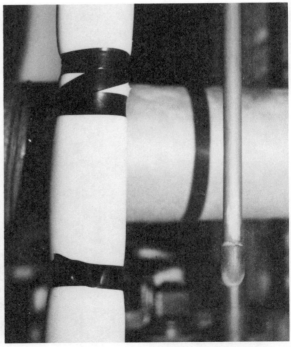

Fig. 11-9. Insulation on hot water pipes is essential for cutting energy costs. Note the uninsulated cold water pipe next to the insulated hot water pipe.

Fig. 11-10. Proper draft is important in both gas- and oil-fired appliances. This figure shows the gas draft hood.

erly insulated hot water pipes. The cost of insulating pipes and the tank is negligible when compared to bills you would have to pay because of heat losses.

DRAFT

Both gas- and oil-fired hot water tanks need an adequate draft for proper combustion. A gas-fired unit should have a draft diverter and an oil-fired unit should have a draft regulator, both of which will provide the proper amount of oxygen needed for combustion. These two types of draft units are pictured in Figs. 11-10 and 11-11.

Check the *draft regulator* (usually found in the flue pipe and sometimes found in the chimney) by moving the swing-plate to see that it swings freely.

Sometimes the regulator is jammed shut because of accumulated rust and soot and/or because of an ignorant owner. You may find anything from a nail to a shim of wood jamming the plate closed. This is mistakenly done to prevent cold air from entering the basement. To check the draft in a gas-fired hot water tank, place your hand near the diverter cover; you should not feel a flow of air on your hand. If you do, there is a blockage in either the flue pipe or the chimney. If this occurs, be sure to record it for further examination by a heating serviceman.

DETERMINING A TANK'S AGE

To determine a tank's remaining useful life, you need to know its age. Most tanks are sold with either a 5- or 10-year warranty, and the data plate on

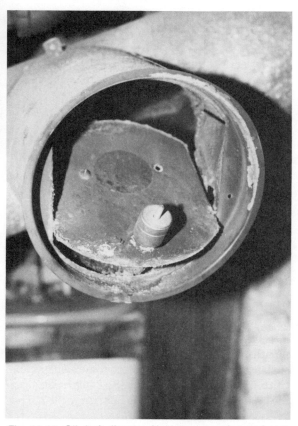

Fig. 11-11. Oil draft diverter. Note the corrosion and soot build-up in the oil draft diverter.

Fig. 11-12. Data plates sometimes give information about when the tank was manufactured, which is important to know to determine how many years it has left. The serial number is sometimes coded to give the month and year of manufacture.

the tank will sometimes give you the age of the unit. (See Fig. 11-12.) Different companies use different letter codes, however both Rheem and Rudd (two major manufacturers) use the first four numbers of the serial number to tell the month and the year that they were manufactured. For example, the number 0383 tells you that the tank was made in March 1983; tanks are usually installed within several months of their manufacture. Other companies, such as A.O. Smith, use a different method of identification. The number 900-B-83-2468 means that the tank was manufactured in February, 1983. This letter code starts with A for January and ends with M for December.

If you find that the tank is 10 years or older, it is likely on borrowed time and replacement will be needed in the near future. An electrically heated tank will last longer, because the heating elements are immersed in the water and do not affect the tank itself.

CHECKPOINTS

- Is the hot water flow from fixtures adequate or restricted?
- Is the amount of hot water sufficient?
- Does the water in the fixtures appear to have sediment or rust particles in it?
- Is there corrosion or rusting on the jacket of the hot water tank or the tankless plate of the boiler?
- Are there signs of deterioration on either the inlet or outlet pipes?
- Are flue pipes properly pitched towards the chimney?
- Are there signs of deterioration in the flue pipe?
- Does the flue pipe have a proper draft regulator or draft diverter?
- Is the flue properly connected to the chimney and the tank?
- Does the tank make unusual sounds as it is operating?
- Is there a relief valve on the unit?
- Does the relief valve have a connecting pipe for safe discharge?
- Are there signs of corrosion on the relief valve or its fittings?
- Are hot and cold water lines reversed?
- Is the tank insulated?
- Are water lines insulated?
- Do burners need cleaning and servicing?
- What is the size of the tank?
- How old is the tank?
- What is the current temperature setting?
- Does the tank look like it is on borrowed time?

Air-Conditioning

Air-conditioning is becoming more and more popular all over the country; it provides a comfort that few homeowners want to do without. The fact that such systems are tied in with electricity does not make your inspection any easier: that they come in three different types, makes it even more complicated. Don't be afraid, though, to venture into this unknown territory. If you have managed to inspect the electrical system, you are going to do just fine.

Cooling systems consist of either *wall-mounted room air conditioners, central air-conditioning systems,* or *heat pumps.* All have elements in common, and each has peculiarities that make it efficient or inefficient. The easiest first.

WALL-MOUNTED ROOM AIR CONDITIONERS

The beauty of room air conditioners is that you can mount them where you need them, and you do not have to go into the major expense of having to outfit the entire house with duct work and registers. Wise positioning and mounting of units in walls or windows can provide comfortable cooling. (See Fig. 12-1.)

Individual units are made up of a *condenser* (the part that is hanging outside), a *compressor, cooling coils,* a *blower,* and a *thermostat.* Figure 12-2 shows the major parts of an air-conditioning unit. The care and maintenance of these parts are important not only for efficiency in cooling but for the life span of the unit as well. Simple annual maintenance, such as replacing filters, will result in years of efficient performance.

Location of the Air Conditioner

Individual units should be placed as far as possible from doors leading to the outside. Distance will prevent drafts from interfering with cooled air. It is also important that no obstructions, such as drapes or furniture, are placed in front of an air conditioner. Outside, the free flow of air is just as important; bushes and shrubs should be cut down to make room for the condenser. It needs to have cool air to disburse the hot air drawn from the inside. As a rule, the cooler the air is around the condenser, the more efficient your unit will be. If you note that an air conditioner is bathed in midday sunshine, con-

135

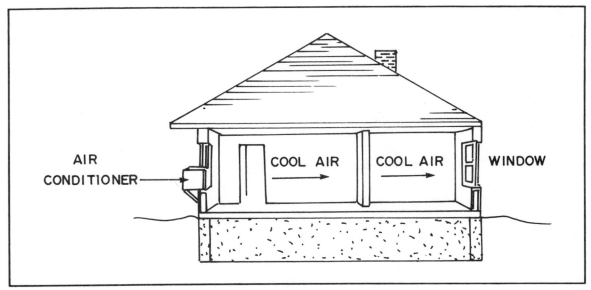

Fig. 12-1. Wise positioning of air conditioning units can provide cool air to several rooms.

sider mounting an awning above it for shade.

General Condition of the Unit

It seems reasonable to assume that you want to know what shape a unit is in, so ask the owner how he maintains it. Then turn on the air conditioner (assuming it is not stored in a closet). Does the unit sound strange or noisy while it is on? If so, check the fan blades and the motor bearings. The blades may be bent or dirty, and the motor bearings may need lubrication. The noise could also stem from the fact that the unit is poorly mounted and needs tightening down. Should the air conditioner blow hot instead of cold air, check the temperature control knob (which is usually the thermostat). It may be faulty and need to be replaced.

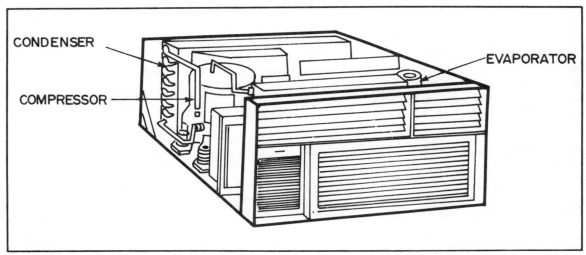

Fig. 12-2. The major parts of a room air conditioner are shown in this figure.

Fig. 12-3. Banged up and damaged room units will not function properly and will need repairs. Note the dented jacket and damaged fins in this window mounted unit.

Of course, the unit may also need a compressor, which will be quite expensive. In Fig. 12-3, note the damaged cover and dented fins of this unit. Be sure to tell the owner about any defects that you may find.

Proper Mounting

A cooling unit should always be mounted in a wall or window in such a way that it tilts toward the outside. Such tilt is important for the removal of condensate. Place your hand on the unit and pull back and forth gently. Is the unit attached firmly, or is it about to fall out of the opening? Check to see if weatherstripping and gaskets are tight and seal out unwanted warm air. Sealing should be done both on the inside and the outside. Are the support brackets that hold the unit in good condition, or do they need to be replaced? Note your findings.

Inspecting the Unit

Shut down the air conditioner and take off the cover so you can see the inside. Check the filter; usually it is loaded with dust and needs to be cleaned or replaced. Cleaning the filter should be done often during the summer. Check mounting screws, nuts, and bolts that may have worked themselves loose because of vibrations. Mark down loose or brittle window seals for future caulking and sealing. Note any oil cups that are low on oil and mention it to the owner. A few drops of oil will work wonders. Coils that are loaded with dust and dirt will be highly inefficient, so note on your worksheet the need for vacuuming. Inspect all motor and fan belts for slippage or deterioration. By pressing a finger against each belt individually, you will be able to tell whether it needs adjustment. A belt should not deflect more than 1/2-inch. A worn out belt should be replaced. Find out how old the unit is—a 10-year-old one is borrowed time.

CENTRAL AIR-CONDITIONING

Inspecting central air-conditioning is a little more complicated when compared to looking at individual units. The first thing you should be concerned with is the system's size. One that is too small may run all the time. This is costly and inefficient. Too large a system is also costly because it cools the house quickly, shuts off, and comes on again in a short period of time. Not only is this *short-cycling* very costly in energy dollars, but it is also very hard on the system's parts.

The square footage of living space is a major consideration in sizing a central air-conditioning system. In addition, the number of windows, their sizes, the directions they face, the amount of insulation, the layout of the house, and the exterior shading are all factors that must be considered. In general, when all are taken into account, a house usually requires 1 ton of cooling capacity for every

600 square feet of air-conditioned space. A typical 1200-square-foot house would require a 2-ton system.

Types of Systems

There are two basic types of systems in use today: *integral* and *split systems.* The integral is self-contained, which means that all of its parts (compressor, condenser, expansion device, evaporator, and electrical controls) are housed in a single unit. Figure 12-4 shows a diagram of a typical integral cycle. This type is less expensive than a split system; but it is noisy because of vibrations from the condenser/compressor, which is located within the house. A much better system is the split system, where the condenser/compressor is located outside the house and the remaining parts (evaporator, coil, blower, and controls) are located either in the attic or in the furnace. In Fig. 12-5, you see a combination warm air furnace and air-conditioning system.

Compressor/Condenser Unit

The compressor/condenser is the part of the air-conditioning system that you normally see outdoors. Figure 12-6 is an example of one. It is the most important part of the system and the most expensive to replace. Generally, they last 8 to 10 years; anything over that should be considered on borrowed time. In addition to the compressor and condenser, this exterior unit also contains the cooling coils and operating controls.

Several things should be checked during your

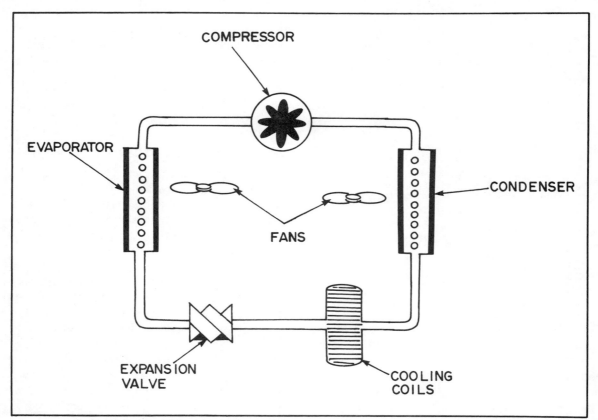

Fig. 12-4. A self-contained system is a simple system. Integral systems such as this are found in older types of air conditioning systems. The major drawback was the noise factor.

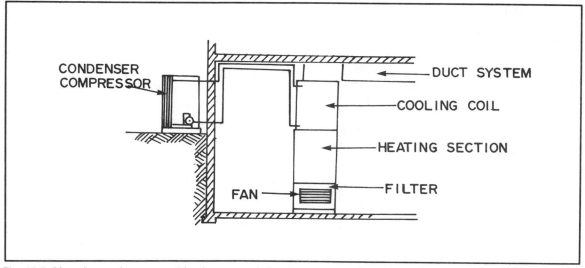

Fig. 12-5. Many homes have a combination warm-air furnace and air conditioning system built into one unit.

survey. First, find the electrical disconnect switch, which should be mounted on the outside wall as shown in Fig. 12-7. Be sure to test it by switching the off and on button. Notify the owner if it is not working. If you can't find the switch, make a note to have one installed because they are required by most codes.

Check the condition of the platform that is supporting the unit. Usually these platforms are made of poured concrete or in some cases, concrete blocks. Look for cracks in the concrete or settlement in the blocks, either of which could cause the unit to make excessive noise while it is running or even fracture the refrigeration lines.

Be sure to note the location of the unit. Does it have overgrown shrubbery all over it, and is it too close to the house? Is there any shade from an awning or a nearby tree? Poor air circulation and direct sunlight will overwork the unit and hasten its demise.

Does the compressor/condenser look like it has been properly maintained? Check to see if leaves or accumulated dust are causing problems. Look for rust and corrosion on the metal parts of the unit. Like any other moving, mechanical apparatus, the compressor/condenser should have periodic servicing and maintenance.

Fig. 12-6. A compressor-condenser unit located on the outside of a house. Note the slab that it is resting on.

139

Fig. 12-7. A fused electrical disconnect located on the outside wall adjacent to the compressor-condenser. This safety shut-off switch is mandatory in most communities.

Evaporator

You will find the evaporator unit either in the attic or in the furnace plenum. Figure 12-8 shows a typical evaporator. It consists of cooling coils, a fan, and the refrigerant lines that connect it to the condenser/compressor unit. The evaporator is used to cool the circulating air. There are specific things to look for here to determine if the unit is working effectively.

If the evaporator is accessible (units in furnaces are not), carefully check the coil and the attached refrigerant lines. Poor circulation of air through the evaporator coil or a low amount of refrigerant liquid in the system will cause frosting and/or the build-up of ice on the coil or the refrigerant lines. This will cause the unit to malfunction. Such conditions should be checked by a refrigeration technician.

At this time, also look for leaks: water will corrode the unit. Directly below the evaporator should be a pan that collects condensate cause by cold air. Its pipe allows the water to discharge (unless it is plugged up, in which case the pan will overflow). Check to see if the pipe is free of any blockage. This is particularly important if the evaporator is in the

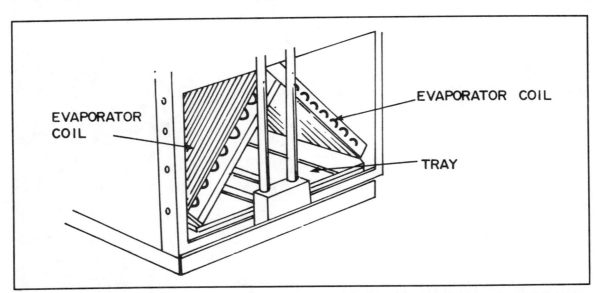

Fig. 12-8. The evaporator is necessary for cooling the air circulating in the system. Any frosting or build-up of ice on the evaporator should be checked out by a qualified technician.

furnace because the heat exchanger could be seriously damaged. If you see corrosion or mineral deposits on the furnace where the evaporator is mounted, have a technician check it out.

Operating the System

If the temperature is below 60° F, you will not be able to turn on the system because if you do, you might seriously damage the compressor. At such a time, have the seller/owner give you a written guarantee that the system is working. At any other time (i.e., above 60° F), be sure to turn on the system by activating its thermostat. Let the system run for a good half hour. This is a good time for you to double-check the condenser/compressor unit outside, as well as the evaporator coil inside. Listen to them carefully and note leaks or defects such as excessive vibration.

Distribution System

After the system has been running for approximately 15 minutes, go from room to room and check the registers to see whether cool air is being discharged. In Fig. 12-9, a typical distribution system is illustrated. If, during your inspection, you find a register that is not doing its job, note that room on your worksheet. The register may not be blowing cold air because the duct may not be fully open, the damper in the duct may be closed, or because there is a heat gain in the duct leading to the register. If the duct is accessible, see whether it needs insulation, and if a damper is partially or fully closed. Other factors that might make it inoperable are that the entire system may be undersized or that the system is low in refrigerant. Again, this will have to be checked out by a serviceman.

The location of registers is also important. The best place for them is on the ceilings or on the upper sections of walls. Low wall or floor registers, although commonly used in a warm air system, are less effective in cooling a house because cool air is heavy and falls rapidly. (Quite contrary to warm air.)

Last but not least, the loss of cooling effectiveness through uninsulated ducts cannot be overemphasized. This is very true of uninsulated ducts that pass through crawl spaces and attics. Heat gains from surrounding areas greatly cut back on the cooling capacity of the system. Also be sure to check for open seams or joints, which are essentially air leaks. These can be inexpensively sealed with duct tape. By insulating ducts and taping seams and joints, you can pick up some big savings on your energy costs. Figure 12-10 shows an uninsulated duct with an open seam.

HEAT PUMPS

A heat pump is an electrically powered device that provides both heating in winter and cooling in

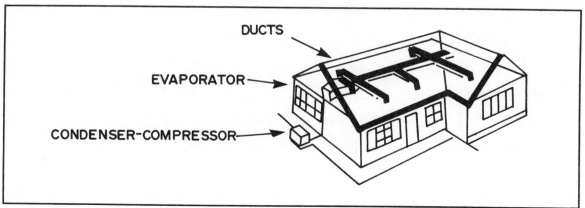

Fig. 12-9. Distribution duct work should be fully insulated to prevent energy losses to heated areas such as attics. Make a note to have any sections that are not fully insulated covered with insulation.

Fig. 12-10. Uninsulated ducts with open seams are costing you valuable energy dollars.

summer. This system is actually an air-conditioning system that is used in reverse during the winter. In winter, heat is extracted from the outdoor air (sometimes water is used) and pumped indoors. In the summer, the cycle is reversed—heat is wrung out of the house air and discharged outdoors. Figure 12-11 shows a heat pump installation. Heat pumps are usually not recommended in climates where temperatures drop below 30° F for any length of time. In northern climates, an auxiliary backup heating system is needed to take over during the long cold spells.

As is true with an air-conditioning system, the heat pump's compressor/condenser is mounted outside, the evaporator inside. The defects found with heat pumps are much the same as those with air-conditioning systems. Thus, your inspection process is not very different. There are some exceptions, however. First, the temperature setting for turning on the unit's air conditioning mode should be 65° F rather than 60° F. For the operation of the heating mode, the temperature should be below 65° F.

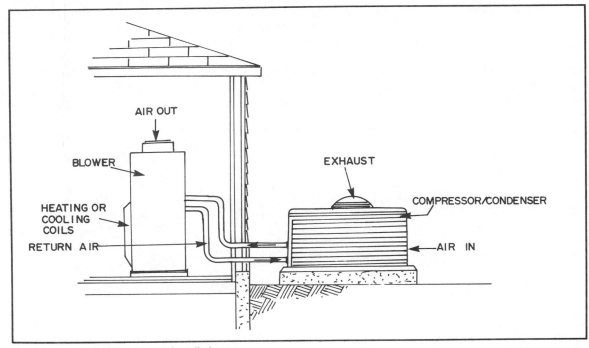

Fig. 12-11. A typical heat pump installation.

Operating the air-conditioning mode during the winter could damage the compressor and vice-versa for operating the heat mode in the summer.

Inspecting the System

Check with the owner on how often the system is inspected and serviced to maintain its efficiency. While you run the appropriate mode to test the system, listen for any unusual sounds and note any strange vibrations. Check the filter for dust accumulations. Note obstacles in the path of the air flow. If the system works in one mode, you can safely assume that it also works in the reverse mode. Because maintaining a heat pump is more technical than caring for the average heating/air-conditioning system, make sure that you have a trained serviceman go over the entire system for you. He may also have some free tips as to how to keep it in good working order. Figure 12-11 shows a typical heat pump installation.

CHECKPOINTS

Individual Wall-Mounted Units

• Check to see how close units are to doors leading to the outdoors.
• Note obstructions in front of air conditioners.
• Is the exterior part (condenser/compressor) in full direct sunlight?
• Turn the unit on to test it and record any unusual noises.
• Examine the mounting brackets. Are they loose or in need of support?
• Does the cooling unit tilt to the exterior?
• Are weatherstripping and gaskets tight, or do they need resealing?
• Does the filter need cleaning or replacement?
• Inspect motors for lack of oil in oil cups.
• Check motor belts for deterioration or defects.

Central Air-Conditioning

• Is the system large enough for the house?
• What type of system is it? (Integral or split?)

• Examine the condenser/compressor for defects or unusual sounds.
• Check the condition of the support platform for the condenser/compressor. Is it cracked or sagging?
• How is the location of the condenser/compressor? (Too much sunlight, not enough free flow of air?)
• Does the unit need cleaning?
• Is there a main electrical disconnect switch and is it working?
• Examine the evaporator cooling coils for signs of frosting or icing.
• Look for leaks in the refrigerant lines leading into and out of the evaporator.
• Is there a pan under the evaporator, and does it have a discharge line connected to a drain?
• Note corrosion and mineral deposits on the evaporator unit.
• Check both registers and ducts to be sure sufficient cold air is reaching all rooms.
• Note the need for insulation on ducts and tape on joints and seams.

Heat Pumps

• Check the air-conditioning mode when the temperature is above 65° F.
• While the system is running, listen for unusual sounds that may indicate problems.
• Inspect the exterior mounted compressor/condenser for signs of corrosion or rust.
• Is the location of the compressor/condenser adequate? (Minimum sunlight, sufficient clearances for free flow or air?)
• Ask the owner how often the system is serviced.
• Examine filters to see whether they need cleaning or replacement.
• Inspect the evaporator for signs of deterioration.
• Does the house have a back-up heating system in case of low temperatures (Temperatures below 30° F)?
• Be sure to have the system serviced and maintained on an annual basis.

Energy

One of the major considerations in buying a home is how energy efficient it is. A house that is as "tight as a drum" will reduce utility bills considerably, which in turn will make owning a home much less expensive. If the subject house is several years old, the chances are that it is not as efficient as it should be. The first thing you should do is have a local utility company make an energy audit after you move in.

An energy audit is a thorough inspection of the house to determine areas that allow excessive heat loses. Most of the improvements suggested by the utility companies are wise investments and will usually pay for themselves in a very short time.

INSULATION

Most homes waste energy because they lack sufficient insulation in ceilings, floors, walls, and basements. Proper insulation will not only cut back on heat losses but will also reduce cooling costs during the warmer months as well.

Checking out insulation can easily be integrated into your general inspection of the house. While in the basement, check ceilings, heat ducts, and water pipes. Also note the lack of insulation on walls, bulkhead doors, or doors leading to garages. While you are in the attic, check for insulation in floors, ceilings, and walls, although in finished attic rooms, this can be next to impossible. In finished areas, take off the cover of a light switch or receptacle on an outside wall. Shine your flashlight into the space between the electrical box and the wall, and you will see whether there is insulation. Note your findings.

Kinds of Insulation

Before you go on your insulation hunt, you should be aware of the fact that there is a great variety of insulation materials available. The three most common types are *batts* or *blankets, loose fill,* and *rigid board*. Figure 13-1 illustrates these types. Batt or blanket insulation usually consists of fiberglass or rock wool. Loose fill can be either fiberglass, rock wool, cellulose, or vermiculite. Rigid

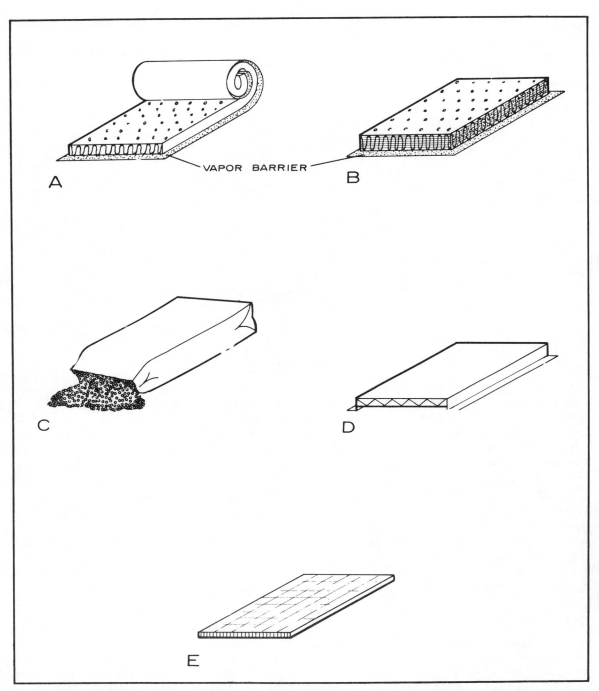

VAPOR BARRIER

A

B

C

D

E

Fig. 13-1. Different kinds of insulation are readily available at most lumber yards and supply stores. (A) and (B) show typical batts and blankets of fiberglass insulation with a vapor barrier, (C) shows a typical pouring insulation, (D) and (E) demonstrate types of rigid insulating board. Courtesy Forest Service, USDA.

board comes in a variety of materials: polystyrene, urethane, and fiberglass are among the more common.

Formaldehyde and Asbestos

Two types of insulation to be on the lookout for are *urea formaldehyde* and *asbestos*. If urea formaldehyde was installed in a house at an incorrect temperature, it could not solidify. The results are noxious odors and toxic fumes. Many lawsuits are still pending in the courts about this potential health hazard. Be sure to ask both the owners and the real estate brokers whether such materials were used in the subject house.

Fig. 13-2. Asbestos insulation on an old coal boiler. This type of insulation is no longer in use, but it is found in many homes. The asbestos fibers are quite dangerous and a qualified contractor should be hired to dispose of this material.

Asbestos insulation was used years ago, primarily on heating boilers and heat pipes. It is no longer used because of the danger of inhaling the asbestos fibers from deteriorating insulation. If, in your inspection, you notice either a boiler or its piping insulated with chalklike material, you can assume that it is asbestos. Figure 13-2 gives a good example of this dangerous material.

WHERE TO INSULATE

There are several areas in any house that should be insulated. (See Fig. 13-3.) Ceilings in attics are great heat losers. So are all exterior walls, particularly in homes in northern climates. Floors over unheated spaces, such as crawl spaces or garages, should have insulation as well. Walls of heated basements need insulation to prevent escaping heat.

Attics

Attic floors are an ideal place to install insulation, especially because they are usually open and accessible for easy installation. In most regions, several inches will be sufficient; in northern climates or in homes using electric heat, 12 inches of insulation is recommended. Note on your worksheet any deficiencies.

Exterior Walls

Depending upon the "expert" you listen to, the perimeter walls of a house can lose anywhere from 32 to 38 percent of your annual heat. The walls take second place, however, when you compare them to the attic floor or leaky windows. With this in mind, first try to find out if the walls have insulation. One way is by asking the owner—an easy one. If the owner does not know, try the electrical outlet trick. Should you still wish to know (and of course you do!) check with a local insulation contractor. Some of them can find out by means of infrared pictures.

Unheated Spaces

Places such as unheated garages and crawl spaces are notorious for losing heat and conducting cold air into the house. As stated before, the cost

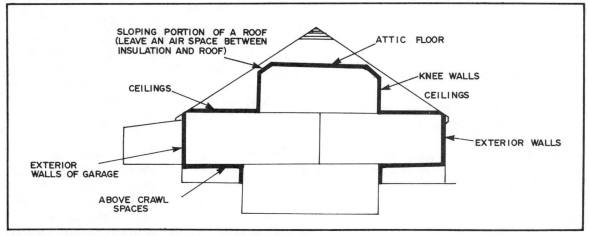

Fig. 13-3. Where to insulate is aptly illustrated in this figure.

of insulating these areas will more than pay off over the long run. If ceilings are finished, a professional will be needed to blow in loose insulation.

Heated Basements

Rigid or batt insulation can easily be attached to basement walls to provide protection. Usually 3 inches of batt insulation or 1 inch of rigid board should be sufficient. If the basement does not have any such insulation, mark it down for a future project.

VAPOR BARRIERS

With the installation of any type of insulation, a proper vapor barrier must also be installed. It is usually attached to the batts or blankets, and the only thing that you have to remember is that the vapor barrier always faces the heated side of the house. (See Fig. 13-4.) For instance, when insulation is installed on an attic floor, there should be a vapor barrier on the floor *between* the insulation and the flooring. On some types of insulation having no vapor barrier, you will have to place a sheet of plastic between the heated side and the insulation.

Vapor barriers come in a variety of materials. Any thin sheet material through which no vapor can pass, such as polyethylene, aluminum foil, or asphalt impregnated kraft paper, will do as a barrier. Should you find accessible areas that have insulation without such a barrier, record it for future correction, because without a vapor barrier moisture from the house will penetrate the insulation and render it ineffective.

There are two ways to put a vapor barrier on already existing insulation. First, you remove the insulation, then install the barrier and replace the insulation. A simpler way, however, is to paint the ceiling or walls on the opposite side of the insulation with a special vapor barrier paint. Most hardware stores carry such a paint. In either case, be sure to record your findings and make necessary corrections once you move in. In Fig. 13-5, you will see a condensation zone map denoting where vapor barriers are required.

ATTIC VENTILATION

Moisture that inevitably builds up in an unvented or poorly vented attic does just as much damage to insulation as it does to everything else. Most of the vapors that escape, condense into water, and drip down on the insulation cause irreparable damage by making the insulation soggy and thus rendering it ineffective. In Fig. 13-6, you see such an instance.

Make certain that there are ample vent openings. A standard rule of thumb is that for every 300

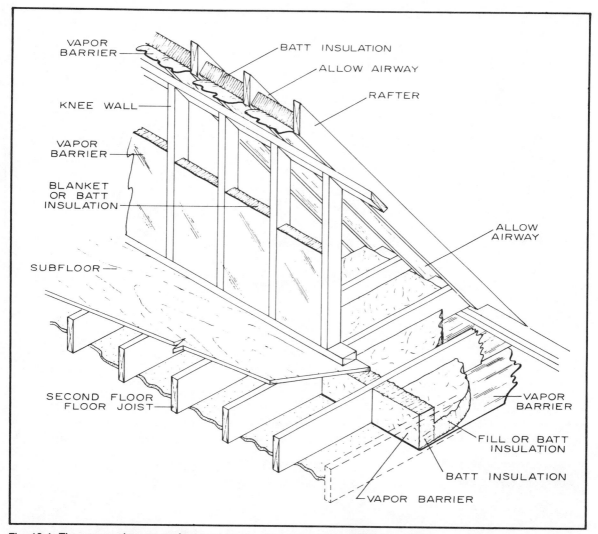

Fig. 13-4. The proper placement of a vapor barrier. Courtesy of Forest Service, USDA.

square feet of floor space, there should be one square foot of ventilation at each end of the attic. Always remember, a properly insulated attic cannot be overventilated. Be sure to note on your worksheet areas that need ventilation. If for some reason vent openings cannot be installed on the gable ends of the attic, consider vents that are mounted on the roof or in the soffit areas. Figure 13-7 show the results of not having soffit vents and the effects of having them.

INSULATING DUCTS AND PIPES

Insulating pipes and ducts throughout the house, particularly in unheated areas, is quite often overlooked. As you inspect the house, check for water pipes or heat ducts that may benefit from insulation. Heating ducts and hot water pipes give off much of their costly heat by warming up areas that do not need to be heated. There is also the chance that water pipes in unheated spaces may freeze

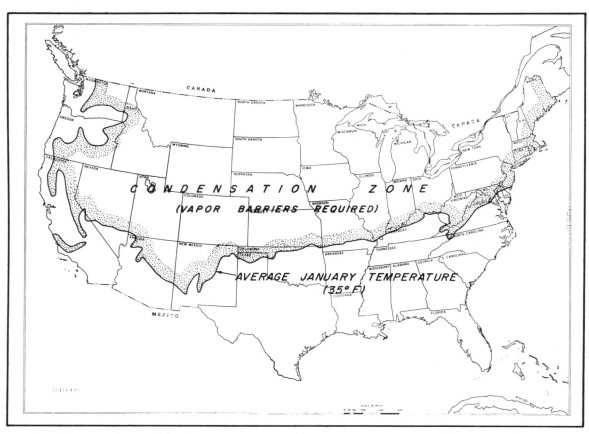

Fig. 13-5. Vapor barriers are required in the condensation zone shown on this map. Courtesy of Forest Service, USDA.

Fig. 13-6. Condensation can soak insulation and cause decay in wood framing. Courtesy Forest Service, USDA.

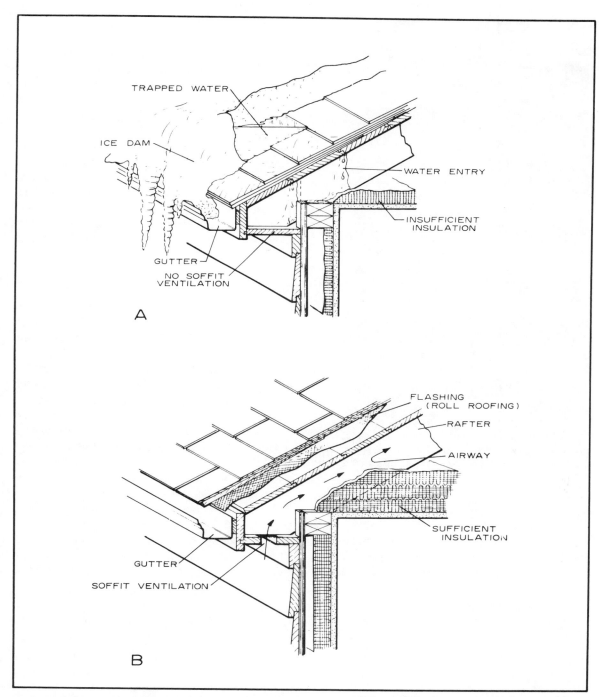

Fig. 13-7. (A) The lack of sufficient insulation and ventilation can be the cause of water penetration to the attic. Sufficient insulation and ventilation (B) prevents ice dams from building up. Courtesy Forest Service, USDA.

151

Fig. 13-8. Uninsulated pipes on exterior walls stand a good chance of freezing. Pipes can easily be insulated and protected.

this is especially true when windows, including those in new homes, let heat escape to the outside. Even homes with storm windows over the regular house windows leak heat to the outside and let cold air enter the house. The best type of windows are tight-fitting double hung ones with either double- or even triple-insulated glass panes.

In many parts of the country, a home should have storm windows. If you see old-fashioned wooden storm windows, don't automatically discount or replace them with new metal ones. Wood frame storms do a good job of keeping out the cold, because the frame itself does not conduct the cold air as does a metal frame. One advantage of metal frame storms is, however, that they can be used all year round.

CAULKING AND WEATHERSTRIPPING

Double-pane glass windows and storm doors won't be helpful in keeping the cold air out unless leaky seams are fully weatherstripped and caulked. (See Fig. 13-9.) Check both the inside and outside of all windows, doors, and hatches leading to attics and crawl spaces. Because, over a period of time, this material deteriorates, note areas that need replacement. Unfortunately, most homeowners do not make necessary maintenance repairs and thus lose many energy dollars.

There are many places that you can inexpensively caulk and seal to prevent energy losses. Check the joints between the exterior siding and the window and door frames. Examine the seam between the siding and the foundation for gaps and inspect storm windows and doors for openings as well. Check the exterior siding for cracks that may need caulking. All outside joints should be inspected on an annual basis as a preventative measure.

HEATING AND AIR-CONDITIONING

If you decide to have the local utility company do an energy audit, it is quite important that the efficiency of your heating and air-conditioning systems be tested. The auditors test the efficiency of these units and submit recommendations on how to make them more efficient.

when the temperature drops-another reason why they should be insulated. Air-conditioning pipes and ducts should also be insulated for the same reason. Figure 13-8 shows a pipe on an exterior wall. This uninsulated pipe is a prime candidate for freezing.

Note on your worksheet the kind and amount of insulation you see and jot down where additional insulation may be needed. Pipes should have at least 1/2-inch of insulation and ducts at least 1-inch. In northern climates, these figures should be doubled.

WINDOWS

You most likely know that practically everyone heats the neighborhood at one time or another, but

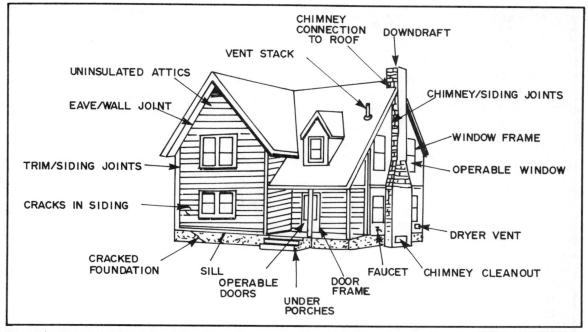

Fig. 13-9. Proper caulking and sealing of joints will cut down substantially energy leaks that are costing the average homeowner hundreds of dollars a year.

During your inspection, don't be afraid to ask the owner questions. Find out when the heating and air-conditioning systems were last cleaned and serviced; both should be done on an annual basis. This is particularly true of oil burning systems because they tend to get dirtier and need more attention than do gas or electric systems. Figure 13-10 gives a good example of poor maintenance given to the draft unit of an oil burning system. You can only surmise what the rest of the system looks like.

Check to see if there is a clock thermostat for the central heating or air-conditioning system. It will automatically turn your heat down at night and turn it up in the morning. This timer can also be used with the cooling of the house. A simple 5 percent turn down each day saves between 15 and 25 percent of your energy costs, depending upon which section of the country you live in.

Closing off unused rooms is just as important in saving on air-conditioning as it is for heating. If the subject house has some extra rooms that you don't intend to use, consider closing them off.

Fig. 13-10. Getting your heating system tuned-up and cleaned is a sound bet for saving money on fuel costs. This chimney draft unit probably hasn't seen a serviceman in quite some time.

153

When checking the house, be sure to examine each window for signs of air leakage. Shake each one to see if it is loose fitting. If latches do not lock properly, make a note to replace them. Also, check the storm windows to see whether they are securely mounted to the window frame. Are they loose? Is there missing caulking? Put your hand along the seams of the windows to see if you can feel a draft. Note all defects.

DOORS

Doors, like windows, can be major heat losers. Be sure to check all exterior doors during your inspection. Look for gaps that allow cold air in and warm air out. In northern climates, all exterior door openings should also have a storm door to provide the necessary air vacuum that greatly reduces heat losses. As with main doors, be sure to check that there is no space between the door and the threshold and that the door itself is weatherstripped. If you find a thermal door used as the main one, a second door is not necessary. Thermal doors are used primarily in colder climates and consist of a metal door filled with an insulating material. In addition, these doors are weatherstripped to make a tight fit in the door frame. Consider this a plus if you find such a door in the house you are purchasing.

Read up on energy conservation. Two books that are highly recommended are *The Energy Wise Home Buyer*, and *In the Bank or Up the Chimney*. Both these publications are published by the Department of Housing and Urban Development. Not only are they reasonably priced, but they are also packed with useful information. Refer to Appendix B for the mailing address.

CHECKPOINTS

- Has an energy audit been done on the house, and if so, what were the results?
- Is there insulation in the basement?
- Are the exterior perimeter walls insulated?
- Is the attic insulated?
- Are unheated areas such as garages and crawl spaces insulated?
- Do the insulation materials have vapor barriers?
- Is there urea formaldehyde in the house?
- Did you find any signs of asbestos insulation?
- Is there sufficient ventilation in the attic and crawl spaces?
- Are heating ducts and water pipes insulated?
- Are the house windows tight and free from air leaks?
- Does the house have storm windows, and if so, what is their condition?
- Are exterior doors tight fitting?
- Does the house have storm doors or thermal doors?
- Will you need to caulk and seal exterior areas?
- Does the heating system or air-conditioning system need servicing?
- Are these systems fully insulated?
- Is there a clock thermostat, and does it work?
- Check with the owners to see what they spent for heat and cooling during the past year. Does it seem reasonable?

Attics

The attic is one of the most important parts of a house to inspect, because it is here that you discover clues about what kinds of ailments you might find with the chimney, vent pipes, skylights, gutters and downspouts, and most importantly, with the roof itself. Water is the cause of all evil, and soggy or deteriorating insulation, stains and rot on rafters, crumbling mortar on the chimney, and decaying roof sheathing all point to the fact that water made its way through the roof, into the attic, and may have gotten into the rest of the house. Be sure to be thorough in your inspection and take all the time you need.

If the house does not have an accessible attic, as shown in Fig. 14-1, make sure that you carefully check the ceilings and walls of the rooms directly below the attic space for water stains, cracks, and loose or flaking plaster. If you see ceilings and walls that are falling apart, you can assume that some water penetrations have occurred over the years. Go back outside and double-check the roof and its members, such as the chimney and gutters, to see

whether they are defective. Check with the owner if there were leaks from the roof at any time. If repairs were made, make sure to get the name of the roofer that did the work in case you need some follow-up work done.

ATTIC CRAWL SPACES

Sometimes finished attics have crawl spaces that can be checked; they are usually in the kneewall sections of the attic, so look around for doors that will lead you to them. Figure 14-2 illustrates such an access. If at all possible, check these spaces because often they are not properly ventilated. Condensation builds up, which may cause wooden members to decay and the insulating material to deteriorate. Be sure to wear a respirator while you are crawling around insulated or dusty areas.

ATTIC ENTRANCES

Because attic openings are notorious heat losers, note on your worksheet all doors or open-

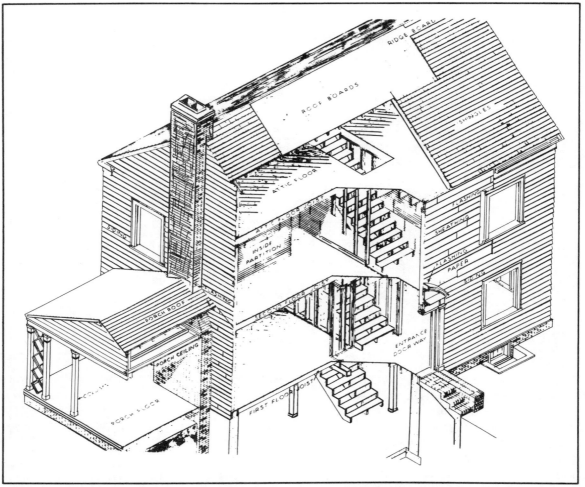

Fig. 14-1. A walk-up attic is a plus for easy access and plenty of storage area. Courtesy of Forest Service, USDA.

ings that are uninsulated. Refer back to Fig. 14-2 and note the lack of insulation on the access door. It is quite possible to find a home that has several inches of insulation on the attic floor but an uninsulated door or hatch. Here the entrance acts like a chimney that draws costly heat from the house.

Although you may have thought you would be able to reach the attic when you looked at the house from the outside, you may be surprised to find yourself shut-off from it once you are inside the house. Don't let the presence of a gable vent (as shown in Fig. 14-3) fool you into believing that you can get to the attic. Sometimes owners have

remodeled and closed off the access to the attic. As you know by now, this is a very serious mistake because roof leaks, condensation, decaying wood, insect activity, deteriorating chimneys, and damaged or insufficient insulation could exist in attics without anyone being aware of these conditions. If the subject house has no entrance, be sure to provide on in order to check the condition of the attic.

UNFINISHED ATTICS

Should the subject house have an unfinished attic, by all means spend plenty of time there to check

Fig. 14-2. A kneewall access panel removed to show a roll of insulation ready to be installed.

nominal costs. (Sometimes the application of roofing cement compound around the culprit roof member's base will cure the ill.) Flashing material that has loosened around chimneys and vents can be tapped down to restore a tight seal. In any event, be sure to record your findings on your worksheet.

RAFTERS

Probably even more important than actual water penetration is structural damage to roof framing members from rain and melting snow. Check each rafter for decay or structural weakness. Does your screwdriver sink into the rafter? Is there a pronounced sag in the rafters? Carefully check the area of the ridge where the rafters meet. Are the opposing rafters tightly secured to a ridge board or to each

Fig. 14-3. Gable vents visible from the exterior do not necessarily mean that the vent is open. In many instances, someone has boarded up the inside and prevented the free flow of air.

it thoroughly. Water that has done damage to the roof and its members will be recorded on rafters, roof, wall sheathing, and floors. Take along your flashlight, your screwdriver, and your worksheets. Look carefully for signs of water penetrations. Examine roof openings such as chimney exits, plumbing vent exits, skylights, and roof ventilating units because that is where leaks will develop first. Shine your flashlight on the adjacent wooden members of these areas. Do you see water stains? Is the wood wet or soggy to the touch? Does your screwdriver penetrate easily, and can you see daylight from where you stand in the attic? If you have to say yes to all or even some of these questions, you may have an active leak. Don't panic: most roof defects can be corrected—usually at

Fig. 14-4. Rafters that are poorly nailed to each other or to a ridge board sometimes pull apart.

other, or are they pulling apart as shown in Fig. 14-4? Sometimes, because the original nailing was done poorly, the rafters will come apart from each other. This could mean a serious structural defect, particularly in areas where heavy snow accumulates on roofs.

ROOF SHEATHING

Check the roof sheathing for defects. Note any missing roof boards or holes in the sheathing. Small openings should not concern you, but openings so large that they could allow someone walking on the roof to fall through should be noted for future restoration. Check also for decay or water penetrations. Note the rusting on exposed nails in the roof

sheathing in Fig. 14-5. Leaks over a long period of time have caused this condition. Try to follow the path of the water stains so you can determine whence the water came. Sometimes it enters several feet away from where you find the stain. But be aware, detecting leaks is difficult, especially on a dry day! If you see water stains and the roof is over 15 years old, you can be reasonably sure that the roof is leaking.

CHIMNEY AREAS IN THE ATTIC

Chimneys are easily inspected from the attic, and since you are up there, be sure to check the condition of both brick and mortar joints. Are the bricks

Fig. 14-5. Water penetrations or condensation will leave their marks on the ends of protruding nails. See the rusted ends of the nails in the roof sheathing.

crumbly to the touch? Is the stucco finish falling off? Look at the wood flooring around the chimney. Do you see water stains? Is the wood around the chimney rotting out? Check to see if the insulation around the chimney is damp or damaged. Can you see daylight from the chimney connection to the roof? Any one of these signs could mean that water is penetrating into the attic. Take your screwdriver and probe the brick joints. Can you put your tool through them, or are there any openings from deteriorated bricks? In Fig. 14-6, note the deteriorating brick, the patched hole in the chimney, and the debris around the base. This attic chimney is a potential fire hazard. Record all your findings, and if any questions remain, have a competent ma-

Fig. 14-6. Chimneys in attics suffer from lack of proper maintenance. Note the end of the tin can sticking out of a hole in the chimney.

son examine the chimney for you.

ATTIC WALLS AND FIRE-STOPS

Check the wall sheathing and wall studs in the attic for signs of decay and/or weakness. Gently place your body against the gable wall and push, but be careful not to puncture yourself with exposed nails. Does the wall seem to give? It shouldn't. Movement in an attic wall tells you that there is structural damage and that you should be concerned. While at the walls, flash your light down between the walls and the flooring. Can you see directly down to the next floor? You shouldn't be able to. Each floor, including the attic, should be separated from the floor below with a fire-stop, usually made of wood studding. This fire-stop prevents rapid flame spread during a fire. (Weak walls, by the way, can be repaired and fire-stops can be installed. This should not turn you off from buying the house.) Record your findings and make sure the owner knows about them. When you later analyze your entire report and you figure out rough costs, you may want to renegotiate the asking price.

ATTIC INSULATION

Is the attic insulated? You will lose quite a bit of heat directly through the attic area if it is not. Check the attic floor for insulation. Anywhere from 6 to 12 inches may be required. In northern climates, 9 to 12 inches are necessary. Use your ruler to determine the amount of insulation. If it is less than 6 inches, it should be increased. Check to see if a vapor barrier was installed with the insulation. The vapor barrier should always face the heated side of the house, and in the attic it should be lying on the attic floor with the insulation over it. (See Fig. 14-7.)

It should be noted here that sometimes improperly installed insulation can cause more problems than it was intended to solve. If you see insulation installed directly on the underside of the roof, it is likely that moisture is being trapped between the insulation and the roof sheathing because air cannot circulate. Unless a 1-inch space between the roof sheathing and the insulation is provided, trapped air will condense and cause typical decay

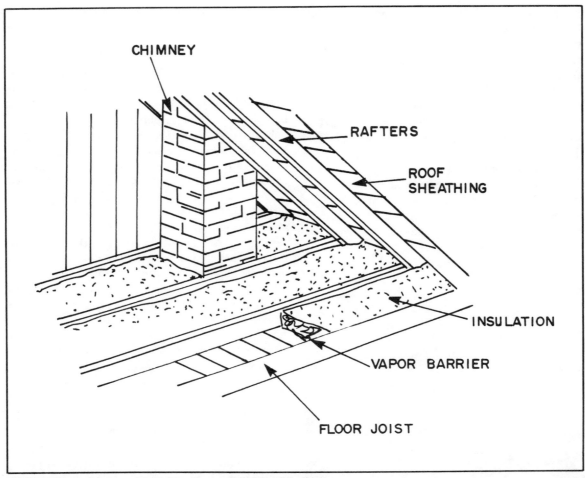

Fig. 14-7. Vapor barriers always face the heated side of the house.

problems with wood members. Make a note to remove any such poorly installed insulation.

ATTIC VENTILATION

Proper ventilation of an attic is a must. It should take place year round, and attic vents should never be closed off. Some people make the mistake of shutting off ventilation openings thinking that they can save on energy costs during the winter. This is a false assumption. Moisture builds up and causes decay and rot in wooden members.

Check the attic for vent openings in the walls, on the roof, or in the eaves. A combination of ridge vent, soffit vents, and gable vents work most effectively. (See Fig. 14-8). Remember that you cannot overventilate an attic, especially one that is heavily insulated. Check the vent openings for signs of water penetrations and general decay. Sometimes you find vents, such as the soffit vents in Fig. 14-9, that are missing screens. Be sure to replace these screens to keep out insects and bats.

VENT PIPES

Before you consider the attic thoroughly inspected, make sure that there are no vents that terminate in the attic—either from the plumbing

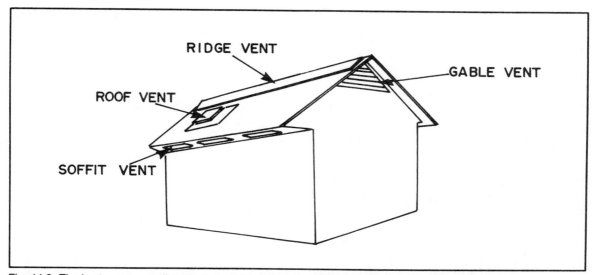

RIDGE VENT

ROOF VENT

GABLE VENT

SOFFIT VENT

Fig. 14-8. The best way to ventilate an attic with sufficient insulation is with a combination of vents.

system, the kitchen, or the bathrooms. (See Fig. 14-10.) All vents should exit to the outside, because plumbing vents carry sewer gases, and bathroom and kitchen vents carry moisture and grease. Return to the living areas of the house and make a mental note of where the kitchen and the bathrooms are located. Upon returning to the attic, locate the area of each and pull back the existing insulation. If you do see moisture- and grease-producing or gas-expelling vent pipes, make a note to have them changed so that they ventilate to the outside of the house.

OTHER TYPES OF DEFECTS

Sometimes attics house parts of electrical or mechanical systems, particularly heating or air-conditioning ducts. Occasionally, you can even find water pipes and electrical junction boxes there as well. All of these could have defects and should be checked. Heating and cooling ducts should be insulated, as should plumbing lines. Electrical junction boxes should have protective covers, and the wiring should not be makeshift. (See Fig. 14-11.) The use of lampcord to provide electricity for lighting or running attic fans is clearly a fire hazard and should be discontinued.

Fig. 14-9. Soffit vents on the underside of an overhanging eave. Note the missing screens that allow in all sorts of flying creatures.

Fig. 14-10. Plumbing vent pipes should not terminate in attics. Their sewer gases will discharge into attic, causing a health hazard.

Some words of caution while inspecting attics: walk carefully, especially on unfinished floors. Walk only on the floor joists—never between them. Stepping between the joists could damage the ceilings below. Move slowly; a sudden move could result in a nail puncture or a bruised head. Be sure to wear a respirator, because most attics contain dust particles and insulation fibers that are hazardous to your health. In testing wooden members or chimneys, be careful: you don't want to damage someone else's property.

CHECKPOINTS

• Do the top floor ceilings and walls have water stains?

• Are there cracks in plaster ceilings or walls?
• Are crawl spaces accessible?
• Is the attic entrance door insulated and weatherstripped?
• Are there signs of deterioration in rafters or roof sheathing?
• Can you see daylight from the attic?
• Are there pronounced sags in the ridge board or rafters?
• Are rafters pulling away from each other at the ridge?
• Are there water stains around the chimney and vent areas?
• Check the chimney for holes or deterioration.
• Are attic walls sturdy and fire-stopped?
• How much insulation is in the attic?
• Does the insulation have a vapor barrier?
• Is there sufficient ventilation in the attic?
• Are there screens in the attic vents?
• Are water pipes, air-conditioning, or heating ducts insulated?
• Check for discharge vents in the attic.
• Are there any electrical hazards in the attic?

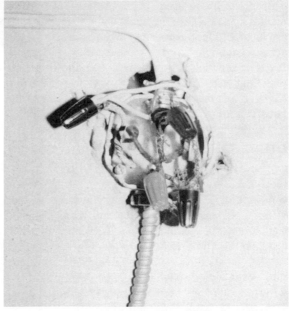

Fig. 14-11. No exposed live wires should be present in the attic. All junction boxes should have covers. The open one shown in this figure presents a potential shock hazard.

Bathrooms and Kitchens

Bathrooms and kitchens undoubtedly suffer the most wear and tear and should be well built and well maintained. Whether or not they are is for you to find out, and because there are very few technical terms to be learned, you can plunge right into the inspection process. Be prepared for many details that you must observe, however.

BATHROOMS

If there is a bath on one of the upper floors, start there. First put on the lights and pull up the shades to give yourself as much light as possible. Also, check the window to see that it is operating properly. If there is a mechanical vent, turn that on. By law, all bathrooms must have either a window or a mechanical vent to allow the free flow of air. Double-check to make sure that the vent is connected to an exterior opening and does not vent directly into the attic, where the moisture is likely to settle and do damage.

Check to see if the electrical outlets are GFI's (ground fault interrupters), because by code they are required in all new construction. If the subject house is an older one (most older homes do not have them), make a note for future electrical updating. Test the outlets with your tester to make sure they are working.

Wall and Floor Coverings

Next, check the tiles, particularly those sections that are directly affected by water. Check the condition of the floor and wall tiles adjacent to the tub. In many homes, poor caulking in the seam between the tub and the tile allows water to penetrate. You are likely to find deteriorated flooring and walls. (See Fig. 15-1.) Gently tap the wall areas to check for weaknesses. If a wall moves inward, repairs may be needed. Press down with your hand along the floor line adjacent to the tub to see that the floor does not give way. If it does, the subflooring may be rotting out. Also look for loose or missing floor tiles. Figure 15-2 shows an extreme case of floor deterioration. Note any defects on your worksheet.

Water Pressure

Check the water pressure in all fixtures by

Fig. 15-1. Proper caulking and sealing of tub/tile joints will prevent deterioration of wall members.

turning on the cold water in the sink and the tub and flushing the toilet, all at the same time. If there are two bathrooms adjacent to each other, do the same thing to both bathrooms simultaneously. No marked drop in pressure should be noted. Then check the hot water lines the same way. If you find a drop in pressure, you may have a defective hot water tank or the water lines may be lined up (deposits of minerals that narrow the water pipe interior), a problem that can be corrected fairly easily by a plumber.

Shut-off Valves

Check to see if there are shut-off valves under the fixtures and if they are working. (See Fig. 15-3.)

Turn the valves on and off and note any that won't operate or don't entirely shut off the water flow in the fixture. Check for leaks in the water pipes and shut-off valves. Note any signs of corrosion or deterioration.

Bathtub

Be sure to fill up the tub and then drain it to see if it drains properly. Gurgling sounds during draining can mean poor venting of the plumbing system, as can odors coming from any of the fixtures. Note whether the tub is chipped or damaged. Tap the side of it with your knuckles; a tinny sound tells you that it is a steel tub and not the best quality. A solid sounding tap tells you that it is cast iron and the more expensive of the two.

Fig. 15-2. Lack of floor maintenance will, in time, result in this advanced case of deterioration.

Fig. 15-3. Shut-off valves under fixtures should be tested to see if they are working. In many instances, the valves have not been opened or closed in such a long time that they are frozen.

Sinks/Vanities

Bathroom sink vanities are common in many bathrooms, and some discussion about them is necessary. One common and typical problem that can be found is a poorly mounted top. These loosely mounted tops, as shown in Fig. 15-4, can easily be damaged by an accidental upward thrust. Gently try to lift the top. If it gives, it needs to be fastened to the base. Also, check the vanity's finish—can you pull its veneer away from the base? If so, it needs to be reglued. The bowl should have no chips or be otherwise damaged, and it should have a working stopper. Check the faucet for leaks. Don't forget

to look under the vanity. Sometimes you may find a hidden surprise—heat registers or exposed live wires, for example. Note on your worksheet all defects.

Shower Enclosures

A poorly maintained shower enclosure can have distinct defects, so scrutinize it carefully. When you are inspecting a metal one, be sure to look for signs of corrosion or rusting, which is sometimes hidden by a coat of fresh paint. Look carefully at all exposed metal parts of the shower (walls and base). Badly deteriorated metal, even though camouflaged, will exhibit telltale signs. The painted areas will usually be bubbled out and blistered, and the adjacent metal areas will appear weak. Gently break off some

Fig. 15-4. Vanity tops are usually put on improperly. After a few good pushes, a broken plumbing connection could occur.

of the bubbled paint, and you may discover extensive corrosion under it.

Tiled shower enclosures with poorly maintained or repaired tile joints are likely to have loose or missing sections of tiles. Make a fist and gently tap the sides of the shower area to see that the walls are not weak and the tiles are not ready to fall off. Gently put pressure against the walls. Do any give way to the pressure? Check the tile floor of the enclosure for missing grout between the tiles. Cover the drain on the shower floor and fill up the base with water and let it stand for 15 minutes. Check the ceilings directly below for water stains. Loose or missing tiles, missing grout, weak or rusted-out walls all could mean water penetrations and hidden damage. Note any such deficiencies and ask the owner about them.

Traps

What king of trap is under the sink? There are P and S types—the P-type is the more effective trap of the two and was illustrated in Chapter 10. Usually S traps, as illustrated in Fig. 15-5, are likely to lose their trap seal easily. When this happens, sewer gases enter the house. This can be best illustrated in Fig. 15-6. The siphoning action that sucks the water out of the sink also drains the protective trap.

This is more of an occurrence when the sink is not properly vented to the exterior. A simple way to reestablish the seal is by letting the faucet run for a few seconds. Water draining out of the sink into the trap makes a new seal.

KITCHENS

Take plenty of time to check the kitchen. There are just too many items that must be checked to rush through it. First, get an overall impression of the kitchen. Is it big enough for your family and lifestyle? Are there enough cabinets and counter spaces? Are there enough outlets in the kitchen to make working there easy? Chapter 8 shows what happens when there are insufficient electrical outlets. An octopus arrangement is extremely hazardous. Check to see if you have sufficient light and ventilation. As you know, the kitchen is one of the most lived-in areas of the house. It should make you feel comfortable; it should be a pleasant area with plenty of natural light and a free flow of air.

Sink

Once you are satisfied with the overall look, check the sink for proper drainage and adequate water pressure. Do the faucets leak, and are they in

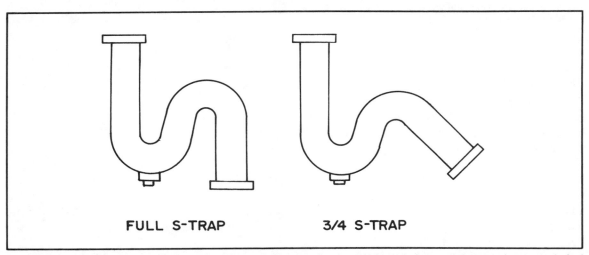

FULL S-TRAP   **3/4 S-TRAP**

Fig. 15-5. S-traps are a poor substitute for a P-trap. S-traps tend to lose their seal: the result in many instances is foul smelling sewer gases entering the house.

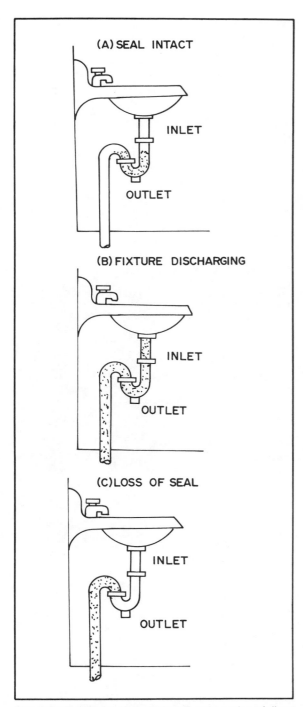

(A) SEAL INTACT

INLET

OUTLET

(B) FIXTURE DISCHARGING

INLET

OUTLET

(C) LOSS OF SEAL

INLET

OUTLET

Fig. 15-6. This figure gives a good demonstration of direct siphonage. Note the loss of seal.

need of repair or replacement? Does the faucet have a sprayer, and is it working? With your flashlight, look under the sink to check for leaks in the water lines, sprayer, and drain. Do the pipes look deteriorated, or do they have temporary patches?

Examine the sink cabinet base and walls for wood decay and insect activity. Are there holes in the rear walls? Do you see exposed wiring that is clearly a hazard? A water leak near electrical wires could spell trouble.

Disposal

If the kitchen has a garbage disposal, you will find it under the sink. Check it carefully for signs of corrosion or deterioration. If there is a switch, turn it on. Be sure to have some cold water running in the sink so the disposal can operate properly. If you hear unusual banging or rattling noises, it may mean that the appliance is defective or a metallic object is in the disposal. Ask the owner about the noises and find out the age of the unit. Most manufacturers project a 8- to 12-year life expectancy for the average appliance. If the disposal is over 8 years of age, you should note that it is on borrowed time. A special note here about septic tank or cesspool systems: if the subject house is serviced by either, the use of a garbage disposal is not advisable because wastes from the disposal put an added burden on the tanks.

Dishwashers

Many homes have dishwashers nowadays. If you find one in the house you are inspecting, run it to see that it is working properly. Look for leaks and listen for strange noises. Because dishwashers should not be drained into private sewage systems (detergents kill the beneficial bacteria found in private tanks), a separate drywell should be provided.

Stove

Inspect the stove by turning on all burners and the oven. Record any that do not work. If it is a gas stove, check the rear to see what king of connection it has. The use of a flexible pipe connection is

167

Fig. 15-7. A flexible gas connection is no longer considered safe in most communities. If you have such a connection, check with your local building department to see if it is still allowable.

no longer legal in most communities, so if you see this type, find out from the local building department what the code regulations are. (See Fig. 15-7.) If the stove is electrical, it should have a 50-amp fuse or circuit breaker on a No. 6 wire, although some communities allow a 40-amp circuit for an electric stove. Be sure to turn off all burners when you are through inspecting the stove. Mark down any missing hardware or inoperable doors, clocks, or lights.

Check the stove vent to see if it vents to the exterior or to a charcoal filter in the hood. Figure 15-8 shows the control knobs on a stove vent. Note the missing middle knob. If the unit is a charcoal filter-type be sure to check the filter. Usually they are loaded with grease and either need a thorough cleaning or replacement.

Refrigerators

In checking a refrigerator, open and close the doors to see if the rubber seal is intact and that the doors fit tight. Check the rear of the refrigerator to make sure that there is enough room between the kitchen wall and the unit for circulation. People have a tendency to push appliances up tight against walls or enclose them in cubby holes. This prevents ventilation of the cooling components and will shorten the life of the appliance. Scrutinize the freezer for frosting or other signs of malfunctioning. Pull off the base panel to check for accumulations of dust. (See Fig. 15-9.) Excessive build-up of dust prevents proper circulation of air and may result in repair calls.

Fig. 15-8. Stove vents can either vent to the exterior or can be self-contained charcoal filter-types. Note the missing knob on this vent.

Fig. 15-9. The base of most refrigerators load up with dust and dirt, so be sure to pull off the base panel to examine its condition. This unit has a slight build-up of dust, which should be dusted off for better coil performance.

Kitchen Floor

Like the bathroom floor, the kitchen floor also carries a great deal of weight. When you stop and think about all the appliances that sit on that floor, you can well appreciate the need to check for structural defects in flooring and supporting members. Eyeball the floor from one side to the other. Does it slant excessively, particularly in corners or spaces where heavy appliances, such as stoves and refrigerators, are located?

Use a level to determine how much the floor is off. Don't be concerned about minor drops; they can be found in most houses. What you should be concerned with are very obvious slants in the flooring.

If you feel as though you were walking up or downhill as you cross the kitchen, return to the basement and check the area under the kitchen. Find the support beams and posts and see if original supports have been removed. The wood supports may have been damaged by water leaks, or they may have sunk into the cellar floor. Look for causes and you may find answers. If the floor and walls are badly aligned and you can't find a plausible reason, you should have an expert check it out. Normal settlement should not be a major concern, but any active structural defect could cause future damage to the house.

Cabinets

Last, but not least, check the kitchen cabinets. Not only the size of the cabinets is important, but also the quality of their construction. Open the doors of all units to check for size and condition. Gently place your hands on the bottoms and sides and press. Properly mounted wall and floor cabinets should not give. Do the same thing to the counter tops. Well installed tops are securely attached to the bases and should not move. Note on your worksheet inoperable doors or drawers and any missing hardware.

CHECKPOINTS

Bathrooms

- Is there adequate ventilation?
- Is there an exhaust fan, and does it exhaust to the exterior?
- Are electrical outlets ground fault interrupters?
- What is the condition of the tile?
- Do the walls or floor need repairs?
- Is the water pressure adequate?
- Is there sufficient hot water?
- Do all fixtures drain properly?
- Are there any leaks in drains or water lines?
- Are the shut-off valves working?
- Check the condition of the vanity.
- Is the counter mounted securely?

- Are there high quality fixtures, and are they in good condition?
- What is the condition of the shower walls and floor?
- Any leaks showing up in the ceilings below?
- Are there any indications of venting problems?

Kitchen

- Is the kitchen large enough?
- Is there sufficient light and ventilation?
- Check for leaks under the sink.
- Does the faucet have a sprayer and is it working?
- Any decay in the kitchen cabinets or counters?
- Are wall units and floor units properly mounted and secured?
- Is there adequate drainage?
- Is the water pressure sufficient?
- What is the condition of the appliances?
- Are appliances over 8 years of age?
- Do all the appliances work?
- What is the condition of the floors and walls?
- Check the support members in the basement for structural soundness.
- Will the kitchen be a pleasant, happy place in which to be?

Chimneys, Fireplaces, and Solid- Fuel Stoves

With the ever-increasing costs of energy, many people have turned to alternative sources to heat their homes. They use wood and coal burning stoves as well as fireplaces to supplement their central heating systems. Stoves and fireplaces are not without their hazards if not in good working order, however, so if you find any such system in the subject house, check it out very carefully.

EXTERIOR CHIMNEY

Part of your inspection of roof-mounted structures is to check the chimney for loose and missing mortar, broken or missing bricks, and loose sections of flashing, which are all signs that the chimney needs repairs.

Chimney height is also important. The chimney should extend at least 3 feet above flat roofs. On pitched roofs, if should be 2 feet higher than any point within 10 feet. (See Fig. 16-1.) Proper height prevents downdrafts and fires caused by flying sparks.

If the chimney is made of metal, be sure to look for signs of corrosion, creosote build-up, holes in the metal, and general deterioration. All-metal chimneys should have a metal cover, as shown in Fig. 16-1. If it is missing, make sure you note it on your worksheet.

CHIMNEY LINERS

Not all chimneys have a flue liner, and most older homes have just a brick interior. If the roof is accessible and safe to walk on, check the chimney to see if it has a liner. Don't be fooled by a liner that only goes down 2 feet and then stops. The remaining section of the chimney may be brick lined, and is as dangerous as a chimney with no lining at all. Figure 16-2 shows a brick lined chimney. Note the deterioration in the brickwork and the chimney cap.

If you cannot get on to the roof, check the fireplace when you are inside. Open up the damper and look up the chimney. If the flue looks smooth and uniform, you have a liner.

Having a liner is by no means a guarantee that the chimney is safe. Flue tiles crack and chip dur-

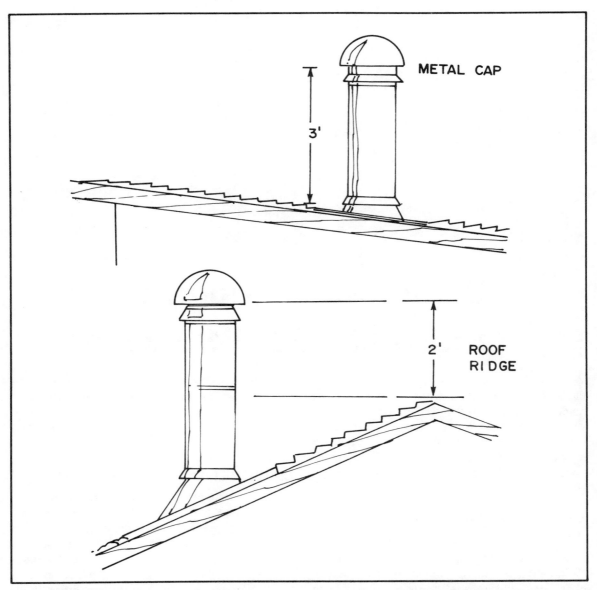

Fig. 16-1. Proper chimney height is essential for good draft and to prevent fires caused by flying sparks. Note the metal hoods on the chimneys.

ing cleaning or may have been damaged by a previous chimney fire, so look for cracks or fire damage. A professional way to check a flue is by doing a *smoke test*. Start a fire in the fireplace or stove and then cover the top of the chimney. If you have cracks or holes in the chimney, the smoke will be forced through them. If you find that the chimney leaks smoke into the house, it must be repaired or it should not be used at all. In Fig. 16-3, an example of a smoke test is shown.

Repairing a chimney flue liner is not as easy as it sounds. An expert mason will have to check the

Fig. 16-2. A brick lined chimney should not be used with a solid fuel appliance. The chances of a chimney fire are magnified by the chances of deterioration in the bricks or mortar joints. Note the deterioration at the chimney cap in this figure.

chimney to see what needs to be done. Sometimes the installation of a metal flue liner will take care of defects in chimneys. These types of liners are not always allowed, however; it will be specified in local building codes, so be sure to check with your local inspector before installing one.

ATTIC AREA

During the inspection of the attic, one of the areas to check is the visible section of the chimney. Any defect in the chimney should be recorded for later repairs. It is also important to bring these defects to the attention of the owner, because most

owners rarely go into the attic. Defects could be hazardous to them as well as to you, the new owner. As was mentioned in Chapter 14, be sure to check for crumbling and deteriorating mortar or brickwork. Holes in the chimney should be repaired with brick and cement. Figure 16-4 shows a chimney that needs the attention of a mason. Soot and carbon has built up on the rim of the opening, and noxious smoke fumes are penetrating the attic. During your inspection, if you find holes that have been plugged up with metal plates, be sure to record their location. Metal plate plugs, as shown in Fig. 16-5, are a potential fire hazard. The pressure

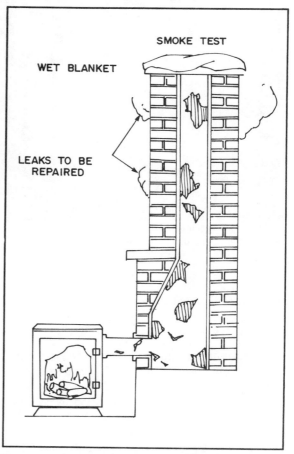

Fig. 16-3. A simple way to perform a smoke test is by placing wet blankets over the chimney flue while it is going. Smoke that is forced through cracks in the chimney into the house can be noted for future repairs.

Fig. 16-4. Neglect causes deterioration in the chimney shown in this figure. This chimney needs a good cleaning and repairs to both the brickwork and mortar joints.

generated by a fire can blow them out and flames could enter the attic area.

BASEMENT

While you are checking the heating system in the basement, also check the chimney portion that is there. As with the exterior and attic areas, be on the lookout for signs of deterioration in both the brickwork and the mortar joints. Check the ash pit's cleanout door, which you should find at the base of the chimney. The door should be made of metal and not of any combustible material. Open and close the door to see if it fits snugly, because loose ones create unwanted drafts. If the ash pit is loaded with soot

deposits, as shown in Fig. 16-6, make a note to have it cleaned. These materials are corrosive and will eventually attack both brick and mortar. Also check the flue pipe connections from the chimney to the heating plant. These connections should be tight. Any openings are a cause for concern because noxious gases can escape into the basement.

FIREPLACES

Fireplaces are, at best, poor heaters. A typical masonry fireplace averages about 10 percent efficiency. The draft created by a fire draws room air up the chimney along with the burning gases in the fireplace. This results in a net heat loss for the whole house. Heat is also lost if the damper is left open after the fire dies out, which happens all too fre-

Fig. 16-5. Metal caps in chimneys are potential fire hazards. The pressure generated by a fire would blow these metal plates out. Areas such as this should be bricked up.

Fig. 16-6. The ash pit has not been cleaned in years. The build-up of these corrosive materials deteriorates both brick and mortar joints. Annual cleaning would avoid this situation.

quently in most houses. Because of its inefficiency, various modifications have been introduced over the years. One is the use of hollow tube grates, which are placed in the fireplace to extract heat. Another modification, metal-lined heat exchangers, are sometimes fitted into the fireplace in order to radiate more heat into the living areas. Yet another, tightly fitted glass doors over the fireplace opening, can cut down on room air losses. Even with all of these modifications, however, a fireplace is still costly to use. Figure 16-7 illustrates a typical fireplace with a clay flue liner.

Fireplace Walls

In your inspection of the fireplace, be sure to check the condition of the bricks on the inside walls. Building codes generally require that the back and sides of the fireplace be made of solid masonry or reinforced concrete at least 8 inches thick. Usually the brick is firebrick. Firebrick can be distinguished from ordinary brick by its yellow color (ordinary brick is red). Firebrick can withstand extreme temperatures without cracking. Because most older homes do not have firebrick, you may find cracked bricks and deteriorating mortar joints. Take your screwdriver and gently probe the joints between the bricks. Is the mortar weak and crumbling? Can you easily move the brick, and are there any visible openings? If your answer is yes to any of these questions, you should consider having the inside walls rebuilt. Note the deterioration in the wall and floor of the fireplace in Fig. 16-8.

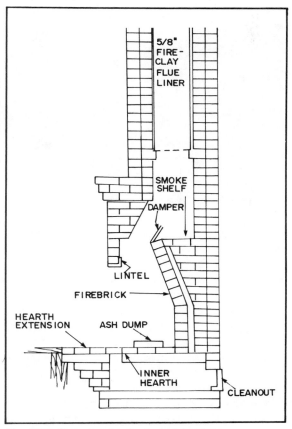

Fig. 16-7. Components of a typical fireplace.

175

Fig. 16-8. Fireplaces need annual repairs to prevent the type of deterioration seen in this figure. Note the left sidewall and the hearth deterioration.

Damper

You would be surprised at the number of fireplaces that have no damper, or one that is not working properly. A damper consists of a cast-iron frame with a hinged lid that opens and closes to vary the amount of air needed for a good draft. Refer back to Fig. 16-7 to see the location of a damper in a fireplace. If the fireplace has no damper, and the opening is not plugged up with some form of insulation, expensive house heat is being sucked up the chimney. If there is a damper but it is loose and/or partially open, you are also heating the neighborhood. Besides that, birds, insects, and even rodents will find it very easy to enter the house through the fireplace.

While checking the damper, you should also look for signs of excessive soot build-up or creosote deposits on the fireplace walls and flue. You can identify creosote by its appearance. If you see black, shiny, tarlike deposits in any section of the fireplace or flue, consider having a chimney sweep clean them. If you find large amounts of creosote, you have an ideal situation for a chimney fire that could not only seriously damage your chimney but also burn down the house. Should any doubt remain, have a mason or chimney sweep double-check it for you.

Combustible Materials

No woodwork should be placed within 6 inches of the fireplace opening. Woodwork above the opening should be a minimum of 12 inches from the top of the opening. Keep in mind that these are minimum requirements and that the further away the wood is the better. (A good publication to read up on is the *Fireplace and Chimney Bulletin,* published by the U.S. Department of Agriculture.)

SOLID-FUEL STOVES

Don't be surprised to find coal- and woodburning stoves in garages, basements, finished attics, and other living areas of the home. Your concern will not be so much about the location as about the code regulations governing their installation.

There are a variety of stoves on the market today that can either burn wood, coal, or both. One of the first things you have to find out from the owner is whether a unit was installed with permission from the local fire department. If the owner can show you an official local fire department permit, you can at least be sure that it was inspected when it was first installed. But don't let that fool you. Sometimes owners will modify a stove after it was inspected. If no permit was issued, insist that the owner secure one from the proper officials; otherwise the stove should not be used.

Stoves must be installed in such a way that specific clearances from combustible materials are carefully observed to prevent fires. Because sides, bottom, and stovepipe each attain such different temperatures, there are specified clearances for each.

Stove Sides

The sides of a stove should be at least 36 inches from any combustible materials. Only if non-combustible material is spaced 1 inch away from the wall, may a stove be positioned closer than 36 inches. That 1 inch space will allow the air to circulate so heat cannot be conducted directly to the wall. Asbestos millboard spaced 1 inch away from a wall will allow an 18-inch stove wall clearance. If 28-gauge sheet metal is installed in the same manner, the acceptable clearance is 12 inches. (See Fig. 16-9.)

Floor Protection

Safe floor clearances are substantially less than those for walls because the heat radiated from the bottom of a stove is generally much less than from either the sides or the top. During a fire, ashes fall to the bottom of the stove and have an insulating effect, resisting the flow of heat downward. Clearances for proper floor protection are classified according to the length of the stove legs and are shown in Fig. 16-10.

Stovepipe

A *stovepipe* is the metal flue that connects the stove to the chimney. When stovepipe is used for

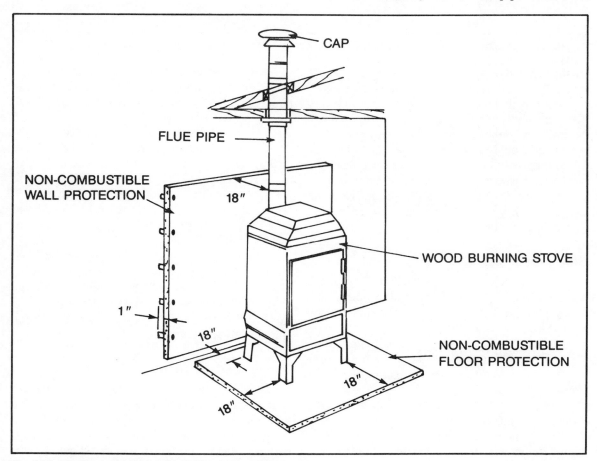

Fig. 16-9. Minimum clearances for safe stove installation.

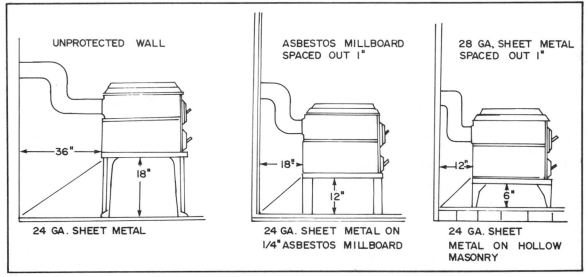

UNPROTECTED WALL

36"

18"

24 GA. SHEET METAL

ASBESTOS MILLBOARD
SPACED OUT 1"

18"

12"

24 GA. SHEET METAL ON
1/4" ASBESTOS MILLBOARD

28 GA. SHEET METAL
SPACED OUT 1"

12"

6"

24 GA. SHEET
METAL ON HOLLOW
MASONRY

Fig. 16-10. Depending upon the material on the floor, the length of the stove legs will vary accordingly.

a chimney, dangerous creosote may build up on the metal and combine with outside moisture (rain or melting snow). This can corrode the pipe in a very short time. Should a chimney fire occur, there would be little to contain it. It is for this reason that stovepipe should not take the place of a chimney, but should only be used as a connector from the stove to a masonry or metal-gauge chimney. Quality chimneys are made of corrosion resistant materials. They do not have to be replaced and are also able to contain a fire.

Stovepipe Installation

A stovepipe must be installed so that there is a good draft to carry the hot gases away quickly and safely. Be sure to check the following guidelines in your inspection of the stovepipe:

• The stovepipe should be short. Long runs tend to build up creosote deposits and provide a poor draft.
• Turns and bends should be kept to a minimum number.
• The horizontal portion of the stovepipe should be no more than 75 percent of the vertical portion.

• The stovepipe should enter the chimney well above the stove outlet. Horizontal portions of the pipe should rise at least 1/4-inch per foot.

Check if the pieces are fitted together tightly. The sections should be permanently joined with two or three metal screws to prevent the pipe from coming loose. Stovepipe does not normally last long, so ask the owner how old the pipe is. If it is over 3 years old and has been used regularly, it may need to be replaced. During your inspection, look for corrosion and holes in the pipe. Blackish stains indicate creosote deposits. If the pipe has not been cleaned at the end of each heating season, heavy deposits of soot and creosote are likely. When you have the chimney cleaned, be sure to have the stovepipe as well as the stove itself cleaned and inspected by the chimney sweep.

Stovepipe Clearances

Care must be taken when a stovepipe is attached to a chimney. Stovepipe clearances must be maintained from all combustible surfaces. Passing a stovepipe through a wall should be avoided if possible. If it cannot, special precautions should be taken. Check to see if there is an insulated *wall thimble*,

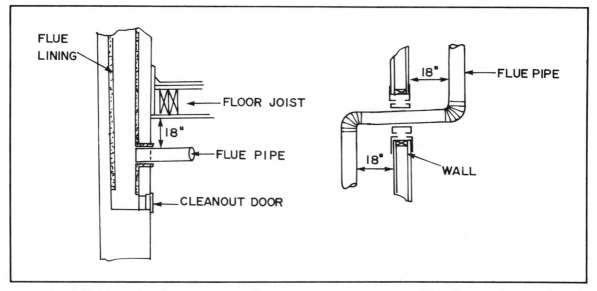

Fig. 16-11. Stovepipe can overheat rapidly, and any combustible materials close to it stand the risk of burning. Be sure to follow the recommendations in this figure for proper installation.

which should be made of sheet metal or asbestos millboard and should be three times the diameter of the stovepipe. (See Fig. 16-11). Stovepipe should never run through concealed places like closets or attics. Note any such findings on your worksheet.

SAFETY PRECAUTIONS

All chimneys and heating appliances are potentially a fire hazard. While you inspect the house, you should be concerned about latent fire traps. Ask the owner how often the chimney has been cleaned. It should be cleaned every year, or as often as necessary to get rid of creosote buildup. Be sure to note the height of the chimney from the outside. Flying sparks could start fires to adjacent combustible areas. Double-check all the important clearances necessary for safe fireplace or solid fuel stove use. Also, see if the house has a sufficient number of smoke detectors to give you and your family plenty of time to escape during a fire. They are able to detect a house fire while it is still smoldering. If the house does not have any, consider installing one on each level. Be sure to check solid fuel stoves for signs of deterioration in the stove or its stovepipe.

If questions or doubts remain about the safety of a chimney, a fireplace, or a stove, call in a professional to check them out for you.

CHECKPOINTS

Chimney (exterior)

• Inspect for loose, missing, cracked, or damaged masonry.
• Look for mortar joints that are deteriorating.
• Does the chimney extend at least 3 feet above the roof and 2 feet above any point within 10 feet?
• On metal chimneys, look for signs of corrosion, rusting, or holes.
• Does the chimney have a flue liner?
• Does the chimney have a protective rain cover?
• How often has the owner had the chimney cleaned?

Chimney (attic)

• Look for holes or deterioration in the chimney wall.

179

- Have metal plates been used to plug holes in the chimney? If so they should be removed and the holes cemented up.

Chimney (basement)

- Check the ash pit cleanouts for accumulations of soot and carbon deposits.
- Are the ash pit doors made of metal, and do they fit snugly?
- What is the condition of stove or boiler flue connections to the chimney?
- Is there any deterioration in the chimney?

Fireplaces

- Inspect the walls of the fireplace for signs of crumbling mortar or damaged bricks.
- Does the fireplace have firebrick or ordinary brick?
- Check to see if the fireplace has a damper and if it is working.
- Are there signs of excessive creosote build-up in the fireplace?

Stoves

- Is there a permit for a solid fuel stove?
- Are the clearances for the sides, bottom, and stovepipes of the stove sufficient to prevent a fire?
- Is the stovepipe installed in accordance with standard safety guidelines?
- What is the condition of the stovepipe?
- Has the stovepipe and stove been cleaned and maintained on an annual basis?

Safety Precautions

- Does the house have smoke detectors on each floor, and are they working?
- Are there any accumulations of creosote in the chimney, fireplace, or solid fuel stove?
- Is there deterioration in the chimney, fireplace, or stove?
- Are the clearances for chimneys, fireplaces, and stoves sufficient?
- Has the owner properly maintained and serviced the chimney, fireplace, and solid fuel stove?

Interior Rooms

The last sections of the house for you to inspect are the interior living quarters. Once you are finished with the attic, methodically examine each and every room from the upper levels to the lower ones, including closets, crawl spaces, halls, stairways, and the living spaces themselves. What you are actually doing is taking the visible damages and defects that you have found, such as a defective gutter outside, for example, and correlating them to conditions inside the house. Clearly, if the exterior, attic, and basement did not show major defects, you should not find them in interior rooms either. What the rooms might need, however, are "cosmetic lifts," which involve repairs that usually do not run into a lot of money. A host of minor defects can be corrected with simple structural repair techniques; for example, sagging floors can be jacked up and supported, or damaged plaster ceilings can be replaced with sheetrock.

Before you examine each room thoroughly, you may want to follow a pattern that will give you a quick overview before you begin your more detailed inspection. First turn on all the lights and pull up all drawn shades to provide plenty of light for you to see. Then check a room from all four sides from a standing position as well as a kneeling one, because you want to get the whole picture of the room. (You would be surprised at the difference in views from one side of a room to another and from a standing position to a kneeling one.) Stand in the center and visually survey the room, taking in the ceiling, walls, windows, doors, and floors. Besides looking, touch areas that appear suspicious. If the walls or ceiling look out of line to you, gently push them outwards. Does the ceiling or wall move? Determine whether it is only loose plaster or whether the wall itself is giving in. As with any area of the house, if you have serious doubt, consult a professional.

CEILINGS

Now you are ready to scan the entire ceiling for bulging or loose plaster. Note on your worksheets

Fig. 17-1. Water stains on ceilings and walls indicate either an exterior or interior leak. Find the cause and see if it is still active.

water stains and their locations. Check the notes you took outside. Do these stains correspond to those areas noted on the exterior? If not, check again; look particularly for areas directly above the stain. Sometimes water from the bathroom or from a leaking radiator may stain the ceiling underneath. (See Fig. 17-1.) If you cannot find a plausible explanation, check with the owner. Also pay particular attention to cracks that you see next to doors or window frames. Such cracks, particularly if they are wider than 1/4-inch, are indicative of a structural fault. Weak or twisted wall framing and sagging floor joists are also often due to a faulty structure. If plaster looks as though it is ready to fall soon, make a note to have repairs done.

From a suspended ceiling, remove a few panels to check the condition of the ceiling above. Using a ladder may make things easier in reaching panels. Don't pull on the metal runners of the ceiling, though, because most of these merely hang by wire and cannot take too much weight. Push up individual panels and use your flashlight. Quite often these ceilings are put up to camouflage falling plaster or the scorched remains of wood framing. Be sure to pay special attention to the use of lampcord for electrical connections. Figure 17-2 shows a lampcord connection to a ceiling fixture. This, as well as evidence of exposed wires or uncovered junction boxes, should be recorded and also brought to the attention of the owner.

WALLS

Expect to find minor cracks in any plaster walls.

Fig. 17-2. Improper wiring should be corrected before any serious consequences occur.

Be aware that what you might think is a crack may only be a vertical or horizontal seam in a sheetrock wall. Very often cracks are merely cosmetic defects and can, in most cases, be easily corrected. It is with cracks that are larger than 1/4-inch, found in corners or next to window or door framing, that you should be concerned. As with similar cracks found in ceilings, they too are indicative of structural failure. If you find several such cracks in rooms throughout the house, it might be wise to call in a professional.

Sometimes walls are covered with paneling that may be poorly attached to the original walls. As you walk around the perimeter of the room, gently push inward on several spots. Noticeable movement means that a panel is not securely nailed and will pull away in time. Once more, this is not a structural problem but rather a cosmetic one. You could choose to ignore it, or you may wish to pull the panel off the wall and renail or reglue it properly.

FLOORS

As you walk around the rooms checking ceilings and walls, be alert to sensory messages that you might get from floors, such as squeaks and springiness, or windows rattling. Here the subflooring may have loosened or the support may be generally poor. Mark down each clue and if possible, try to check out the areas directly under each section that are questionable.

Check the flooring itself, and if there are rugs, get down on your hands and knees and closely examine them. Is the rug worn and in need of replacement? Check the joints of tile floors. Can you easily dislodge tiles, as seen in Fig. 17-3? If so, a new floor may be in order.

Wood floors should be checked for spaces between individual sections. The wood may have shrunk and formed gaps that are hard to repair. Look for protruding nail heads. They are not only a physical hazard but also may ruin a good sanding machine.

WINDOWS

All windows should be checked no matter where they are located. Are there broken or cracked panes such as in Fig. 17-4? Do all windows have properly locking latches? Does the window glass need putty, or does the frame need repair? Do the windows open and close easily and properly? Look for broken sash cords, rot in window frames and sills, and peeling paint. If windows do not fit tightly, they will let cold air in and warm air out.

Metal casement windows, as seen in Fig. 17-5, are not good insulators and therefore draw in cold air during the winter. They also rust easily, because condensation builds up on them in a short time. Corrosion and peeling paint are constant companions to these windows. Because most of these windows are crank operated, check the cranking mechanism.

Fig. 17-3. Loose tiles indicate moisture problems. Before you install a new floor, be sure the cause of the previous damage has been corrected.

183

Fig. 17-4. Broken windows should be repaired immediately to prevent anyone from injuring themselves.

Don't be surprised to find that the gears are worn out and that you can't open or close these windows.

Does the house have storm windows? In northern climates, you should have snugly fitted storm windows or insulated glass windows. Usually, a double-pane insulated glass window will prove to be a better insulator than the typical aluminum storm window. Note all defects on storm or insulated windows. On storm windows, be sure to check the outside perimeter for proper caulking. To do this, just open the inside house window and look where the storm window joins the house. If you can see daylight between that and the frame, mark it down on your worksheet. A simple caulking job will correct this. On insulated glass, check whether the seal

between the double panes is broken. Droplets of water or a cloudy section will tell you that it is and that it is now an ineffective window.

DOORS

Open and close every door in the house. Some that do not close tightly may just be swollen because of the humidity in the house. Once this is gone, the doors are fine again. Other doors, as well as windows and floors, may not be aligned properly because the house has settled to a considerable degree or may still be in the process of doing so.

Do all rooms in the house have doors? It may not be necessary, but it would be nice for privacy. Look the doors over generally. Do you see deteriora-

Fig. 17-5. Metal windows are very poor insulators. To compound the problem, the condensation that usually forms on them rusts them out. Metal windows of this kind need annual attention.

Fig. 17-6. Doors, like windows, will need annual attention. Lack of maintenance can only lead to further deterioration and costly replacements.

tion or neglect, as shown in Fig. 17-6? Record all your findings.

TRIM

Trim members such as ceiling moldings, floor baseboards, and window and door casings should be looked over for defects. Record missing, cracked, or broken sections as well as shoddy workmanship. Make the necessary repairs after you have moved into the house.

HEAT

As you check every room, note those that do not have a source of heat (radiator or register). Usually in new additions, enclosed porches, or even in renovated attic areas, people fail to add a heat source. You certainly need one, particularly if you plan to use such an area as a bedroom. Because the cost for piping or duct work could be high, it would be wise to tell the owner before the sale that a radiator or register is needed. Also, because it is most efficient to place radiators or registers on exterior walls, preferably directly below a window, make a note of heat sources that are located elsewhere.

ELECTRICAL SOURCES

All rooms should have electrical power sources, such as wall outlets and overhead lighting. Many state codes require a minimum of two wall outlets or one wall outlet and one overhead light. In new houses, outlets must be located no more than 6 feet horizontally from another outlet.

Use your electrical outlet analyzer to check each outlet in every room. It will tell you which are not grounded or where wiring is incorrectly wired. Under no circumstances should you have ungrounded outlets in kitchens, bathrooms, or laundry rooms. During your inspection, look for "octopus" connections, wires running under rugs, and improperly

Fig. 17-7. Makeshift wiring is not only a potential physical hazard to anyone using this light fixture, but also a fire hazard. Be sure to make the necessary repairs to correct this type of wiring.

used lamp cord. Figure 17-7 is a good example on how not to wire a light fixture.

HALLWAYS AND STAIRS

Check hallways as if you were checking a living area: ceilings for cracks and/or sagging plaster, walls for buckled or warped sections, floors for deterioration and safety hazards. Test the hall lights to see if they are functional. Are there smoke detectors mounted on the ceilings? (See Fig. 17-8.) Many states require them before a new owner can move in. These detectors need to be positioned on ceilings away from dead air spaces or corners. If they have testers, activate them to see if they work. Mark down any that need replacement.

Fig. 17-9. Any stairs over three risers high should have a railing. The stairway shown should have a railing from top to bottom. The chances of someone falling off these steps is great.

Stairways leading to and from halls should also be checked. As you walk up the steps, note potential hazards such as weak or missing railings, uneven risers, and defective steps. Figure 17-9 illustrates a prime candidate for an accident. Low windows adjacent to stairs are another potential hazard. Note on your worksheet whether a protective grille should be installed to prevent anyone from crashing through a window. Check the height of ceilings to stairway landings. Are they high enough to avoid a nasty bump on your or anyone else's head?

Fig. 17-8. Smoke detectors are probably the least expensive safety devices any home can have. Be sure that you have several in your home (at least one on each level) and that they are functional.

CLOSETS

Look at each closet in the house as you come

Fig. 17-10. Broken or missing sections of plaster should be replaced immediately. Flame spread during a fire through such a wall is rapid. Both fire and sanitary codes require that this type of damage be repaired.

to it during your tour. Note unusually wide cracks in ceilings or walls, look for hanging plaster, and broken or missing sections of walls or ceilings. (See Fig. 17-10.) Note any improper use of lamp cord. If there are lights in the closet, check them by turning them on and off. When you open the door, does a cold blast of air hit you? If so, you may wish to insulate the exterior walls. Are the closets large enough to meet your storage needs, or will you have to go through the expense of having additional ones built? Look for water stains on ceilings, walls, or floors. Note all defects on your worksheet.

CRAWL SPACES

Crawl spaces that lead off of rooms often do not

get rid of condensation because of faulty ventilation. Check the condition of visible insulation. Have roof leaks or condensation ruined it? Is it adequate to keep out the cold air and keep in the heat? Are there any uninsulated water pipes running through these areas, and if so, will they freeze during a cold spell? Burst pipes are more than a nuisance; the water can seriously damage ceilings and floors. Check visible wiring for frayed or exposed sections that could be a hazard to anyone entering the area. Use your flashlight to see if there are any rodent droppings. Mice love dark, uninhabited areas. Remember, no one likes to admit to having such unwelcomed tenants.

CHECKPOINTS

• Look for loose, cracked, or damaged plaster walls and ceilings.
• Check for water stains on walls and ceilings, and try to determine if they are active.
• Examine cracks to see whether they are wider than 1/4-inch.
• Push back suspended ceiling panels to examine hidden areas for signs of deterioration in ceilings or walls.
• Note cosmetic defects as well as structural ones.
• Do the floors squeak or have unusual springiness to them?
• Do the underpinnings of the floors need additional support?
• What is the condition of the finished floors? Do they need repairs or replacement?
• Inspect windows for weathertightness. Are there gaps that allow heat losses?
• What is the general condition of the windows? Broken sash cords, cracked windows, and decaying frames all should be recorded.
• Does the house have metal casement windows? Are there signs of condensation?
• Do all windows operate properly? Check for missing latches and warped frames.
• Are there storm windows on the house, and in what condition are they?

- Does the house have double- or triple-pane insulated glass? Check to see whether the seal is still intact.
- Do the doors in the house open and close easily?
- Do the doors require repairs or replacement?
- Record missing, broken, or deteriorating trim members.
- Be sure to check each room for a source of heat.
- Are there sufficient electrical outlets and overhead lights in all rooms?
- Are all outlets properly grounded, or are there potential shock hazards?
- Look for safety hazards in hallways and stairways.
- Are there properly installed smoke detectors in hallways, and are they working?
- Check both closets and crawl spaces for defects and potential hazards.

Solar Energy

Although the claims are high for considerable savings, easy installation, and low maintenance, it is still relatively seldom that you encounter a house with a solar energy installation. Just in case you do, the following passages will give you some insight into what to look for and what to expect of such systems.

To catch the radiant energy from the sun, most systems use a lot of outside glass backed by large quantities of heat-absorbing materials. But what happens when the sun does not shine, and there is no energy to collect? All residential solar energy systems require a supplemental system of the conventional-type which, needless to say, should be in good working condition.

TYPES OF SOLAR-ENERGY SYSTEMS

There are two basic ways the sun can be used to heat a home or provide domestic hot water: by *passive solar energy* or by *active solar energy.* A passive system only means that it does not require new hardware but relies instead on the parts of the house that are already there, such as south-facing windows that are used as heat collectors and masonry walls or floors that are used as storage and distribution areas. Figure 18-1 shows a typical passive solar energy system.

An active system requires a series of large flat panels, called *collectors,* which sit on the roof or ground next to the house. In such collectors, the sun heats up either air or a water-antifreeze mixture that takes heat into a storage tank. A good example of this is shown in Fig. 18-2. The tank is then used as a source of heat for the home heating system or the domestic hot water. Keep in mind that the tank only carries enough heat or hot water to get the house through a few overcast days and nights; after that, your conventional system must carry the load.

Every active solar system has basic components: *solar collectors,* a *distribution system* (pipes or ducts), *storage tanks, heat exchangers,* a *heat transfer medium* (antifreeze solution or air), and *temperature gauges* and *safety valves.* A solar collector is an assembly especially designed to absorb the sun's heat. A *closed loop system* circulates a liquid

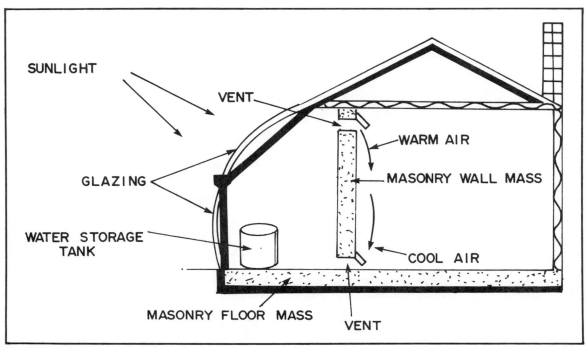

Fig. 18-1. A typical passive solar system.

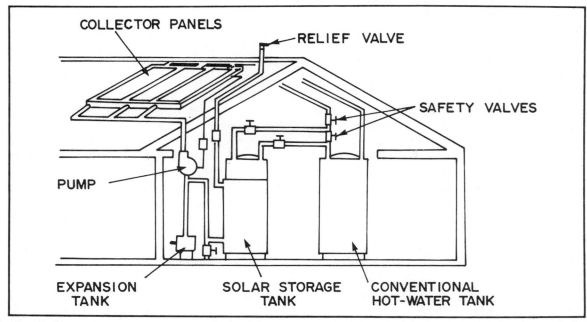

Fig. 18-2. An active system employs several components to gather and store solar energy. Note the use of a conventional heating unit as a back-up for the solar system.

solution or air from the collectors to the storage tank, which stores the heat until it is needed. The heat exchanger, with the help of electronic controls and pumps, moves the heat into the house. Although it is basically a very simple system, there are some important things to watch out for.

SOLAR COLLECTORS

Solar collectors are large panels, usually placed on a south-facing roof. (See Fig. 18-3). They collect the sun's rays and heat the fluid that passes through them. The size of the collectors is important: a typical home will require 60 square feet of collectors to provide 70 percent of a household's needs. They should be mounted on the roof at an angle between 35 and 45 degrees in order to be perpendicular to the sun's rays. In addition, in order for them to be most efficient, the collectors should face true south. Deviations of more than 30 degrees from true south will cause a significant reduction in efficiency. Collectors with moving parts, such as those that track the sun, require continued maintenance and should be checked annually.

Because each collector weighs about 75 pounds, some consideration must be given to the strength of the roof. During your inspection of the attic, be sure to check the areas directly below the collec-tors. Are the rafters sagging, and is there visible damage to the roof sheathing? Record such defects for future strengthening. Also note how the panels are attached to the roof. Installing panels on roofs can be tricky, because winds can seriously damage panels and roofing. The best way to mount collector panels on a roof is with *spanners,* as shown in Fig. 18-4. Either a 2×6-inch wood spanner or a metal one bolted to rafters should do. In addition, *unistruts* (galvanized steel pipe with a flange) are installed to tie the panels to the roof and to provide an air space. This space is important because it allows rain and melting snow to flow under the panels and not pile up against them.

Solar collectors should not be placed above entrances or exits. Melting snow could slide off after a storm and injure someone. A slowing device, such as a metal lip, should be installed to prevent this from happening, no matter where the panels are located.

DISTRIBUTION SYSTEMS

Although most active solar systems use a fluid for carrying the heat from the collectors to the storage tank, some employ an air system. Each system has its disadvantages. Water must be treated with antifreeze to prevent freezing of pipes, while air re-

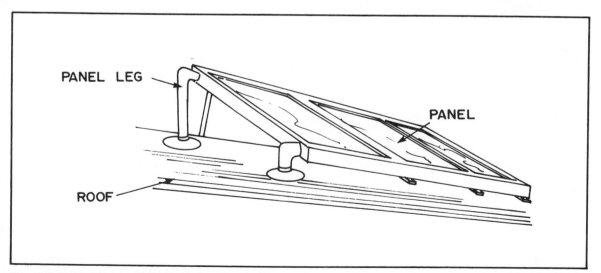

Fig. 18-3. Solar panels mounted on a roof act as collectors of solar energy. Correct positioning of these panels is vital.

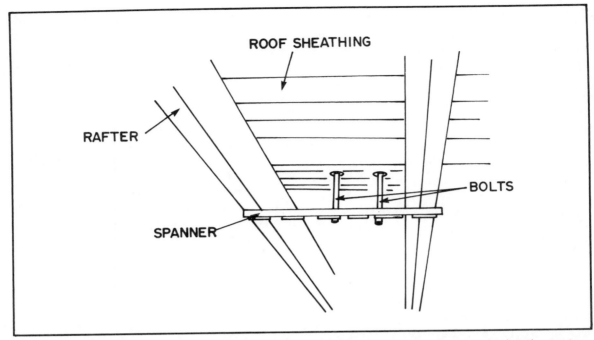

Fig. 18-4. Spanners are special wood or metal units tied into the roof framing to hold the collectors securely to the structure.

quires an electric fan for efficient movement through the systems ducts. Both systems require annual maintenance.

Air Systems

Like a conventional air heating system, a solar air system should have a filter on the return run, behind the blower. Filters should be checked and replaced if found to be loaded with dirt. Because dampers are also critical parts of solar air systems, they should likewise close tightly during cold days to prevent cold air from reaching the storage tank. See whether they are dirty or dusty; dirt can prevent a damper from closing tightly. Periodic cleaning of dampers will result in a more efficient system. As with any air system, be sure that the duct work is properly insulated and that all joints are sealed tightly. A standard air system is illustrated in Fig. 18-5.

Water Systems

About 80 percent of all solar installations are

fluid systems, and the majority of those are closed loop systems. A closed loop system circulates a nontoxic pressurized antifreeze solution through the collectors and the tanks. There is no air in such a system, and it offers the most positive type of freeze protection. One of the major disadvantages of using an antifreeze solution is that it slowly changes into *glycolic acid,* a substance that corrodes the pumps, pipes, and valves. For this reason, it is imperative that the entire fluid be replaced every 5 years. In your inspection, be sure to look for the use of dissimilar metals in piping. Corrosion and leaks are almost a guarantee. If you find plastic pipe, ask the owner if they are designed for high temperatures and high pressure. Regular plastic piping will not stand up under the vascillating temperature found in solar systems. If there is any doubt, have a solar heating technician check it out for you. Figure 18-6 shows a water system.

STORAGE TANKS

The storage tank is designed to hold the work-

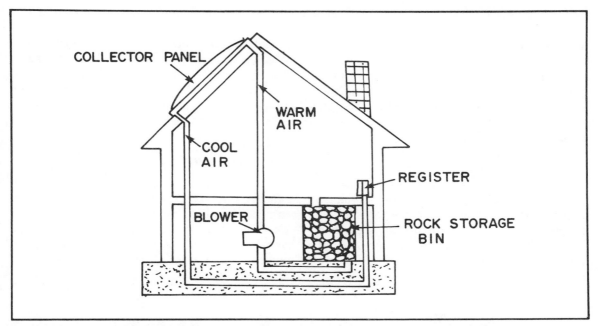

Fig. 18-5. Air systems are similar to warm air heating systems except that the fuel is the sun's rays.

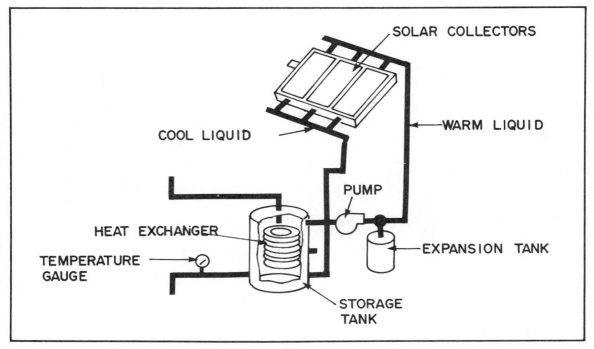

Fig. 18-6. In a water system, a liquid is pumped through the pipes. As it passes through the collector panels, it is heated, and this heated liquid passes on throughout the house releasing its heat as it flows.

ing fluid heated by the sun for use during the night or any other time when the sun's rays are few. Solar water heaters may use one or two tanks. The two-tank system allows more solar energy to be collected and stored and makes life easier during cloudy days. The two main types of storage media are *rocks* and *water*. Rocks hold heat well but require a large storage space; water does not need as large an area but corrodes the tank. So, if there is plenty of space, rocks might be a good medium; where there is little, water may be a better choice.

Check the holding tank carefully for obvious defects such as corrosion and/or rust. Is the tank properly supported? Because the weight of the tank is considerable, it should be placed where it can cause no structural damage to floors or walls. Figure 18-7 is a good example of a rock solar storage tank. While you are examining the tank check the amount of insulation on it. The more the tank is insulated, the less heat will be lost through its walls. At least 6 inches of insulation should be on the tank. If it is buried in soil, the insulation should be waterproof as well. Check the connections going into and out of the tank. Are there signs of deterioration or leaks? Note any questionable areas on your worksheet.

HEAT EXCHANGERS

In the heat exchanger, the heated substance transfers heat to the distribution system, which in turn uses it to heat the house or the domestic hot water for the house. The method of distribution of the solar energy varies with how the heat is to be applied. Space heating distribution systems can in-

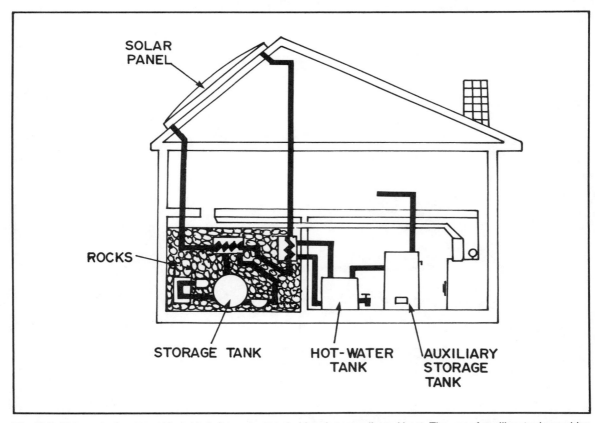

Fig. 18-7. Storage tanks are employed in solar systems to hold and store collected heat. The use of auxiliary tanks enables the storage of more heat, which can be utilized during cloudy days.

194

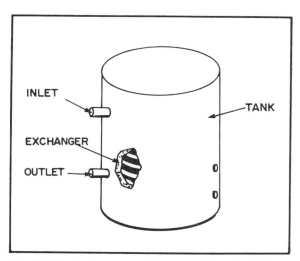

Fig. 18-8. Typical heat exchanger located in a storage tank. Since most heat exchangers are not visible, all you can really check is any related piping adjacent to the exchanger and tank.

volve duct work (for warm air) or pipes and radiators (for hot water). While some systems require pumps or fans to transport heat, others use gravity and convection. In Fig. 18-8, you can see the heat exchanger in the storage tank and the related distribution pipes.

During your inspection of the storage tank and its heat exchanger and piping arrangement, be sure to check all visible pipes for leaks and signs of deterioration. Check whether adjacent pumps need oil and if fans need cleaning. Run the system to see if the heat is evenly distributed. If the solar system is just for hot water, run it to see if the water is sufficiently hot. Are the distribution lines fully insulated? You should expect to find at least 1 inch of insulation on pipes and ducts. The insulation not only conserves heat during winter, but also helps to prevent overheating during the summer.

TEMPERATURE GAUGES AND SAFETY VALVES

Most solar system experts recommend that temperature gauges be installed both on the inlet and outlet lines of the system so temperatures can be monitored in the various areas of the system. Defects in the system can also be much more easi-

ly pinpointed with such gauges. *Check-valves* should be installed on the collector loop to prevent backflow of liquid at night or on cloudy days. An *expansion tank* with a *relief valve* should be included in the system as a buffer against major expansion in the system. Without this safety device, possible overheating could cause an explosion in the system. Safety gauges and valves are illustrated in Fig. 18-9.

In any form of solar installation, whether it be for heat or for domestic hot water, local building and plumbing codes must be adhered to. Consider the cost of such a system and the potential for something to go wrong with it. In fact, think of the whole complexity of such a system, and you will conclude that it might be wise to have an expert come in to thoroughly check it out. In any event, keep in mind that a solar system (as of yet) is not meant to meet the total energy needs of a family but is merely an adjunct to a conventional system.

Because solar energy has such high potential

Fig. 18-9. Temperature gauges are important features of an active solar system. Most experts concur that safety and temperature gauges should be on both the inlet and outlet lines of the major distribution lines.

to meet future energy needs, and because the entire solar energy field is so complex, the government has established a clearing house for information on it. The National Solar Heating and Cooling Information Center offers a wide variety of information on solar space and domestic hot water heating. Write for information to Solar Heating, P.O. Box 1607, Rockville, MD 20850.

CHECKPOINTS

• What type of solar system does the house have? Active or passive?

• If it is a passive system, do most of the windows face south?

• Are there large enough masonry areas next to or adjacent to south windows that can store solar heat?

• If the system is an active one, are there enough solar collectors?

• Do collectors face true south, and are they mounted perpendicular to the sun's rays?

• Inspect the framing in the attic directly under the solar panels for signs of deterioration.

• Check the panels. Are they mounted properly? Will there be problems with melting snow falling from the roof?

• If the system uses an antifreeze solution, find out when it was last changed.

• In an air heating system, check the filters and fans for dust build-up.

• Inspect dampers in air heating systems to make sure that they are functioning properly.

• Are ducts and joints properly insulated and taped?

• Are water pipes insulated?

• Examine pipes and joints for signs of rusting or deterioration.

• Note dissimilar connected metals found in the system.

• Check the condition of plastic pipes.

• Are storage tanks fully insulated?

• Look for signs of deterioration in tanks, temperature gauges, and safety valves.

• Does the system have an expansion tank to prevent water pressure problems?

• Is there sufficient hot water and heat?

19

Condominiums

Although this book is chiefly with single family homes, much of the information in the text also applies to condominiums. Because this type of home ownership has been growing steadily during the past decade and probably will continue to do so in the coming years, I believe that some discussion about it should be included here.

A condominium can be part of a multiunit development or half of a duplex. One thing to remember from the outset is that you, the owner of a condo unit, also own part of the common areas that make up the total development. Thus, you are responsible for the upkeep and maintenance of such areas as well. As a cautious buyer, therefore, you should study the condo agreement very carefully before you buy and thoroughly inspect the dwelling itself.

Check to see what you will actually own. Some condominium developers retain ownership of recreational facilities and lease these to you for steep fees. Often these "recreational leases" contain *escalator clauses* that permit the developer to raise the fees with the increased cost of living.

Another item to watch out for is *low balling*, a procedure whereby monthly maintenance fees are estimated on the low side. After you have become the proud owner of a condominium, you find that the fees rise dramatically, sometimes as much as $50 to $75 per month. Check with current owners to see what they pay in monthly fees and, if possible, look over the condominium association's operating budget. After you see the budget, you can decide whether the monthly fee is realistic.

Buying a condominium requires more paperwork than the purchase of a "regular" house. The basic documents that you should receive are: *the master deed, the condominium sales contract,* the *bylaws of the owner association,* and the *management contract.* All of these will give you the buyer/owner information about what you really own.

The first contract for you to sign is most likely the sales contract. It should fully describe the unit, the purchase price, and the method of payment. Before you sign it, however, look over the master deed, which provides you with information about the owner's association, how each individual unit is used, and the assessments and charges that you have to pay. At the same time, check the by-laws, which determine the administration of the dwelling complex, and which also gives you an insight as to what you are and are not allowed to do. If you think the restrictions are too severe to live with, try another development. Finally, check the management contract. Good management will make condo living a pleasure, whereas poor management or none at all can prove disastrous. The best way to head off a poor investment is for you to hire an attorney familiar with condominium real estate who will go over each document with you.

If the condominium that you have fallen in love with is part of a former apartment building, you will want to make sure that the renovations are not merely cosmetic. All too often building codes in many communities are inadequate or not enforced, particularly those concerning fireproofing and soundproofing.

FIRE SAFETY

All structures should be built in such a way that they provide two exits in case of fire. The second exit may even be a window if it is close to the ground. Spatial layout generally should be such that smoke and fire will not spread rapidly throughout the unit. All sleeping quarters should have tight fitting doors that would prevent rapid flame and smoke spread.

Smoke detectors are excellent lifesavers, provided they are placed correctly and are in good working order. Most codes stipulate that they be installed outside of each sleeping area, at the top of basement stairs, and on the ceilings of each stairway landing.

Fire-stopping must be provided in condominiums just as it must in single family dwellings. Building codes require barriers installed vertically inside walls and horizontally through ceiling spaces. Barriers must be made of noncombustible materials such as sheet metal, gypsum board, plaster, brick, and noncombustible insulation. In wood frame construction a 2-inch thick piece of lumber may do. Be sure to check whether your condo is properly protected.

SOUNDPROOFING

Nothing is more annoying than having to listen to your neighbor's noises morning, noon, and night. So be thorough in testing noise levels coming from the adjacent condominium units. Should any adjacent units be vacant, ask the broker for the keys so you can send a friend there to make all the noises possible. Of course, you will be listening intently for running faucets, toilets being flushed, and blaring radios. This should give you some idea of what you will be living with.

If the adjacent condo units are occupied, visit the subject unit at different times to hear what you may have to live with. If normal conversation blasts through the walls, you will have two choices: you can go through the expense of soundproofing, or just walk away from the transaction.

Soundproofing a condominium is costly and not always successful. Not only are expensive ceiling and wall renovations necessary, but bathrooms and kitchens with common walls are next to impossible to soundproof because of the built-in cabinets, bathroom tiled walls, and various plumbing fixtures. If your apartment entrance is from a common hallway, you will also have to soundproof the doors. All together then, soundproofing is overwhelmingly expensive, and you might as well accept the fact that the unit is not worth all the trouble, unless of course, you can stand the noise.

COMMON AREAS

Remember, buying a condominium is different from buying your own house. You not only own your unit, but you also share in the responsibility of maintaining common areas including the roof, the exterior walls, the corridor, the basement with all of its mechanical systems, and the exterior grounds and parking facilities. Even though you may not participate in the various recreational facilities, such as swimming pools or tennis courts, you still are responsible for their maintenance and upkeep. If something goes wrong with any of these areas, you are responsible for paying your share of the repair costs.

It is therefore essential that you thoroughly

check the entire complex. If you find that the mechanical systems are too complex for you, by all means hire a professional to inspect them. In the long run, it will have been worth it. Remember too, that the larger a complex is, the greater the demand, usage, and thus the strain on mechanical and electrical systems. If you can get hold of an engineering report, study it carefully. Very often you will find a listing on how long systems are expected to last. There are many sad condominium owners "holding the tab" for thousands of dollars of repair work and replacements that should have been done by the developer in the first place, but was not. Don't be one of those owners.

Talk to people who own units in the complex. See what they have to say about the quality of workmanship delivered by the developer. Are they satisfied or disgruntled? Has the assessed value of the condominium gone up dramatically since they bought theirs? Are there small print restrictions against children or pets? What are their impressions of the management company? Is the maintenance work done promptly and properly, and are the fees reasonable? Were there major repairs done to the heating, plumbing, electrical, or air-conditioning systems? If so, are they completed? Finally, will you be able to park your car without purchasing or renting a parking space?

As with any real estate, check the location. Is it a good area, or is it starting to "go down?" Will you be able to get back your investment in a few years? Make sure you understand everything before you make the final commitment.

Because this chapter only covers the highlights of condominium ownership, you may wish to do some additional reading on the topic. An excellent source is the booklet, *Questions About Condominiums*, published by the U.S. Department of Housing and Urban Development. Write to Consumer Information Center, Pueblo, CO 81009, for a free copy.

CHECKPOINTS

- Are use of recreational facilities an extra cost?
- Do the maintenance fees seem realistic?
- Does the condominium development have a reliable maintenance firm?
- Do you understand all of the condo paperwork? It is important to have an attorney go over these papers with you.
- Have sound fire safety precautions been built into the unit?
- Are there smoke detectors in strategic locations?
- Has the condo unit been soundproofed?
- Do you fully understand the full extent of your responsibility in regards to the upkeep and maintenance of all common areas?
- What is the present condition of the electro-mechanical systems?
- Is the building structurally sound?
- Are the grounds and recreational areas well maintained?
- In what kind of a location is the development?
- What is your overall "gut" feeling about the condominium?

Quality

Two almost identical houses can vary greatly in the quality of materials that were used to build them, in the mechanical systems and appliances, and in the proficiency of workmanship. The concept of quality is an important one when inspecting and appraising houses. Keep in mind, however, that there is no such thing as a perfect house. All houses need repairs and continued maintenance. It is the initial value of materials and the proficiency of workmanship that determines the amount of future repairs and maintenance; that is what we are concerned with here.

What is good construction, and how can you tell? This chapter will help you know what to look for, and what should influence your final appraisal of a house. In addition, there are two very good sources of information for you to read: the Federal Housing Authority book *Minimum Property Standards*, and the building code of your local community. You can obtain the FHA book by writing to the U.S. Government Printing Office, Washington, D.C. The code can be picked up either at your town hall or at the state capital printing office. Figures 20-1

and 20-2 show the difference between good house design and poor house design.

FOUNDATIONS

The worst type of foundation you can encounter is a concrete block foundation, because the blocks are hollow and there are so many joints. Unless the cores are filled with cement, they give termites easy access to the house framing, and unless the joints between each block are properly cemented, they deteriorate easily. Weak or deteriorating joints mean water penetrations. If you are planning to buy a house or presently own one that does have such a foundation, be sure to have an annual termite inspection and to promptly make the necessary repairs to weakened joints.

FOUNDATION WINDOWS

Because some foundation windows are situated low enough to almost touch the soil, metal windows instead of wooden windows would be a great plus. Wood-boring insects do not like to chew through

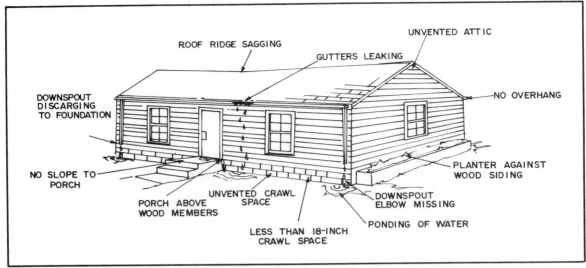

Fig. 20-1. This figure aptly illustrates poor design features. Note all of the water related problems.

metal. Keep in mind, however, that the metal will rust and will need periodic painting. A bit of paint far outweighs the damage wood-boring insects can cause.

EXTERIOR WALLS

The highest quality siding is undoubtedly that which is made of materials that will resist decay and withstand the deteriorating effects of weather. Stain-ed cedar shingles meets these requirements. Top quality shingles are free from knots and pitch pockets, and you can differentiate them from poorer quality ones by their clear and regular grain. Vinyl and aluminum sidings are quite popular today. You have to be careful, though, about houses that have had their original siding covered with this low-maintenance material. Very often, the original siding is suffocating under the tightly installed new siding. If no ventilation is provided, major decay will set

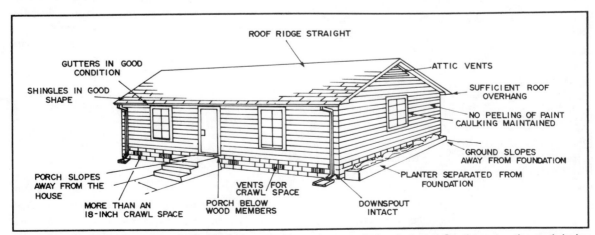

Fig. 20-2. In this figure, you see the same house but without the poor design features. Good construction and design have avoided the defects found in Fig. 20-1.

in, not only in the original wood siding but also in the wall sheathing. Proper ventilation must be provided.

WINDOWS

Windows come in many shapes, sizes, types, and styles. Brand names such as Anderson and Biltwell indicate good quality. The difference in dollars between cheap quality and better quality is seen in less condensation and longer life of window parts. Those made of steel rust and corrode and will require periodic repair. If you are looking at *jalousie* (louvered) windows, keep in mind that they are quite leaky and ill-advised in northern climates. They do not belong in bedrooms either, because they make escape in case of fire almost impossible. Figure 20-3 shows this type of window.

Fig. 20-3. Jalousie windows make poor insulators against the weather and poorer exits in case of fire.

ROOFS

Asphalt shingles are most commonly used to cover roofs. Top-quality roofing requires shingles that last 25 or more years. Lesser-quality construction makes use of lighter-grade shingles that last only up to 15 years. Good-quality construction does not require that one worn layer of shingles be stripped down to the bare roof sheathing before a new layer of shingles be applied. When new shingles are put over one worn but not warped layer, you have less expensive work, and additional insulation value. Remember that two layers are the maximum that most building codes recommend. Anything over that amount could cause serious structural damage to the roof framing. Another quality feature that distinguishes good roofing appearances is the use of a metal drip edge at the eaves. The drip edge is used chiefly for cosmetic reasons, but it does provide some protection against wind-blown rain.

CHIMNEYS

Chimney flashing will eventually need repairs and/or replacement. Flashing that is cemented over with roofing cement will soon open, so a quality repair job would be to replace it with new flashing. Mortar in the joints also deteriorates and will need repairs. An amateur simply plasters over the bricks and joints so that the chimney will appear to be nothing more than a vertical stuccoed mess similar to that shown in Fig. 20-4. If the job had been done correctly, no one would be able to notice the repair work, at least not when looking up from the street.

GUTTERS AND DOWNSPOUTS

It is interesting to see so many new homes being built today without gutters and downspouts. The usual reason given by the builder is that the house does not need them or that it is more trouble to maintain them than they are worth. Wrong! All houses should have roof drainage; it inhibits paint from peeling, reduces damage done to siding and trim, and prevents water from entering the basement. A high quality system will have very few seams with few leaks and no costly repairs caused by rain or melting snow. In addition, a quality drain-

Fig. 20-4. How not to repair a chimney. It won't be long before the stucco and asphalt patches start to flake off, and the entire cycle of repairs starts anew.

age system allows the roof runoff to flow away from the house, preferably 3 feet or more.

LOW WOOD QUALITY

Good quality construction and design is evident when all low wood members are up off the soil by at least several inches, because decay and insect activity is greatly lessened when the distance between wood and soil is considerable. Poor quality construction will often have wooden posts, stairs, and even siding directly in contact with the soil or a few inches away from grade. In new construction, this is unforgivable and some form of preventative measure should have been taken by the builder.

The use of pressure-treated wood in direct contact with the soil, for example is one such measure. You should require a very special inspection of those areas, because the chances of major deterioration are great indeed.

HEATING SYSTEMS

A boiler is either made of steel or cast iron; one made of iron lasts longer because it does not rust as easily as steel. If the heating system is gravity fed, consider it very poor quality. All new boilers and furnaces have either blowers or circulating pumps to make them more efficient. Insulation on the heating plant and the branch lines also adds to their quality because, if not insulated, heat will be lost. The brand name of the unit can be checked with local dealers to see if it is a "dog." If the house is large, check to see if the heating system has separate zones that control the amount of heat in any given area. Give the house a minus if it only has one zone and has more than one level of living space.

ELECTRICAL

Most building codes require a minimum of 100 amperes for a new home. Builders often provide just that. On new construction, however, you should not accept anything less than 150 amperes. The cost is only a few hundred dollars more when installed at the time of construction. With 150 amperes you can provide for any electrical needs that your family will ever have without fear of overloading the system. In older homes, you should insist on a minimum of 100 amperes. Anything less will just not take care of the demands of a modern family. Good construction stipulates that every room in the house have a minimum of one electrical outlet on each wall and that all outlets be properly grounded. Ground fault interrupters in bathrooms, kitchens, garages, and outdoor receptacles are evidence of quality work.

PLUMBING

Brass and copper water pipes are a sign of quality; iron and steel tend to corrode and will not last as long. An "XH" printed on plumbing waste and drain pipes indicates extra heavy material and lasts

10 times longer than lighter types of drain pipes. A good quality plumbing system will have adequate water pressure even when all fixtures are turned on simultaneously. A top quality plumbing system will have good drainage in all fixtures and accessible cleanout plugs for periodic sewer cleaning.

HOT-WATER TANKS

Brand names are important, particularly those of well established companies because they stand for quality. If the tank's name is unfamiliar, a plumber might be able to tell whether it is a good or bad one. A quality tank, in addition to being warrantied anywhere from 5 to 10 years, also should have an energy rating guide on the tank (as shown in Fig. 20-5). This helpful guide gives you an idea of the cost of providing hot water in your home.

Fig. 20-5. If you are considering buying an appliance, be sure to check to see if it has an energy guide label.

AIR-CONDITIONING

Central air conditioning is always a more favored system compared to individual room units. Individual units are not as efficient as a central system and are more expensive to run and maintain. A certification seal of the Air Conditioning Refrigeration Institute means the system is a quality one. A quality system, when turned on, will cool the entire house in a very short time.

BASEMENT FRAMING

It is a fact of life that in the housing business most contractors try to shave costs by cutting back to bare minimum requirements at the cost of quality. Even if you have the good fortune to look at a new house, don't be surprised to find deficiencies that may appall you. Be sure to familiarize yourself with the local building codes so you are quite clear on what to look for in your inspection.

GIRDERS

The main girder that supports the center load of the house is probably sized correctly. A 6-by-10-foot girder is generally considered a minimum size: less than that should be properly supported at closer intervals, say every 6 feet or less. The problem, however, is not usually with the size but rather with the installation. It is often only after the walls are poured that the builder realizes that the recess for the girder is too low or that insufficient space was provided for the girder. What some builders do to make up the difference is a crime. A girder should have at least a 4-inch bearing on the foundation wall and at least a 1-inch breather space on both sides and at the end. You may find the ends of girders just barely sitting on the foundation walls or girders that look as if they were poured into the recess of the wall. Both examples are the mark of very poor quality workmanship. There is not too much you can do about too tight a fit, but you should insist on additional support columns under any suspect girder to prevent disaster. In Fig. 20-6 a typical girder installation is shown.

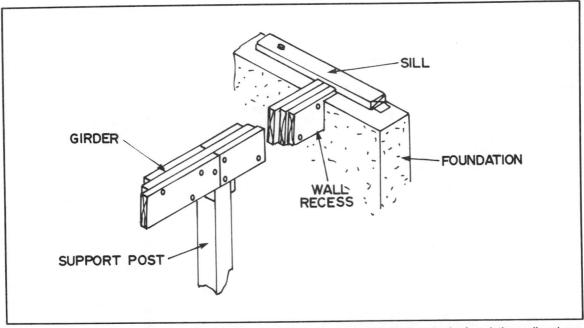

Fig. 20-6. Good girder construction calls for correct sized lumber resting a full 4 inches on the foundation wall and supported every several feet by sturdy support posts.

CROSS BRIDGING OR BLOCKING

Cross bridging or blocking under floors (visible at the basement ceiling) will help prevent bouncy floors. (See Fig. 20-7.) If you do not see such bracing, walk on those floors. You will see why they should have been installed. If the ceiling in the basement is not finished, you can easily have bracing members installed.

WET BASEMENTS

One reason for wet basements is that drain titles were not laid around the foundation perimeter when they were supposed to have been laid: namely, at the time of construction. Adding them after a house is built is expensive, because the entire perimeter of the house has to be dug up. It is particularly important to have foundation drainage in areas where wet basements are common. Top quality construction dictates that the system be installed during the time the house is being built. The owner or builder should be able to tell you whether such a system was provided.

ATTICS

Framing in an attic is very important. Builders who skimp on materials are usually not around when you start having problems. Rafters should have cross braces between every third rafter pair to give added strength and to prevent outward thrust from heavy roof loads.

Insulation and ventilation go hand in hand. Quality construction requires sufficient insulation to cut costs of heating and air conditioning. In the north, a minimum of 6 inches is required—9 to 12 inches represents top quality. To get rid of moisture, however, you need ventilation and plenty of it, which includes not only the standard gable vents but also a combination of soffit and ridge venting.

There are houses on the market selling for hundreds of thousands of dollars, but when you get to their attics you need a ladder to get in and a flashlight to see because the builder could not afford to install a pull-down staircase and a light. Such negligence certainly makes you wonder about the overall quality of the house.

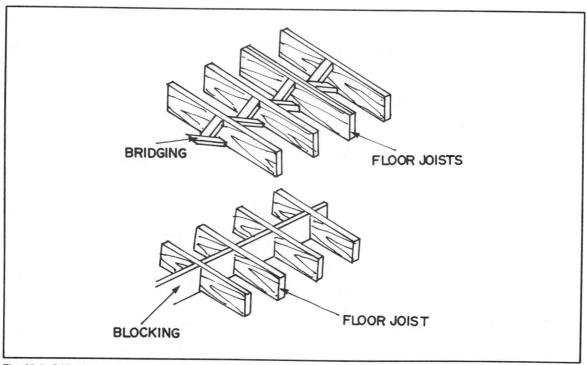

BRIDGING

FLOOR JOISTS

BLOCKING

FLOOR JOIST

Fig. 20-7. Stiffening members, such as cross bridging or blocking, are essential for floor bracing. Lack of such wood or metal members indicates poor construction on the part of the builder.

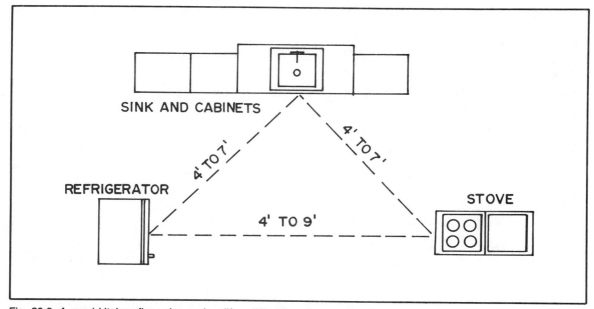

SINK AND CABINETS

4' TO 7'

4' TO 7'

REFRIGERATOR

STOVE

4' TO 9'

Fig. 20-8. A good kitchen floor plan makes life a little bit easier.

BATHROOMS

If you are still uncertain about the quality of a house, a check of the bathrooms will do the trick. Simple things that save the builder a few dollars but will cost you, the owner, tenfold can be found there. The tile work is a good example. Did the installer take time to strike all the tile joints or did he leave extra thick grout joints? Were the tiles expertly cut with little space left between tile and fixtures, or are there large gaps that will have to be caulked and sealed annually? Was a good quality ceramic tile used or a cheap plastic imitation?

Another example is the quality of the fixtures. A quality tub is one made of cast iron rather than

Table 20-1. High versus Low Quality in Major Areas of a House.

Building Area	High Quality	Low Quality
Foundation	Poured concrete	Concrete Block
Foundation windows	Metal	Wood
Exterior walls	Stained cedar shingles	Aluminum or vinyl with little or no building ventilation
Windows	Double- or Triple-glazed windows	Steel or jalousie
Roofs	25 or more years life	15 years or less
Chimneys	Mortar joints in good repair, flashing tightly sealed	Mortar crumbling, Flashing loose
Gutters	Few seams/tight joints	No gutters
Downspouts	Lead at least 3 feet from foundation	Discharge to foundation
Low Wood	Several inches from soil, use of treated wood	In direct contact with soil, untreated wood few inches from soil
Heating system	Cast-iron Boiler, Known Brand, More than 1 zone	Steel Boiler, Unknown Brand, Only 1 zone
Electrical	150-200 amp main, Sufficient outlets, Ground Fault Interrupters	Under 100 amp main, Insufficient outlets, No Ground Fault Interrupters
Hot water tank	Brand name, 10-year warranty	Unknown brand 5-year warranty
Air-Conditioning	Central air-conditioning, brand name	Room units, unknown brand
Girder	4-inch bearing on foundation walls	Less than 4-inch bearing
Cross-bridging or blocking	installed	none
Wet basements	perimeter drainage	none
Attic	cross braces, sufficient insulation, plenty of ventilation, pull-down attic door, attic lighting	little or none, need ladder, need flashlight
Bathrooms	high quality tile work quality fixtures tub/shower access panel	poor tile work, mongrel brands, none
Kitchen	good arrangement of appliances, brand name/quality, model appliances, warranty	poor arrangement of appliances, unknown name, low-cost model, no warranty

steel. Often less expensive vanity sinks have, in addition to poor base material, flimsy cementing of surface finishes. This easily delaminates after a short period of time. Does the brand name of the toilet sound familiar to you, or is it a name that no one has heard of? Does the overhead exhaust vent to the exterior or directly into the attic, where moisture is sure to cause its havoc? Do the fixtures each have their separate shut-off valves? In a high quality construction bathroom, the tub/shower wall has an access panel so you can check the condition of the water pipes and drains.

KITCHENS

If there were more builders of the female gender, there would undoubtedly be many more efficient kitchens than there are. Some are so poorly designed that to work in them amounts to running a marathon every day. Refrigerator, sink, and stove should all be within working distance. They should form a triangle and not be more than 4 to 9 feet apart. See Fig. 20-8.

Is the kitchen well equipped with appliances, and are they manufactured by reputable companies? Will you be able to buy spare parts for future repairs? Developers of housing tracts are notorious for selecting cheaper models of known brands. You should be able to look over the warranties to determine what you are getting. If the house is in the process of being built, make sure that you have a say in the selection of models and brands of appliances. Even though good quality is more costly, in the long run it will be well worth it.

CLASSIFYING HOUSE FLAWS

House flaws can be classified as *major, serious, or minor.* A major one would be a badly twisted house frame that would require costly repairs, a fact that may deter you from buying the house. A serious flaw would be that a boiler needs to be replaced. Although here the cost would be high, it would be unlikely to "kill" the sale. Minor flaws are such that you may need an additional outlet, or the relief valve on the hot water tank has to be replaced. After you have inspected the house and appraised the different kinds and degrees of flaws, you should be able to get an idea of whether or not the asking price is reasonable. If you feel it is too high, give your reasons. A well documented cost analysis of repairs will surely make an impression on the owners and their representatives. Table 20-1 compares building areas in regards to their quality.

Maintenance

Keeping your house "shipshape" takes a maintenance program that goes on forever. Most of the upkeep chores of any house, however, are basically easy and require only the simplest of tools. Information on how to make simple repairs can be obtained from a limitless supply of books, articles, and do-it-yourself pamphlets. Included at the end of this book is a list of excellent sources and guides that will be helpful to you. (See Appendix B.)

Some preventative maintenance work is seasonal: cleaning leaves out of gutters and tuning up the old boiler before the new heating season begins, for example. Much of the work should be done at regular intervals during the course of the year: like regrouting tile joints and making sure downspouts are doing their job. Putting off upkeep until you have a free weekend will not only result in overloading yourself with work but will probably result in a "a lick with a promise" repairs. You will be much better off scheduling these tasks over the course of the year. Smaller jobs done on a weekly or monthly basis won't overwhelm you.

Failure to routinely maintain the home will end in costly repairs. Water-caused decay in wooden members, if not repaired, will in time spread to adjacent wooden members and may even invite wood-boring insects to do their job. What started out as simple surface damage, in time becomes a serious structural defect. As you can see, the potential for expensive repairs is always present. The key word to remember then is prevention.

The entries in this chapter are divided into two major categories: the exterior and the interior. When working on equipment or appliances, be sure to consult manufacturer's manuals or guides. Remember, too, not all equipment or appliances should be serviced or maintained by you. Some annual preventative maintenance requires very special skills that only trained technicians have. They should be called in at the appropriate time to service an air conditioner, for example, or tune-up an oil burner. Servicing these requires special knowledge and special tools. It is best to leave the more complicated chores to those who are specially trained.

EXTERIOR

The most important exterior maintenance begins at the top and works its way down. If, after regular seasonal maintenance, major repairs or replacements are still needed (reshingling a roof, etc.) be sure to get a professional appraisal and estimate before tackling the job yourself.

Roof

In spring, after all the winter battering is over, check the roof shingles. Be sure to use caution if you are balancing on a ladder or on the roof. Look for broken or missing shingles and deterioration caused by winds, snow, and ice. Replace damaged shingles to prevent water getting into the attic. Sometimes small holes can be easily patched up with a dab of roofing cement. Exposed roofing nailheads rust out and cause problems, so coat rusted or missing sections with roof cement as well.

Chimney

When you see loose or crumbling mortar between the joints of bricks, you know it is time for repairs. Scrape out loose debris, wet down the joint, and apply fresh mortar to the open "wounds." If your chimney is high and you are afraid of heights, hire a mason to do the job.

If your chimney has a flue that is connected to a woodburning stove, be sure to have it checked and cleaned by a professional chimney sweep. If the flue for the stove is free-standing, have the sweep check the integrity of the pipe. Sometimes the mounting brackets come loose and need to be secured back to the house.

Flashing

The flashing around chimneys, skylights, vent pipes, ventilation units, and roof edges will loosen over a period of time, and water will very quickly find its way through these small grooves. Therefore, all flashing should be checked and repaired annually. Usually a thorough coating of roof cement both under and over the flashing material will suffice. Use a trowel to spread the cement under loose sec-

tions and then nail them back down. Finish off by applying a liberal coat of roof cement over the flashing surface.

Gutters and Downspouts

As you already know by now, water is the most deadly of enemies to property. Thousands of gallons of it flow off your roof each year. If you do not have a system to drain it away from your house, you are in big trouble. Defective gutters or improperly aligned downspouts can cause havoc with both the outside and the inside of the house. As a bare minimum, gutters and downspouts should be looked at twice a year; in the fall and in the spring.

The gutter joints (where they butt into each other) are the most important parts. Decay in wood gutters sets in first in the joints, and preventative measures can greatly reduce serious damage. Again, all you need is roofing cement.

Semiannual treatment of gutters with a 50/50 solution of linseed oil and turpentine will help extend their life span. This solution, applied in spring and fall, not only coats the wood but penetrates it so that the gutters become resistant to typical rot and decay. Metal gutters should also have their joints sealed to prevent problems. Silicone or butyl caulking will do the job nicely.

During the checkup of the gutters, be sure to remove all debris that has settled there. With trees close to the house, consider checking the gutters more than twice a year. Leaves easily accumulate and cause back-ups. Water will stay on the roof and possibly seep through the roof. If you have a particularly large amount of debris (leaves and twigs), and the gutters are in bad shape, check the adjacent fascia boards as well. Decayed wood members should be ripped out and replaced. Be sure to paint new wood: two coats on both sides should do the job.

Check the downspouts at the time you check the gutters. If you find that sections are rusted out or that seams have opened up, replace those pieces rather than repair them; it will be just as economical. Once deterioration sets in, it will only increase as time passes. If you find that the ends of the downspouts discharge directly to the foundation, make sure you add an elbow and a section of pipe to carry the runoff at least 3 feet away from the foundation. Many basements are flooded because of faulty gutters or downspouts.

Siding

Peeling paint should be scraped down to the bare wood, and the wood should be primed with a good quality primer followed by two coats of paint. Don't be afraid to scrape and sand undamaged areas. This actually makes the bond of the paint hold better. Allowing paint to peel will increase damage to the siding and wall sheathing itself. Sanding, priming, and painting have to be annual chores; if they are done each spring or fall, you will be able to contain them as such. If you let the paint go unchecked for years, you may have to lay out a large amount of cash and labor.

Masonry walls should be checked for cracks or open mortar joints. All loose mortar or stucco should be scraped away and fresh mortar applied. Because dry walls will draw out moisture from the new mortar and cause it to fail, hose down all areas that will be repaired. In addition to making the repairs, however, also find the cause for the mortar failure. Sometimes vines, such as ivy, work their way between joints or under a stucco finish and cause damage. The simple solution is to cut the culprits or at least trim them away from the walls. Mildew and moss also cause siding deterioration. They should also be removed. A commercial solution of trisodium phosphate or any bleaching compound will do the trick.

Ventilation Units

Check the screens for needed repairs at the end of winter. If they are not in good shape, the chances of having little uninvited winged guests and even some four-legged ones are great. Rusted out screens can be replaced by new screening nailed over the old damaged sections. While you are checking the vents, look over the flashing and caulking as well. Seal and caulk open joints to keep out the weather.

Windows

Windows suffer a host of ailments that, if not corrected, can result in serious consequences. Each year you should check the condition of all your storm windows. If there are no weep holes between the windows and the sill, be sure to drill one in each end. Weep holes allow trapped moisture to escape before it causes damage to wood sills or trim. Remove loose or cracked caulking from the joints between the frames and the siding. Seal and caulk these areas with a quality flexible butyl-based or silicone caulking compound. At the same time, be sure to screw back in loose or popped screws that hold the storm to the house frame.

Loose, deteriorating putty on the main windows should be scraped off and new glazing compound applied. A common "trick of the trade" is to apply some linseed oil to the wood frame where the putty will be applied. It will prevent the dry wood from absorbing oil from the putty. Again, decayed wood should be repaired or replaced. Paint should be applied to the sills to act as a preservative. Linseed oil should be applied in window tracks to keep them from drying out. Window latches should be screwed back down if loose, and broken sash cords should be repaired or replaced.

Doors

Flat, level wood outside, such as door sills, will rot first. Be sure to paint the sills annually, or seal them with protective spar varnish. If the doors need painting, don't put it off for too long for they will buckle and warp and heat will seep through the open gaps. Before the onset of winter, double-check the weatherstripping around the doors to make sure it is not damaged. Oil hinges with a light lubricating oil, and spray graphite dust on the locks for better performance.

Foundations

Patch and repair all cracks or openings in the foundation walls. Plug up and seal all gaps around utility entrances in the foundation. Repair and replace all deteriorated foundation windows. All shrubs next to the foundation should be cut back to provide a better view and to retard unnatural accumulations of moisture against low wood members.

As a protective measure, seal the natural masonry finishes against the weather with a coat of silicone sealer.

Entrances

Each year you should check all entrances to the house: front, rear, bulkhead, and garage entrances. All will develop problems that you must attend to if you want to avoid major repairs. Check metal railings for rusting or deterioration. Sometime in the spring plan on wire brushing, priming (with a metal primer), and applying a generous coat of a good quality metal paint for a finish coat on all metal surfaces. If the rails are wood and you see signs of decay, remove and replace the rotted sections. Sand, prime, and paint to keep them in good condition. Make necessary repairs to steps and platforms. Replace and repair damaged flooring and steps as well. Keep all exposed areas protected with a coat of good stain or paint. An even better idea for wood steps is to give them a good coating of one part oil-based paint (color of your choice) and nine parts linseed oil. This will not only coat them but will penetrate the wood for better protection.

Bulkheads

Bulkheads should be checked for possible water leaks. If found, they should be caulked and sealed. Replace decayed wood members and wire brush rusted metal sections. Prime and paint the doors and trim. Check low areas for possible water damage to either wood or metal, and correct any ponding of water by grading the adjacent soil away from the bulkhead.

Walks and Patios

After every winter, double-check masonry walks and patios for cracks and deterioration. Simple repairs will prevent further damage. Chip out all loose material, widen narrow cracks in order to fill them with mortar, dust and wet down, and then trowel in the mortar. Use a wood tool called a *float* to give a rough finish to the cement. This will prevent slipping.

Decks and Porches

Rain, snow, and ice will seriously damage exposed wood decks and porches. Be sure to apply a wood preservative every year. Replace all decayed wood members and, if possible, use treated wood that resists rot and decay. The cost per foot will be more than the cost of normal wood, but the payback will be in never having to replace the wood again.

Driveways

Cracks in asphalt driveways give water a perfect chance to stay there, freeze, and expand in winter. This causes further cracking and deterioration. If this process takes place for a few winters in a row, your driveway will look like a bombed-out runway. Annual maintenance consists of patching cracks with a cold-mix asphalt compound and sealing the surface with an asphalt liquid coating. If there is a catch basin at the base of the driveway, be sure to clean out leaves and sediment twice a year or whenever necessary.

Garages

Repair all missing or broken shingles both on the roof and on the siding. Clean and repair all gutters and realign all downspouts so that water discharges 3 feet from the garage. Check all low surfaces for signs of decay or insect activity and make necessary repairs. Scrape and paint exterior trim and siding where necessary. Service windows by replacing deteriorating or missing putty and by repairing broken panes of glass. Check to see whether the doors are working properly. Lubricate the garage doors with a silicone spray and lay some axle grease on the door tracks for better performance. Double-check the tightness of the door's weatherstripping and replace if necessary.

Fencing

Look over the wood posts for rot and insect activity. Replace seriously damaged posts or rails. Consider using pressure-treated posts and railings that have a far greater resistance to decay than untreated wood. Metal fences should be painted using a heavy nap roller, which allows an easier application of paint to chain link or similar types of metal fences.

INTERIOR

Interior maintenance is important not only for appearance's sake, but to maintain the structural integrity and overall value of your home. Most interior repairs are well within the scope of the average homeowner.

Framing

At least once a year check all exposed wood members for signs of decay or termite activity. The basement, crawl spaces, and attics of a house will be the major areas to check. all accessible wood framing should be probed with a screwdriver or other pointed tool to test the soundness of the wood. Repairs and replacements should be made where necessary. Evidence of insect damage should be checked by a pest exterminator.

Fireplace

When cement is loose or there are missing mortar joints between fireplace bricks, have the fireplace flue cleaned by a professional chimney sweep to rid the flue of soot or creosote. Clean the damper rim to permit a tight seal when the damper is closed. Be sure to clean out the fireplace ash pit. (If you have a garden, dump wood ashes into it, because the ashes contain minerals that will increase the soil productivity.)

Bathroom Tile

Be sure to double-check the tile joints on the tub walls. Loose or missing grout should be replaced to prevent water from getting behind the tile and causing damage to the walls and floors. When the joints are regrouted, seal them with a silicone waterproofing sealer.

Electrical

The electrical system of a house does not require an annual maintenance schedule, but you should check the following for safety reasons. Circuit breakers should be tripped every 6 months to make sure that they are functional. If you find one that will not shut off, have a licensed electrician troubleshoot it for you. Ground fault interrupters should be tripped once a month. If you find that you continually blow the same fuses, have an electrician check it out. Rather than using lamp cord to provide needed extensions, have additional circuits installed.

Plumbing

If you have any doubts about the quality of your water, have it tested by your local health department. Purifying filters on water lines should be changed every 6 months, and built-in screens on faucets, which filter out sediments, should be cleaned every year. If you have pipes that run through unheated areas, double-check the condition of the insulation before each winter. Corrosion and rusting on pipes and pipe joints should be continuously monitored for leaks. If there is any question in your mind about the possibility of a leak in a pipe or a joint, have it repaired. Condensation on pipes can be corrected with a foam adhesive tape. Sump pump strainer screens should be cleaned annually. Also check the sump pump float to see that it can rise and fall freely. Once a year, check all shut-off valves to make sure that they are functional.

Heating

Oil burners should be cleaned, serviced and tuned-up every year by your oil company. Gas burners only need to be serviced every third year by your local utility company. On a warm air system, you should replace fiberglass-type filters before they clog up with dirt and dust. Permanent filters should be washed and cleaned every 6 months.

Vacuum warm air registers and grilles to keep them free from dust. Inspect the blower during the heating season and replace any deteriorated belts. Be sure to oil and lubricate where required. On a hot water system, be sure to bleed all radiator valves before the heating season to rid the pipes of accumulated air. Do this by opening the valve on the radiator and holding a cup under it to catch any water that may spurt out. Once the air is purged from the radiator, simply close the valve. Be sure to dust all radiators and baseboard units for optimum heat transfer. Circulating pumps on a hot water system will need a few drops of light oil in each cup once a year.

The most important maintenance feature in a steam system is to blow off the low water cutoff valve once a month. Some manufacturers require this to be done twice a month during the heating season. Also make sure that the air valves on the radiators are in good working order.

Domestic Hot Water

If a hot water tank is properly maintained, it will last longer than the average 5- or 10-year warranties given by the manufacturers. A simple maintenance chore is to open the drain valve at the base of the tank to remove accumulated sediment. Drain a bucket of water out every 6 months. if the water in your area has a high mineral content, you may have to do this every 3 months.

Once a year the pressure relief valve on the tank should be tripped. If the valve is working, a spurt of water should be emitted. If it is not working, the valve should be replaced.

Many people pay extra dollars each month for energy that is wasted because the hot water tank and the hot water lines are not insulated. If yours is not, seriously consider spending a few dollars to do it; the cost will be repaid in a very short time.

Air-Conditioning

Be sure to turn off the power before you work on the unit. If the filters are disposable, replace them; permanant ones should be washed. Clean exterior and interior grilles, condenser fins, and blades. Check insulation to make sure all ducts are tightly sealed. Have a serviceman go over the entire system before the summer season starts.

Appliances

On a monthly basis, be sure to clean and remove debris and residue that may accumulate in your gar-

Table 21-1. Exterior Maintenance Chart for Spring and Fall.

Date	Spring										Fall				Notes
	Roof Shingles	Chimney & Flashing	Gutters & Spouts	Windows & Ventilation	Foundation	Entrances — Walks & Patio	Decks & Porches	Catch Basins	Garage	Gutters & Downspouts	Sidings	Catch Basins	Fence		

Table 21-2. Interior Maintenance Chart for 3 Months, 6 Months, and for Monthly Maintenance Chores.

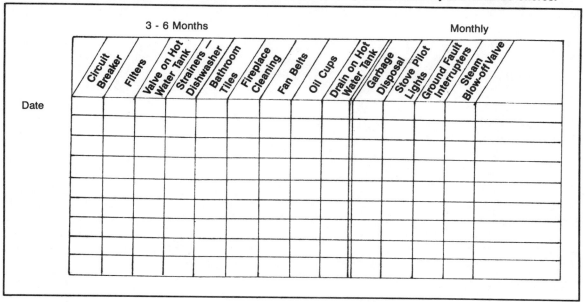

| Date | 3 - 6 Months | | | | | | | | | | Monthly | | | | | |
---	Circuit Breaker	Filters	Valve on Hot Water Tank	Strainers — Dishwasher	Bathroom Tiles	Fireplace Cleaning	Fan Belts	Oil Cups	Drain on Hot Water Tank	Garbage Disposal	Stove Pilot Lights	Ground Fault Interrupters	Steam Blow-off Valve

bage disposal. Every 6 months check the nuts on the disposal to make sure they are tight. Clean and remove any food particles from around stove pilot lights and orifices. Periodically clean the oven door gasket to provide a tight seal when the door is closed. Dishwasher strainers located at the base of a washer compartment should be flushed with water every 3 or 4 months. Remove vent panels from your refrigerator and freezer to vacuum dust accumulations. This can be done on an annual basis. Test the tightness of refrigerator and freezer doors by closing a single thickness of paper between the door and the edge of the unit. If the unit has a tight seal the paper should tear before slipping out. If you can remove it easily, the gasket may need to be replaced.

MAINTENANCE CHARTS

Included at the end of this chapter are some sample maintenance charts (Tables 21-1 and 21-2). You can make up your own charts to accommodate what you wish to accomplish over the course of the year. Use these samples as a guide for making your own. By keeping records of what has to be done and when, you will be able to spread out your workload over the course of the year.

Appendices

Appendix A

Selecting an Inspector

The following may help you find out whether or not an inspector is qualified. Consult with several inspectors until you have a good "gut" reaction about one of them.

LICENSES

Often, an inspector may be a licensed builder but may not have adequate knowledge of the mechanical systems of a house. The reverse can also be true; an inspector may be licensed in plumbing and heating but may not have a strong background in house construction.

BUSINESS ASSOCIATES

Affiliations with either could mean a conflict of interest. Sometimes real estate agents recommend inspectors who give positive reports on the houses that they inspect and barely touch upon critical areas. In other instances, inspectors who also do contracting work have been known to stress the need for repairs that they would be "willing" to do for a reasonable price.

PROFESSIONAL ORGANIZATIONS

Membership in a professional group such as the American Society of Home Inspectors (ASHI) means that the inspector has passed rigid entrance qualifications and that he adheres to a strict code of ethics.

LIABILITY INSURANCE

Most inspectors carry some form of professional liability insurance. In the event of human error, the buyer and the inspector are protected.

SCOPE OF INSPECTION

Buyers should have the inspectors give details about what is to be inspected. For example, will he check all of the appliances in the house? Will he inspect attics and crawl spaces? Does he activate mechanical units such as heating systems? Also, the home buyer should find out how long the inspection is going to be; on the average it should take a minimum of three hours. Any time less than that could mean that the inspection is not a thorough one but merely a walk-through.

ORAL AND WRITTEN REPORTS

The home buyer is entitled to receive an oral report at the inspection site and a written follow-up report detailing the findings of the inspection as soon as possible. Promptness is important, because the sale may be contingent upon the report. Finally, buyers should always be present during an inspection to see what the inspector is doing, whether he is checking all the areas he said he would, and to get as many maintenance tips as possible.

INSPECTOR'S REPUTATION

The reputation of an inspector is as equally important as his qualifications. A list of references of real estate attorneys and home sellers should be made available to the buyers if they so wish. Home buyers should be cautioned about any referrals from real estate agents. Most often the agent represents the seller, thus a potential conflict of interest may arise. An inspector should only represent the buyer, and his opinions must be totally impartial and honest.

CHECKPOINTS

- What licenses does the inspector have?
- Is the inspector associated with a real estate firm or repair contracting business?
- Does the inspector belong to any professional organization?
- Does the inspector carry liability insurance?
- Does the inspector provide details as to what is to be inspected?
- Does the inspector give oral and written reports?
- What is the inspector's reputation?

Appendix B

Additional Reading

Appraisal and Rehabilitation of Old Dwellings. U.S. Department of Agriculture. Handbook No. 481.

Basic Housing Inspection. U.S. Department of Health, Education, And Welfare. HEW Publication No. 80-8315.

Chimneys, Fireplaces, Vents, and Solid Fuel Burning Appliances. Standard No. 211. Fire Protection Association. Batterymarch Plaza, Quincy, MA. 02269

Concrete and Masonry. U.S. Department of the Army. Handbook No. TM 5-742.

Condensation Problems in Your House. U.S. Department of Agriculture. Handbook No. 373.

Drainage Around Your Home. U.S. Department of Agriculture. Handbook No. 64.

Electrical Code for One- and Two-Family Dwellings. Fire Protection Association. Batterymarch Plaza, Quincy, MA. 02269

Finding and Keeping a Healthy House. U.S. Department of Agriculture. Handbook No. 1284.

Fire Safety in Housing. U.S. Department of Housing and Urban Development. Handbook No. H-2176R.

Home Heating Systems. U.S. Department of Agriculture.

In the Bank or Up the Chimney. U.S. Department of Housing and Urban Development. HUD-PDR-89.

Principles for Protecting Wood Buildings From Decay. U.S. Department of Agriculture.

Septic Tank Care. U.S. Department of Health, Education, and Welfare.

Simple Plumbing Repairs. U.S. Department of Agriculture. Handbook No. 1034.

Solar Hot Water and Your Home. National Solar Heating and Cooling Information Center.

Subterranean Termites. U.S. Department of Agriculture. Bulletin No. 64.

The Energy-Wise Home Buyer. U.S. Department of Housing and Urban Development. HUD-H-2648.

Wood-Frame House Construction. U.S. Department of Agriculture. Handbook No. 73

Government publications can be purchased by writing to:

Superintendent of Documents
U.S. Government Printing Office
Washington, D.C. 20402

Appendix C
Inspection Worksheet

EXTERIOR

1. Roof: *Type* _____. *Shingles* (missing/cracking/damage). *Framing* (sagging ridge/bowed sheathing).

2. Chimney: *Condition* (crumbling brickwork/missing mortar/damaged bricks). *Flashing* (needs repair/cemented over/open gaps).

3. Gutters: *Type* _____. *Condition* (leaking/decaying/damaged).

4. Downspouts: *Condition* (open seams/rusting/missing sections). *Discharging to foundation* (yes/no).

5. Roof Vents: *Flashing* (defective/leaking/needs repairs). *Condition* (broken/missing/damaged).

6. Siding: *Type* _____. *Condition* (decaying/dented/cracked). *Repairs needed* (peeling paint/rusting/replace missing sections).

7. Trim: *Condition* (peeling paint/decaying wood/missing sections).

8. Windows: *Type* _____. *Condition* (broken glass/missing putty/missing latches/need caulking).

9. Foundation: *Type* ———————————. *Condition* (cracked/open holes/missing mortar in joints/not visible).

10. Foundation Windows: *Type* ———————————. *Condition* (rusting/decaying).

11. Skylights: *Damage* (missing putty/cracked glass/decaying frame).

12. Garage: *Attached/Detached. Condition* (needs repairs/winterizing).

13. Porches: *Location* ———————————. *Condition* (decaying wood/evidence of wood-boring insects/need for repairs).

14. Entrances: *Condition of doors* (fair/needs repairs). *Condition of steps* (decaying/deteriorating brickwork/hazardous to use). *Rails* (yes/no).

15. Low Wood Members: *Location* ———————————. *Condition* (decaying/insect activity/needs replacement).

16. Grade: *Surface water flows towards house* (location ———————————). *Drywells* (yes/no). *Possibility of flooding* (yes/no).

17. Driveway: *Condition* (cracking/heaving/deterioration). *Needs repairs* (minor/major).

18. Energy Losses: *Location* ———————————. *Type* (open gaps in siding/trim needs caulking/loose trim/need weatherstripping around windows and doors).

19. Fences: *Type* ———————————. *Condition* (rusting/decaying).

20. Landscaping: *Overgrown shrubs* (yes/no). *Ivy on house* (yes/no). *Overhanging tree branches* (yes/no). *Location* ———————————.

21. Retaining Walls: *Type* ———————————. *Weep holes* (yes/no). *Condition* (decaying/in need of repair).

22. Paths: *Condition* (cracked/settled/hazardous to user).

23. Structural Pests: *Evidence of* (carpenter ants/powder-post beetles/termites). *Location of damage* ———————————.

BASEMENT INTERIOR

1. Water Penetrations: *Location* ———————————. *Efflorescence* (yes/no). *See page* (major/minor). *Sump pump working* (yes/no).

2. Foundation Walls: (Accessible/inaccessible). *Condition* (poor/good).

3. Cellar Floor: *Condition* (cracks/holes/evidence of water/needs repairs).

4. Insect   Activity: *Type*   _____. *Extent   of   damage* _____. *Location* _____.

5. Main Girder: *Condition* (resting on foundation/needs repairs). *Evidence of decay or insect activity* (yes/no). *Extent* _____.

6. Posts: *Type* _____. *Condition* (fair/good/repairs needed).

7. Floor Joists: *Condition* (rotting/damaged/sagging).

8. Crawl   Spaces: (yes/no).   *Location*   _____.   *Condition* _____.

9. Insulation: *Type*   _____. *Condition* _____. *Location* _____. *Amount of insulation* _____. *Vapor barrier* (yes/no).

MECHANICAL SYSTEMS

1. Heating: *Type* _____. *Condition* (needs repairs/working). *Type of fuel* (oil/gas). *Fire-stopping needed* (yes/no). *Safety valves/shut-offs working* (yes/no). *Sufficient heat* (yes/no). *Zones* (1/2/3). *Needs servicing/cleaning* (yes/no).

2. Electrical: *How many amps* (60/100/150/200). *Main disconnect working* (yes/no). *Serviced grounded* (yes/no). *Use of* (lamp cord/knob and tube wiring). *Aluminum wiring* (yes/no). *Ground fault interrupters* (yes/no). *Location* _____.

3. Plumbing: *Drainage* (good/fair/poor). *Water pressure* (adequate/inadequate). *Leaks* (yes/no). *Septic or cesspool system* (yes/no). *Use of lead water lines or lead traps* (yes/no). *Sufficient amount of shut-off valves* (yes/no). *Working* (yes/no).

4. Domestic Hot Water: *Type* _____. *Condition of tank* (leaking/corrosion/needs replacement). *Type of fuel* (gas/oil/electricity). *Safety valves working* (yes/no). *Size of tank* _____. *Sufficient hot water* (yes/no).

5. Air Conditioner: *Condition* (fair/needs repairs). *Size of unit* _____. *Type* (split/integral). *Last servicing* _____.

6. Solar: *Type* (active/passive) (heat or hot water). *Working* (yes/no). *Fully insulated* (yes/no). *Condition of pipes* _____. *Solar collector location* _____.

ATTIC

1. Insulation: *Type* _____. *Amount* _____.
Location _____. *Condition* (damaged/needs replacement).

2. Ventilation: *Kind* (soffit/gable/roof/ridge). *Needs repairs* (yes/no). *Sufficient ventilation* (yes/no). *Signs of condensation* (yes/no).

3. Framing: *Condition* (structurally sound/decaying/insect activity).

4. Leaks: *Around chimney* (yes/no). *Vent pipe leaks* (yes/no). *Daylight visible from attic* (yes/no). *Location* _____.

5. Improper venting into attic: *Location* (kitchen vents/bathroom vents).

BATHROOMS

1. Fixtures: *Condition* (fair/poor/good). *Leaks* (yes/no). *Chipped or damaged fixtures* (yes/no). *Faucets dripping* (yes/no).

2. Tile: *Condition* (falling off of wall/broken/missing).

3. Ventilation: *Type* (windows/mechanical vents).

4. Heat: (yes/no).

5. Ceilings: *Need repairs* (yes/no).

6. Floors: *Condition* (decaying/tile pulling up/needs replacement).

7. Ground Fault Interrupter: (yes/no). *Working* (yes/no).

8. Walls: *Condition* (loose plaster/damaged walls from water/needs repairs).

9. Water Pressure: (adequate/inadequate).

10. Drainage: (normal/sluggish).

KITCHEN

1. Sink: *Condition* (good/fair/poor). *Piping* (leaks/needs replacement).

2. Stove: *Type of fuel* (oil/gas/electricity). *Working* (yes/no).

3. Appliances: *Type* _____. *Age* _____.
Condition _____. *Working* (yes/no).

4. Ceilings: *Condition* _____.

5. Floors: *Needs replacement* (yes/no).

6. Walls: *Need repairs* (yes/no).

7. Cabinets/Counter Space: (sufficient/insufficient).

8. Ventilation and Light: (adequate/inadequate).

9. Heat: (yes/no).

10. Electrical outlets: (sufficient/need more).

FIREPLACE OR STOVE

1. Needs Cleaning: (yes/no).

2. Safety Hazards: *Location* _____.
Type _____.

3. Permit for Stove: (yes/no).

4. Condition of Flue Pipe: (good/needs replacement).

5. Proximity to Combustible Materials: *Location* _____.

6. Last Cleaning and Servicing Date: _____.

ROOMS

1. Ceilings: (cracks/damaged areas/water stains/sagging plaster).

2. Walls: (need repairs/holes/missing sections).

3. Floors: (replace/refinish/install new floor).

4. Windows: (need repairs/new storm windows/general tightening up).

5. Doors: (missing/damaged/need repairs).

6. Heating: (radiator/register/none).

7. Electrical: (need additional outlets/overhead lights).

8. Closets: (sufficient size/insufficient size) (need more closets).

9. General Comments: _____.

Glossary

Glossary

attic ventilators—In house, screen openings provided to ventilate an attic space. They are located in the soffit area as inlet ventilators and in the gable end or along the ridge as outlet ventilators.

basement floor slab—The 4- or 5-inch layer of concrete that forms the basement floor.

bearing wall—A wall that supports any vertical load in addition to its own weight.

bridging—Cross bridging or solid. Members at the middle or third points of floor joist spans used to brace one to the next and to prevent their twisting.

burner—A device that provides the mixing of fuel, air, and ignition in a combustion chamber.

chimney—A vertical masonry shaft of reinforced concrete or other approved noncombustible material enclosing one or more flues. It removes the products of combustion from solid, liquid, or gaseous fuel.

circuit—The flow of electricity through two or more wires from the supply source to one or more outlets, and back to the source.

clean-out door—The door to the ash pit or the bottom of a chimney through which the chimney can be cleaned.

collar beam—Wood member connecting opposite roof rafters. They serve to stiffen the roof structure.

collector—A device used to collect solar radiation and convert it into heat.

condensation—In a building, beads or drops of water (and frequently frost in extremely cold weather) that accumulate on the inside of the exterior covering of a building when warm, moisture-laden air from the interior reaches a point where the temperature no longer permits the air to sustain the moisture it holds.

corner brace—Diagonal braces at the corners of frame construction to stiffen and strengthen the wall.

crawl space—A shallow space below the living quarters of a basementless house.

cross connection—Any physical connection or arrangement between two otherwise separate piping systems, one of which contains potable water and the other either water of unknown or questionable safety.

damper—A valve for regulating the draft in a stove or a stovepipe.

decay—Disintegration of wood or other substance through the action of fungi.

disposal field—An area containing a series of one or more trenches lined with coarse aggregate and conveying the effluent from a septic tank through clay pipe.

double-glazed—Two panes of glass or transparent plastic with approximately a 1-inch space between them to provide an insulating pocket of air.

downspout—A pipe, usually of metal, for carrying rainwater from roof gutters.

draft hood—A device placed in and made part of the vent connector, chimney connector, or smokepipe, from an appliance, or in the appliance itself. It is designed to ensure the ready escape of the products of combustion.

draft regulator—A device that functions to maintain a desired draft in oil-fired appliances by automatically reducing the chimney draft to the desired value.

drain—Any pipe that carries waste water or waterborne waste in a building (house) drainage system.

ducts—In a house, usually round or rectangular metal pipes that distribute warm air from the heating plant or cool air from an air conditioning system.

evaporator—The cooling unit of an air conditioning system; found in the attic or in the plenum of a furnace.

fire-stop—A solid, tight closure of a concealed space, placed to prevent the spread of fire and smoke through such a space. In a frame wall, this will usually consist of a 2 × 4-inch cross blocking between studs.

flue liner—The flue is the hole in the chimney. The liner, usually made of clay, protects the brick from harmful smoke gases.

footing—The concrete pad that carries the entire weight of the house upon the earth.

foundation wall—The wall of poured concrete or concrete blocks that rests on the footing and supports the remainder of the house.

fuse—A safety device that cuts off the flow of electricity when the current flowing through the fuse exceeds its rated capacity.

gable—The triangular end of a building with a sloping roof.

girder—A main beam upon which floor joists rest. Usually of wood, but sometimes of steel.

ground—To connect with the earth—as to *ground* an electric wire directly to the earth or indirectly through a water pipe or some other metal conductor.

gutter—A shallow channel or conduit of metal or wood set below and along the eaves of a house to catch and carry off rainwater from the roof.

humidifier—A device designed to increase the humidity within a room or a house by means of the discharge of water vapor.

jamb—The side and head lining of a doorway, window, or other opening.

joist—One of a series of parallel beams, usually 2 inches thick, used to support floor and ceiling loads. They are supported in turn by larger beams, girders, or bearing walls.

main vent—The principal artery of the venting system, to which vent branches may be connected.

masonry—Stone, brick, concrete, concrete block, or other similar building units or materials.

P trap—A trap with a vertical inlet and a horizontal outlet.

pier—A column of masonry used to support other structural members.

plumb—A term used to denote exact perpendicular or vertical lines.

potable water—Water having no impurities present in amounts sufficient to cause disease or harmful physiological effects.

rafter—One of a series of structural members of a roof designed to support roof loads. The rafters of a flat roof are sometimes called *roof joists*.

reinforcing rods—Steel rods or metal fabric placed in concrete slabs to increase their strength.

ridge—The horizontal line at the junction of the top edges of two sloping roof surfaces.

ridge board—The board placed on edge at the ridge of the roof into which the upper ends of the rafters are fastened.

riser—Each of the vertical boards closing the spaces between the treads of a stairway.

roof sheathing—The boards of sheet material fastened to the roof rafters on which the shingle or other roof covering is laid.

septic tank—A watertight receptacle that receives the discharge of a building's sanitary drain system.

siding—The finish covering of the outside wall of a frame building.

sill—The board that is laid first on the foundation, and on which the frame rests.

soffit—Usually the underside of an overhanging cornice.

soil pipe—The pipe that directs sewage from a house to the receiving sewer, building drain, or building sewer.

solar system (active)—Any solar heating or cooling system that requires mechanical devices, such as pumps or fans, to transport heated air or heated liquid.

stud—The vertical wood members of the house, usually 2 × 4s, generally spaced every 6 inches on center.

termites—Insects that resemble ants in size and appearance. They eat out the woodwork of a house, leaving only a shell.

trap—A fitting or device that provides a liquid seal to prevent the emission of sewer gases, without materially affecting the flow of sewage or waste water through it.

trim—The finish materials in a building, such as moldings, applied around openings (windows and doors) or at the floor and ceiling of rooms (baseboard and other moldings).

vapor barrier—Material used to retard the movement of water vapor into walls and prevent condensation in them.

vent—A pipe or duct that allows flow of air. An inlet or outlet.

weatherstrip—Narrow or jamb-width sections of thin metal or other material that prevents infiltration of air and moisture around windows and doors.

Epilogue

The purchase of a home will probably be the largest investment you will ever make. Paying too much for a house or buying one that has serious structural or mechanical defects are minimized if you know what to look for and what questions to ask. Armed with the information that this book provides, you should have no trouble arriving at a fair estimate of what the property is worth and determining what major repairs are needed.

In the event that you do find a serious defect (such as a cracked foundation), and you do not want to let go of the subject house, by all means, hire a professional to get an expert opinion. If you do decide to hire a professional inspector, do it after after you have read the appendix. See Appendix A.

After the inspection and appraisal process is over, there should be little that stands in the way of your buying the house of your dreams. To make sure that you have made the right decision, however, try to arrange for a last walk-through tour of the subject house shortly before you pass papers. It will most likely heighten your sense of determination and anticipation to live in your newly acquired property.

Index

Index

Other Bestsellers From TAB

Other Bestsellers From TAB

☐ **DO-IT YOURSELF DESIGNER WINDOWS—Boyle**

If the cost of custom-made draperies puts you in a state of shock . . . if you don't know what to do with a problem window or what type of window decor would look right in your home . . . here's all the advice and information you've been searching for. It's a complete, hands-on guide to selecting, measuring, making, and installing just about any type of window treatment imaginable. 272 pp., 414 illus., 7″ × 10″.

Paper $14.95   **Hard $21.95**
Book No. 1922

☐ **PRACTICAL LANDSCAPING AND LAWN CARE—Webb**

Make your lawn the envy of the entire neighborhood . . . without spending a fortune or putting in never-ending hours of maintenance time! Here's absolutely everything you need to successfully plan, plant, and maintain lawn grasses and groundcovers, vines, and flowering ornamentals . . . annual, biennial, and perennial flowers . . . shade trees, lawn trees . . . even decorative (and delicious) fruits and berries. It doesn't matter whether your climate is cold and damp or hot and dry . . . whether your soil is sandy, rocky, or gummy clay . . . *everything* you need is here! 240 pp., 84 illus. 7″ × 10″.

Paper $13.95   **Book No. 1818**

☐ **HOW TO BE YOUR OWN ARCHITECT—2nd Edition—Goddard and Wolverton**

The completely revised version of a long-time bestseller gives you all the expert assistance needed to design your own dream house like a professional. You'll save the money that most custom-home builders put out in architects' fees—an estimated 12% to 15% of the total construction costs—to pay for more of those "extras" you'd like your new home to include! 288 pp., 369 illus., 7″ × 10″.

Paper $14.95   **Hard $22.95**
Book No. 1790

☐ **BE YOUR OWN CONTRACTOR: THE AFFORDABLE WAY TO HOME OWNERSHIP—Alth**

If you've put your dreams of home ownership on "hold" because of today's sky-high building costs, this single guidebook can change all that! It shows you can save thousands of dollars on the cost of a new home by becoming your own contractor. It shows how to build an attractive, secure, comfortable home at minimum cost. 256 pp., 207 illus. 7″ × 10″.

Paper $12.95   **Book No. 1554**

☐ **DO YOUR OWN DRYWALL— AN ILLUSTRATED GUIDE—Kozloski**

Professional expertise for the amateur builder and remodeler! Proper installation of interior plasterboard or drywall is a must-have skill for successful home building or remodeling. Now, there's a new time- and money-saving alternative: this excellent step-by-step guide to achieving professional-quality drywalling results, the first time and every time! Even joint finishing, the drywalling step most dreaded by do-it-yourselfers, is a snap when you know what you're doing. And this is a guide that leaves absolutely nothing to chance and that leaves no question unanswered. 160 pp., 161 illus.

Paper $10.95   **Book No. 1838**

☐ **TROUBLE-FREE SWIMMING POOLS**

Here is the ideal sourcebook for anyone thinking of installing a swimming pool—inground or above ground from wading pool size to large indoor public pool. It shows how to plan, excavate, construct, and safely maintain all types of sizes of pools. You'll find out how to have your own pool for as little as $1,000 . . . or how to get more pool for the money no matter how much you're able to spend! 176 pp., 306 illus., 7″ × 10″.

Paper $11.95   **Hard $18.95**
Book No. 1808

☐ **PROFESSIONAL PLUMBING TECHNIQUES— ILLUSTRATED AND SIMPLIFIED—Smith**

This plumber's companion includes literally everything about plumbing you'll ever need! From changing a washer to installing new fixtures, it covers installing water heaters, water softeners, dishwashers, gas stoves, gas dryers, grease traps, clean outs, and more. Includes piping diagrams, tables, charts, and arranged alphabetically. 294 pp., 222 illus.

Hard $16.95   **Book No. 1763**

☐ **HOME REMODELING—A MONEY-SAVING HANDBOOK—Wahlfeldt**

Join the ranks of in-the-know home owners who've discovered that today's best and most affordable home buy is an *older* house. This is a sourcebook that outlines the key things to look for when buying an older home (which faults are easily fixable and which ones can mean major renovation work). You'll find information on everything from finances to location and utilities. 400 pp., 505 illus. 7″ × 10″.

Paper $16.95   **Book No. 1515**

*Prices subject to change without notice.

Look for these and other TAB books at your local bookstore.

TAB BOOKS Inc.
P.O. Box 40
Blue Ridge Summit, PA 17214

Send for FREE TAB catalog describing over 1200 current titles in print.